Marian Barry

SUCCESS

International English Skills

for Cambridge IGCSE®

Teacher's Book

Fourth edition

CAMBRIDGE
UNIVERSITY PRESS

CAMBRIDGE
UNIVERSITY PRESS

University Printing House, Cambridge CB2 8BS, United Kingdom

One Liberty Plaza, 20th Floor, New York, NY 10006, USA

477 Williamstown Road, Port Melbourne, VIC 3207, Australia

4843/24, 2nd Floor, Ansari Road, Daryaganj, Delhi – 110002, India

79 Anson Road, #06–04/06, Singapore 079906

Cambridge University Press is part of the University of Cambridge.

It furthers the University's mission by disseminating knowledge in the pursuit of education, learning and research at the highest international levels of excellence.

Information on this title: cambridge.org/cie

© Marian Barry 2017

First published by Georgian Press (Jersey) Limited 1998
Second edition 2015
Reprinted and published by Cambridge University Press, Cambridge 2010
Third edition 2015
Fourth edition 2017

20 19 18 17 16 15 14 13 12 11 10 9 8 7 6 5 4 3

Printed in Great Britain by CPI Group (UK) Ltd, Croydon CR0 4YY

A catalogue record for this publication is available from the British Library

ISBN 9781316637104 Paperback

···

···

IGCSE® is the registered trademark of Cambridge International Examinations

Contents

Below are the criteria for Cambridge IGCSE English as a Second Language writing and speaking. For full details, go to the Cambridge International Examinations website.

Writing

Marks	Content (maximum 8 marks)	Marks	Language (maximum 8 marks)
7–8	**Relevance** • Instructions are followed. • Consistently appropriate style and tone for the text type. • Excellent sense of purpose and audience. **Development of ideas** • Writing is very well developed, at an appropriate length. • Meaning is communicated skilfully and effectively.	7–8	**Range and accuracy** • A varied range of high and low frequency vocabulary used competently. • A varied level of complex and simple sentence structures used appropriately. • A considerable level of language accuracy throughout. Some errors may remain, but these do not hinder communication of ideas or meaning. • The errors present relate to low frequency vocabulary and more complicated structures. **Organisation** • Consistently well-organised and ordered. • A varied range of connecting words and other cohesive methods, used consistently well.
5–6	**Relevance** • Instructions are followed. • Generally appropriate style and tone for the text type. • Generally good sense of purpose and audience. **Development of ideas** • Writing is developed, at an appropriate length. • Meaning is generally communicated clearly.	5–6	**Range and accuracy** • A good range of high frequency vocabulary used competently. Attempts to use some lower frequency vocabulary. • A good range of simple sentence structures used competently. Attempts to use some more complex sentence structures. • A good accuracy level throughout. Some errors are present, but these usually do not hinder communication. • The errors present usually relate to low frequency vocabulary or more complex sentence structures. **Organisation** • Often well-organised and ordered. • A varied range of connecting words and other cohesive methods, used appropriately.

Marks	Content (maximum 8 marks)	Marks	Language (maximum 8 marks)
3–4	**Relevance** • Instructions are generally followed. • Reasonably appropriate style and tone for the text type, but this may not be consistent. • Some sense of purpose and audience. **Development of ideas** • Some development of writing, but it may be repetitive or insufficient in some areas. • Meaning is communicated, but may lack clarity in places	3–4	**Range and accuracy** • Mostly uses high frequency vocabulary, reasonably appropriately. • Mostly uses simple sentence structures, usually appropriately. • Reasonable accuracy level throughout. Some errors may hinder communication. • Errors are present when using some high frequency vocabulary or simple sentence structures. **Organisation** • Reasonably organised and sequenced. • Some connecting words and other cohesive methods, used reasonably appropriately.
1–2	**Relevance** • Instructions may only be partially followed. • Style and tone for the text type may be inappropriate. • Inappropriate sense of purpose and audience. **Development of ideas** • Limited attempt to develop writing, there may be gaps, irrelevance and/or repetition. • Limited attempt to communicate meaning, it lacks clarity in places.	1–2	**Range and accuracy** • Limited use of vocabulary. • Limited use of sentence structures. • Lack of control of vocabulary. Meaning is generally unclear. • Errors occur when using common vocabulary and simple sentence structures. **Organisation** • Organisation lacks order. • Limited attempt to use connecting words and other cohesive methods.
0	• No response worthy of credit.	0	• No response worthy of credit.

v

Speaking

Give a mark out of 10 for each category (structure, vocabulary, development and fluency), and then add these marks to give an overall total out of 30.

Mark	Structure	Vocabulary	Development and fluency
9–10	The student demonstrates their ability to use a range of sentence structures accurately, confidently and consistently.	The student demonstrates enough command of vocabulary to respond to questions with accuracy and understanding. Meaning is conveyed with precision, and some sophisticated ideas are communicated.	The student demonstrates a continued ability to maintain a conversation and to contribute appropriately. The student can respond to changes in the direction of conversation. There is clarity in pronunciation and intonation.
7–8	Sentence structures are usually sound, but are not used entirely accurately or with confidence. There are some errors when more complex sentence structures are attempted.	The student has a sufficient range of vocabulary to convey meaning and ideas with competence.	The student responds relevantly and at length which makes frequent prompting unnecessary. The student can hold a competent conversation, and pronunciation and intonation are generally clear.
5–6	The student can use simple structures efficiently but has some difficulty venturing beyond them.	Vocabulary conveys simple ideas and information with clarity. Errors are somewhat noticeable, and only partial competence is achieved.	The student attempts to respond to questions and prompts. Effort and additional prompting is necessary to develop the conversation. There is some lack of clarity of pronunciation and intonation, but it is unlikely to impede communication.
3–4	Sentence structures will largely be very simple, limited and with some errors, which will hinder communication.	Vocabulary is not particularly varied and there is difficulty in conveying simple ideas. There is hesitation and repetition.	Responses are short and widely spaced. The student has to be encouraged to develop brief responses and continue the conversation. Pronunciation and intonation cause some difficulties in communication.
1–2	Some attempt at a response will be made during the conversation. Attempts at structured sentences will rarely achieve satisfactory communication.	Vocabulary will generally be insufficient to convey simple ideas.	Responses are so brief that little is communicated. The student hardly engages in conversation. Pronunciation and intonation patterns cause difficulty for the listener.
0	Completely limited/no attempt at a response.	Completely limited/no attempt at a response.	Completely limited/no attempt at a response.

Introduction

This course provides detailed preparation for Cambridge IGCSE English as a Second Language.

The redesigned Student's Book has been revised to bring it in line with the revised Cambridge syllabus for examination from 2019. There are some changes in every unit. These include:

- new reading tasks to further support reading skills and, in particular, to prepare for multiple matching reading exercises

- several additional writing tasks to prepare for writing formal reports

- several additional exercises in the exam-style questions at the end of every unit, to consolidate preparation for the revised syllabus

- several new example answers to the exam-style questions for compositions, emails, reports, note-making and summarising.

There are also:

- five additional exam-style listening tasks to reflect the updated syllabus

- stimulating new photographs to increase the enjoyment of learning.

The Workbook consolidates and tests understanding of the language and themes in the Student's Book, with a range of exercises suitable for classroom use or homework. The Workbook has also been revised and extended to include several new exercises reflecting the developments in the syllabus. It also now includes photos. The final section of this Teacher's Book contains the answers to the Workbook exercises.

How the course reflects the exam

The course reflects the integrated skills basis of the exam, independently of each other. For example, a listening exercise may also be exploited to develop topic and vocabulary knowledge and to practise functional language and intonation.

The holistic nature of Cambridge IGCSE English as a Second Language is based on the expectation that students are receiving their education through the medium of English, or living in a country where English is widely spoken. Students will therefore be more comfortable with English than will 'pure' EFL students at a similar level. Unlike other language exams for non-native speakers, there is no isolated testing of freestanding structures.

Care has been taken in the course to highlight the structures and vocabulary that would be useful for a particular topic. In addition, the *Grammar Spotlight* at the end of each unit clarifies the purpose of a key structure, but the emphasis throughout is on how grammar can be applied in natural English.

Educational aims and objectives

The material is intended to develop students both intellectually and linguistically, to increase personal awareness and to encourage an understanding of the world. An investigative approach is taken, and students use initiative to solve problems. They apply skills, knowledge and understanding, and are encouraged to undertake individual projects and to work as part of a team. It is important that teachers develop these broader skills if the material is to work as intended. The educational aims and objectives of this course also make it suitable for courses other than Cambridge IGCSE English as a Second Language.

Age range

The course is designed to be used by young people in the age range 14–18. Unit themes reflect the interests of teenagers and aim to promote maturity of thought and outlook. This approach reflects the aims of the syllabus.

Time allocation

The course can be used over a period of up to two years, which is the recommended period of time suggested to prepare for Cambridge IGCSE English as a Second Language. This takes into account young people's rate of intellectual and emotional development. Alternatively, the material can be adapted to be covered in one year if this is the time available. The progression of language work, and the selection and treatment of topics, have been carefully chosen to reflect these factors.

Ability range

The two-tier Core and Extended structure embraces a wide ability range, from lower-intermediate through to upper-intermediate. The material in the course covers all the aspects of exams that Core and Extended students could be expected to meet. The emphasis is on the more challenging aspects of the syllabus.

Course structure

The course is organised into ten topic-based units, each systematically and gradually developing the four skills. Exam-style listening and reading exercises are introduced early in the units and fully exploited. Speaking and writing skills are developed at various stages within a unit, but students are not expected to try exam-style writing or speaking tasks until the end of a unit, on the basis that these, the productive skills, are the most demanding. Teachers should encourage students to combine everything they learn in terms of language and understanding of topics before expecting them to do exam-style writing and speaking tasks without help.

The units offer in-depth topic coverage, with shifts of focus indicated by theme headings. By studying a topic from many angles, students will be better prepared for exam questions where new angles are set on familiar topics, and a certain depth of thought is rewarded.

Each unit has a number of regular features including structural work, vocabulary building, spelling, functions, model texts, example answers and an *International overview*. The language study grows out of the texts that are being studied, to maximise relevance, accessibility and practical application.

Language study also takes account of Cambridge IGCSE examiner reports (available on the Cambridge Teacher Support website), which highlight those areas where improvements are needed, or where students have shown encouraging signs which should be further developed. These include: tone/register and audience awareness, vocabulary enlargement, understanding of topic, spelling, idioms, punctuation, paragraphing, and range of structures.

How to use the Student's Book units

Lead-in

Each unit starts with a student-centred lead-in, which introduces the topic and presents language and concepts. Students engage in stimulating group and pair work, in which they share experience and acquire new insights. Teachers should use the lead-in to discover gaps in student's knowledge, such as key vocabulary needed for later work in the unit. The teacher's notes always provide a full backup to support the lead-in. The photos supplied with the lead-in provide an opportunity to engage students across the ability range.

Developing reading skills

Most units have two substantial reading texts from a variety of authentic sources, representing a wide range of styles but staying within what teenagers could be expected to experience or imagine. Texts are chosen specifically to practise skills such as skimming, scanning and detailed reading and matching.

Texts are introduced through a range of structured exercises, including speculation and prediction, and vocabulary and language checks. They are often enhanced by a visual image to help students focus fully on the topic.

Developing writing skills

Writing skills receive particular treatment. The overall aim is to develop a more mature writing style necessary for both a wide range of real-life situations and for exams, whilst stimulating individuality of style and expression.

Developing listening skills

There are 16 recorded listening passages with tasks in the exam style, including monologues, announcements, interviews and conversations. In addition, there are two 'model' conversations which students can listen to and read at the same time. There are also seven recordings addressing phonology, and eight exercises developing language functions. Young voices have been used in a few of the recordings for greater authenticity, and a few voices are *very lightly* accented with non-British accents, including Australian and American, to reflect the new use of such accents in the exam.

Listening texts are multi-purpose. Not only do they build specific skills, such as listening for a specific point or listening for attitude, they also demonstrate a range of linguistic strategies including functional language (e.g. interrupting, expressing disagreement, blaming) and phonological features (pronunciation, stress and intonation) which will be tested in the Speaking Test.

Developing speaking skills

Oral work is encouraged at every opportunity, through whole-class interaction, pair work, reading aloud and so on. Structured exercises develop more understanding of functions, pronunciation, intonation and stress, giving talks effectively, responding to an audience and interacting with a speaker. The exercises will work at different levels, and with less outgoing students, if teachers give credibility to oral work by making time for it in the classroom. The oral work leads up to exam-style speaking exercises at the end of every unit.

Language study and grammar

The language study includes structural work, vocabulary, spelling, punctuation, paragraphing, and idiomatic and figurative language. The work is based on deductive reasoning, so teachers should build on students' prior knowledge and experience. Students should be encouraged to study the examples in the Student's Book and to work out meanings, patterns, rules and exceptions. This principle should be applied whether students are working on spelling, grammar or punctuation, or building vocabulary.

The space given to grammar teaching in the course is balanced against the need to develop a range of skills, and the priority given to such skills in the exam. For example, a grammatically correct letter of welcome which sounds unwelcoming in tone would be less acceptable than a letter which is slightly flawed grammatically but which is warm and inviting, on the grounds that the first letter does not communicate effectively. A letter packed with spelling errors would not receive the highest marks even if the grammar was perfect.

The *Grammar spotlight* highlights one or two key grammatical structures encountered but not focused on earlier in the unit. It provides clear, concise explanations and examples, and directs students to look back in the unit for further examples, to consolidate their knowledge.

International overview

This feature of each unit provides a range of factual and statistical information of global interest and concern, which has been carefully researched from respected sources and is presented via charts, tables and quizzes. It is a device to introduce students to a range of sensitive issues and raise international awareness, and can be delivered in a way the teacher thinks best in his/her particular situation. The teacher's notes provide detailed backup.

Advice for success

The *Advice for success* sections at the end of each unit provide general tips and exam techniques. The first group rounds off the learning aims and objectives of the unit. They build student independence by developing learning strategies, and allow students to identify individual learning weaknesses and to see what they need to study in more detail or revise. It is important to discuss the key advice fully in class and to ask students to highlight or underline points of special relevance. The advice also contains suggestions for language development outside the class, to further strengthen learner autonomy and responsibility.

The exam techniques provide practical guidance about tackling specific types of exam questions and make a useful reference section.

Exam focus

The *Exam focus* provides a summary of the primary learning aims of the unit. Students should be encouraged to familiarise themselves with the *Exam focus* so as not to be surprised during an exam.

The Contents Chart on pages iv and v of the Student's Book, the *Exam focus* sections that appear at the end of each unit in the Student's Book, and the Overview of Cambridge IGCSE English as a Second Language seen on pages vi and vii of the

Student's Book, show how this course helps students develop the skills required for their exam.

Supporting students in mixed-ability classes

There are many ideas throughout the Teacher's Book to help students develop their skills to the best of their ability. However, as every class will be mixed, care needs to be taken to ensure that all students benefit from the work that is done. The following suggestions offer some general ways of supporting students in mixed-ability classes.

- Use your knowledge of students when setting a word length for writing tasks, and where appropriate, give students shorter tasks which gradually build up to the word length required in the exam.

- Simpler words can be added to replace some of the more difficult words on the spelling lists.

When setting a problem solving exercise for the class, include an extra element of challenge for the more able (e.g. something extra, or harder, to do in the same time frame) and for the less able make the task simpler with more scaffolding, fewer actions to carry out, etc.

At the start of a lesson, differentiate your recapping of key points from the previous lesson: to support students, do a quick run-through of an exercise which is the same or very similar to one from last time, while for the more able, offer a new and more challenging context for the same language.

- If students in your class need support with a listening exercise, some of the gaps in gapped notes can be filled in by the teacher beforehand.

- Some of the more challenging questions on reading and listening texts can be answered by a pair or group of students working together under the direction of the teacher, rather than individually.

- An exercise can simply be divided in half and allocated to two groups in the class so there is less for each group to do.

- Students can be encouraged to learn a few selected items on a list of phrasal verbs, for example, rather than trying to learn the complete list.

- A vocabulary list can be cut down, and only selected items taught.

- The 'jigsaw technique' can be used to break a whole task down into component parts. The class is put into groups and each one is assigned a component to complete, with groups of students who require more support being given easier tasks. New groups are then formed, consisting of one representative from each of the original groups. Each representative is responsible for reporting the answers for his/her component part of the task. In the end, all the students have a complete set of answers.

Throughout this book, a range of ideas for prompting students are given. The extent to which the prompts are used can be adjusted to suit the level of the students.

Learning Support and Teaching Support

Throughout the Teacher's Book you will find *Learning Support and Teaching Support* panels. These offer help with the material by providing:

- ideas for how to approach some of the more challenging tasks

- suggestions for making some of the tasks more accessible.

- insight into aspects of grammar and vocabulary

- explanations of language content.

Some of the *Teaching Support* panels direct teachers to the information that follows, which offers a general approach to the four skills as well as to the study of vocabulary and grammar.

A general approach to teaching reading skills

Preparing to read

- Establish the topic (use pictures and headings to encourage students to make predictions about the subject matter).

- Focus on the type of text that students are going to read: Is it an article, an advertisement, a report?

Reading the text

- Ask students to read the text quietly to themselves (as they progress through the course, ask them to read within a given time limit to prepare them for what they are likely to have to do in exams.)

- Encourage students to skim read a text to get its general meaning and scan it to find specific information.

- Tell students to read the easiest parts of the text quickly and to take their time over the more complex parts.

- Encourage students to either use context to work out the meaning of new words, or look them up in a dictionary.

Dealing with the exercises

- Tell students to both identify the key words in a text and think about how those words relate to questions in comprehension exercises. This means understanding paraphrase, which means saying the same thing in a different way.

- **Support students** by telling them in which paragraph an answer can be found or reduce the number of questions they have to answer.

- Encourage students to move on if they don't know an answer to a question; they can come back to it at the end.

- **Challenge students** to give fuller answers to questions about the text.

Discussing the text

- Analyse the style of the text: Is the language formal or informal? How does the way a text is written affect our reading of it?

- Examine the way that information has been ordered into paragraphs and how one paragraph flows into another. This means that students must understand how words and phrases connect one part of a text to another, e.g. *However, Although, Having said that, In addition.*

- Focus on the intention of the writer. Ask students: *'What is the angle of the piece?' 'Who is the target audience?'*

Encourage students to look for what is *not being said*: students need to develop their ability to infer meaning. You can help them to do this by drawing their attention to things the writer has left out and the bias he or she might show against something.

A general approach to teaching writing skills

Preparing to write

- Ask students to think about the type of text they are going to write. For example, if it is a report, focus on its distinctive features: the neutral tone, its use of headings and so on.

- Elicit the vocabulary that students will need.

- Examine ways of beginning and ending the composition.

- Discuss the way information can be arranged into paragraphs which follow a logical sequence of ideas.

- Discuss style, formality, tone, register and target audience: who is the piece of writing for?

- Study an example of the composition type from the unit.

- Encourage students to make notes before they begin writing. Support students by giving them more guidance with the content of their writing.

Writing the first draft

- Encourage students to refer to the model texts in the unit. Writing is imitative – everyone learns by copying from someone who knows what they are doing.

- Tell students to get their ideas down on the page – that is what matters most at the first draft stage.

- Tell students they should aim to capture the reader's imagination.

- As writing is a complex skill, and one about which students can feel nervous and unsure, support students when they are planning their ideas, and help with any vocabulary they may require.

Rewriting the composition

- Tell students to think about how they can improve the organisation of information on the page.

- Support your students by giving them more guidance with the form of their writing.

- Tell students that their aim is to be clear in their writing – remind them that they are trying to communicate a particular message.

- Encourage students to read aloud what they have written: they should concentrate on the rhythm and flow of their sentences.

- Tell students to check the grammar, punctuation and spelling of their work before they finish it.

5

A general approach to teaching listening skills

Preparing to listen

- Focus on the type of recording that students are going to hear: Is it a conversation, an announcement, a discussion?

- Elicit vocabulary that will feature in the recording, especially if you think it will be new to the students. Put this vocabulary into context and make sure students are clear about its meaning.

- Encourage students to think about how we listen for key words – nobody listens to every single word that someone says.

Listening to a recording

- Play a recording several times, if necessary.

- Tell students to listen first to get the general meaning.

- Tell students to listen again to make notes or answer questions.

- In the early stages of the course and with particularly demanding listening tasks, give students the tapescript to read while they listen.

Dealing with the exercises

- Encourage students to identify the key words in a recording and to think about how these relate to questions in comprehension exercises – this means understanding inference and paraphrase.

- Help support students by replaying the part of a recording that contains the answer to a particular question.

- With the most demanding listening tasks, do the exercise with the whole class, pausing the recording as necessary and asking students specific questions to guide them to the answers to a question.

Discussing the listening

- Analyse the recording with the class: How did the person or people speak? What was easy to understand; what was more difficult? Are there any particular accents that students found hard to understand?

- Suggest ideas for further practise: listening to a variety of radio programmes and podcasts offers excellent general practice.

A general approach to teaching speaking skills

Preparing to do a speaking exercise

- Make sure that students understand what they are going to talk about or which part they are going to play if they are doing a roleplay.

- Elicit vocabulary needed for the speaking exercise. Put this up on the board and encourage students to refer to it.

- Remind students that it doesn't matter if they make a few mistakes with grammar and vocabulary in a speaking exercise as long as they communicate clearly and are easy to understand.

- Give students a couple of minutes to prepare beforehand – they can make a few notes and ask you any questions they may have.

Doing a speaking exercise

- Support your students by giving them prompts so that they are not lost for something to say, e.g. In a conversation about happiness you could give one student a piece of paper upon which is written the statement *'Nobody can be happy all the time.'* A student can then make use of this statement in their discussion.

- You could agree beforehand to make a recording of students. If so, record unobtrusively.

- Don't let any speaking exercise go on too long – five to ten minutes is fine.

- Monitor while students are doing the speaking exercise and make a note of common errors. You can go through these with the class at the end.

Analysing a speaking exercise

- When the speaking exercise is over, ask students to analyse their own performance and that of their peers: What did they do well? What did they do less well? What did they find easy or difficult? How could they improve?

- If you made a recording, listen back to it with the class as a whole and then discuss what went well and what could be improved.

A general approach to teaching vocabulary

Presenting vocabulary

- Put the word into context, then ask students to think of a context of their own.

- Drill the pronunciation of the word – make sure that students are familiar with the sound of the word right at the beginning.

- Focus on the spelling: does it contain any silent letters or double consonants?

- Make sure that students understand the social and cultural context of new words.

- Encourage students to learn complete phrases rather than words in isolation. Instead of simply learning the adjective *close-knit*, for example, students can learn *close-knit family* or *close knit-community*, as those noun and adjective combinations are common.

- Ask students to translate the word into their own language.

Recording vocabulary

- Encourage students to keep a vocabulary notebook in which they write example sentences using new words. At the end of a lesson, encourage students to test each other on the meanings of the words they have written down.

- Ask students to make cards. On one side is a word, on the other, its meaning and pronunciation. These cards can then be used in vocabulary games that can be played at the end of a lesson.

Using vocabulary

- Make sure that students feel comfortable with new language by giving them an opportunity to use new words as soon as possible – this can be in the form of simple conversation, debate or games.

- When new vocabulary reappears in later exercises or units, test students' understanding of its spelling, pronunciation and meaning: How much do they remember?

A general approach to teaching grammar

Presenting grammar

- Write the grammar structure on the board.

- Elicit ideas from the students with regard to the form and use of the structure in question.

- Go through the information about the grammar so that students are able to check it against what they themselves have said.

- Encourage students to learn grammatical terms – knowing how to talk about language will help them to master it.

- Set each exercise in turn, setting a time limit for the completion of the exercises if you find it helps. Students can work on exercises in pairs, in small groups or alone: vary your approach here.

- If students have to complete a gap with the correct grammatical structure, tell them to look at the words around the gap to help them decide how to complete it.

Recording grammar

- Encourage students to keep their own grammar reference notebook: they can include within it the information they think is the most important.

- Encourage students to write a correct example sentence in their grammar notebook for each grammar point learned.

- Encourage students to compare and contrast the grammar of their own language with English: What is similar? What is completely different?

Using grammar

- Do a speaking activity to practise the grammar even if it is a basic one. What matters is that you give students the chance to both use the grammar and to see it as something they can make use of.

- Encourage students to revise what they know regularly.

- Tell students to record themselves saying sentences using the new grammar structures. When they listen back to the recording they can analyse their performance: Did they make any mistakes? How could they improve their sentences?

Wider practice

Each unit in the Teacher's Book ends with suggestions for further ways to develop and extend the themes and skills practised. These include suggestions for mini-projects, including internet research on extension topics, ideas for role-plays and student presentations to the group, writing leaflets or blogs, contributing to online forums, listening to the radio and watching relevant TV programmes, and making posters and videos.

These *Wider practice* sections are intended to:

- Allow students to follow their own enthusiasms, the point being that students make better progress when they find a meaningful personal connection to what they are learning.

- Encourage students to take responsibility for what they learn. At university, students will have to manage their own learning – the *Wider practice* sections encourage students to take the initiative.

- Develop links with other areas of the curriculum so that students understand that what they learn is interconnected.

- Encourage students to see how an idea can be developed.

- Ensure that students do not solely concentrate on their exam but see the opportunity for the emphasis to also be on other things.

Example answers for exam-style writing questions

The exam-style writing questions reflect the language and topics learned in the unit. Students should provide sufficient detail and offer examples to support their ideas.

Exams are likely to include two writing tasks. In this Teacher's Book you will find an example answer for each of the different kinds of writing tasks (e.g. report, article, review). Each one shows how exam-style questions could be answered.

And finally . . .

I would like to thank the teachers who have tried and tested this course over many years. Your views and comments have given me great encouragement to persevere with this work. I hope everyone will continue to find this course a helpful aid to teaching and exam preparation.

Marian Barry, 2017

Unit 1
Happiness and success

Overview

The main aims of this unit are to help students study more effectively by developing their spelling strategies, to help them keep work organised, and to encourage them to choose a good dictionary. This will develop their comprehension skills to improve their ability to write descriptions of friends, close relatives and people they admire from a distance.

Theme and skills

The theme of this unit is happiness. The main areas for discussion are:

a   personal:

* What makes you happy?
* If you are feeling unhappy, what kind of things can you do about it?
* Would setting goals give you more control of your life or make you feel more pressurised?

b   more abstract:

* Should the right to happiness be placed above other considerations?
* What are the principles of a happy life?
* Do achievement and success bring happiness, or does happiness come from inside you?

The reading items are a quiz on happiness from a popular magazine, a magazine article about one woman's way of being happy, an interview with someone who didn't learn to read until she was an adult, and comments about a high-flying young entrepreneur who supports small businesses.

Students also listen to a radio interviewer asking a journalist whether the sacrifice of personal happiness is the 'price of greatness'.

Reading comprehension is extended through work on deductive reasoning skills. Students are encouraged to describe people in a way that reveals personality and character. They learn to use more complex clauses and a wider vocabulary, and give evidence to support opinions. A wide range of reading techniques are introduced including skim reading, scanning and reading for detailed meaning.

Language work

Students' vocabulary is enlarged through work on homophones, figurative language, adjectival collocations and colour imagery.

Spelling is made easier to understand through consideration of the links between speech sounds and spelling patterns, spelling rules and silent letters. The 'look, say, cover, write, check' method is introduced as an approach to learning new spellings quickly.

The *Grammar spotlight* contrasts uses of the present simple and continuous tenses, using examples students have encountered in reading texts in the unit.

Before you begin

As this is the first lesson in the course, you may like to use a little time before you start the unit to answer students' main queries about the IGCSE in ESL course, what it involves and how the course can help them build the skills needed for success. Let them know that the end of each unit has a section of exam-style questions, followed by advice and a summary of the main areas focused on in the unit.

A What is happiness?

1 Quiz

The topic of happiness is introduced through a quiz. Tell students not to worry about each individual word but to try to understand the gist of the language. However, students may need some help with the following vocabulary: *approval, ideal, hidden motive, light-hearted, hurtful, sacrifices, nasty, pursue, purpose*. You could either pick this vocabulary out before students do the quiz and check its meaning with your class or encourage students to look up the meaning of these words in a dictionary. The scores are at the end of the unit.

TEACHING SUPPORT

Happiness is an abstract concept which means different things to different people. For this reason, you could introduce it by writing the question, 'What is happiness?' on the board before students look at the quiz. This will give them an opportunity to begin thinking about the major theme of the unit. At this stage, you may need to guide students towards ideas by asking questions, e.g. *'Does happiness come from spending time with your family or by being successful?'*

LEARNING SUPPORT

Offer readers who require more support the opportunity to prepare the quiz in advance at home by reading it to check understanding and looking up any unknown vocabulary but not answering the questions, which they should still do with a partner in class. Alternatively, it may be helpful to provide a glossary for language which might hold students up (e.g. *make up* = stop arguing and become friendly again, *my heart lifts* = I become happy, *go for* = choose).

2 Discussion

A   The quiz suggests that people who are living their life by a set of clear personal values are the happiest. However, as this belief may not be held in all cultures you might like to ask:

'Is self-sacrifice necessary for the benefit of family or community?'

'Is it right to put your own happiness before anything else?

B & C   Encourage students to discuss the things which make them feel happy. You could suggest some specific things which make you feel happy as examples first.

D   It's interesting to explore what students can do if they *don't* feel happy. You could start by asking them to identify specific causes of unhappiness, e.g. being refused permission to stay out late, not being chosen for the school team. You could ask: *'What can help you feel better?'*. Answers might be: talking to a close friend about how he/she coped in a similar situation, or deciding to forget about it by doing something enjoyable, such as absorbing yourself in a favourite hobby.

LEARNING SUPPORT

Before students discuss the questions, revise the language of discussion. Ask students how you might ask someone for their opinion, offer your opinion, agree or disagree –

e.g. What do *you think about?, In my view …, I disagree with you, I don't see it like that, to me …* and so on. You can **support** students by encouraging them to make use of this language in their discussion on happiness. Monitor to check that they are doing so. You can **challenge** students by focusing on extending conversations beyond the questions on the page by asking other questions related to the theme under discussion, e.g. *'What do we seem to have become obsessed by the idea of happiness?' 'Can anyone be happy all the time?' 'Why?' 'Why not?'*

Students who struggle with discussion activities may benefit from a list of statements to agree or disagree with rather than the more open discussion offered in A. For example: *It is better never to worry about what other people think of you.; If you are too individualistic, you will have no friends.; People who think only about their own happiness are selfish.* These students may also need some time to think through what they will say and make notes.

When doing questions B–C, encourage students to follow the language model provided by beginning each item in their list with a gerund form.

3 Formal and informal styles

Students will be developing their awareness of formal and informal styles throughout the course. As an introduction, ask them when they think it is appropriate to use the different styles (informal for friends, school newsletters and family; more formal for newspapers and factual writing). It's also worth reminding them that serious writing will use occasional colloquialisms and idiomatic expressions.

Answers

1 B   **2** D   **3** A   **4** C

4 Spelling patterns and speech sounds

Students need to be able to spell high-frequency words without difficulty, e.g. *book, magazine, people*. However, English spelling is a complex area and the occasional spelling mistake is not disastrous and will not prevent a highly able student performing well.

The letter *q* in English is always followed by the letter *u*. The sound is usually /kw/ but you may like to elicit some exceptions, e.g. *cheque, quay, quiche, queue*, after the students have completed the exercise.

Answers

1   queen
2   quotation
3   quack
4   banquet

Elicit examples of other speech sounds and spelling patterns.

Examples:

ck at the end of words, pronounced /k/: *lock, tick, sock*
ch pronounced /tʃ/: *church, patch, change*
ch pronounced /k/: *chemist, technology, mechanic*
sh pronounced /ʃ/: *shout, push, mushroom*

5 Approaches to spelling

The aim here is to elicit students' previous knowledge of spelling patterns. After they have ticked the strategies they use to help them spell, ask them what they do about words they always misspell.

6 Look, say, cover, write, check

This is an uncomplicated method of memorising spellings. There is a similar exercise in every unit. It's a good idea to emphasise the simplicity of the method. When they get the hang of it, students can learn spellings effectively and with a lower failure rate than with many other methods. Of course, they'll also be using other methods, such as spelling rules and how speech sounds are linked to spelling patterns.

7 Tricky words

These tricky words are often spelled wrongly by students. Ask them to say each word aloud clearly to check pronunciation. It's useful to ask for a definition or example sentence for each word.

Students should go through the 'look, say, cover, write, check' method to memorise the spelling of each tricky word. It's important they don't miss out any steps. Once they feel confident that they have imprinted the image of the word on their mind, they should write it three times.

8 Why are words misspelt?

This exercise highlights a few of the most common problems as a starting point. You can start by asking: '*Which words do you always misspell?*' Students are often aware of their own weak points, such as confusing the endings of words which have similar sounds but a different spelling.

Encourage them to work together to brainstorm all their ideas and encourage them to think about the root of the problem.

When *ps* or *pn* begin a word, the *p* is silent. Other examples: *psalm, pseudonym, pneumonia.*

Words like *truthful* are often spelled wrongly because the addition of the suffix to *truth* sounds like '*full*'. Other examples: *peaceful, hopeful, playful.*

Activities is sometimes misspelled because students forget the rule that a *-y* ending changes to *-ies* if the preceding letter is a consonant. Other examples: *ceremonies, lorries, factories, families, babies, ladies.* Words with a vowel before the final *-y* simply add *s* to make a plural: *boys, holidays, highways.*

The ending of *responsible* is often misspelled '*able*'. Other adjectives ending in *-ible* are *edible, incredible, invisible.* But many words end in *-able*, e.g. *washable, reliable, advisable, excitable, approachable.* There is no simple rule for choosing the right ending. Tell students it's better to learn each spelling through the 'look, say, cover, write, check' method.

Calm has a silent '*l*'. Other examples: *talk, yolk, almond.*

Committee presents problems because students are not sure whether to use a single or double *m* and *t.*

Embarrassment presents similar difficulties to *committee*, as does *accommodation.* Each of these words has *two* sets of double consonants.

Wrist has a silent *w*. Other examples of a silent *w*: *write, wrap, wrinkle, wrestle.*

Encourage students to proofread their work for careless spelling errors, paying particular attention to words that present difficulties for them as individuals.

9 How helpful is your dictionary?

You may like to bring in a variety of dictionaries, or get students to pool and compare their own dictionaries, using the brief checklist as a guide.

It might be helpful to do some follow-up work on the abbreviations used in dictionaries, and the extra features some dictionaries have. These might include a key to pronunciation, tables of weights and measures, or explanations of common acronyms.

You can integrate dictionary work with other projects and in other curriculum areas. Students sometimes respond best to dictionary work which is linked to practical applications (as part of a reading comprehension or during a writing task, for example) rather than work on a dictionary for its own sake.

10 Getting organised

When students start a new course of study, they need to be well-organised. Remind students that the work in the course is sequential and they need to keep lesson notes carefully, as they will need them later. Showing how a file can be organised (e.g. with dividers), perhaps using a well-kept file as an example, can be very helpful.

Some teachers like to set a special, regular time for organisation of course notes and spelling/vocabulary books.

B Happy not to be a high-flyer

1 Before you read

A   Eliciting students' responses to the photograph is a good way to introduce the topic of describing people. Tina has a warm smile. You might like to elicit other collocations for smile, e.g. *a shy smile, a bright smile, a friendly smile*.

   You could ask students to study Tina's eyes for clues to her character, e.g. *'Does she look confident/cold/secretive/shy/warm/nervous?'*

B   The articles comes from a women's magazine and features an interview with a woman who doesn't believe in sacrificing everything to achieve success.

Vocabulary check: answers

a priority: something you think is more important than other things

insignificant: of little importance

trivial: similar in meaning to insignificant

2 Comprehension check
Answers

1   They feel she could achieve more / she is only an assistant.

2   her family

3   because she realises more responsibility at work would involve too many personal sacrifices

4   Her attitude to life is positive. She makes the most of the life she has.

3 Principles of a happy life

Explain to students how to skim read, if necessary. It requires reading quickly to get the main idea, without pausing to focus on individual detail. Students may disagree about some of the principles in the list, and it will be interesting to explore why. For example, you could ask:

'Is it really a bad idea to try to impress other people?'

'Is it always harmful to regret decisions you made in the past?'

> **LEARNING SUPPORT**
>
> Check whether all students understand and can explain to their peers the word *principle* – if necessary, explain that a *principle* is a rule or belief that someone lives by, e.g. *John doesn't believe in putting money before people. He won't compromise his principles just to be successful.* As a means of checking understanding, elicit examples of other principles, e.g. being kind to others. Once students have skim read the list of principles, you may want to check that they understand **key language** including *regret something* (to be sorry or sad about something you did), *envy someone* (to feel that you want something that someone else has), *status, material possessions and achieve*.

4 Finding examples

Remind students that scanning a text means a search through the text looking to spot evidence, sometimes going back as well as forward. (The comparison with having a brain scan or baby scan in hospital might be useful.)

The discussion will be useful as students often find matching abstract ideas to concrete examples hard because it involves thinking about how theories can be applied in practice. Ask them to concentrate on getting their message across in the group, rather than on grammatical accuracy. After the groups have thought through their ideas, you may like to elicit the main points and write them up for everybody.

Possible answers

She says her mother wanted her to have a job with more status but this hasn't troubled her. This shows she doesn't hold resentment against her parents.

She says her relationships are more important to her than academic or career success, which shows she doesn't value status or material things more than people.

She says she realises how tied down she is when friends go off travelling, but she accepts that she cannot do this. This shows she doesn't envy other people.

She says she doesn't want a more senior role at work because that would mean another part of her life would suffer. This shows she is realistic about what she can achieve.

The pleasure of her job comes from feeling it's worthwhile rather than the status of it, which shows she has chosen a job which gives her real satisfaction.

5 Sharing ideas

The concept of 'happiness principles' will vary according to the interests and maturity of your group. Extra ideas to discuss could be:

Don't let small worries take over your life.

Do try to take responsibility for solving your problems.

Do give the important people in your life most of your attention.

Don't spend time with people who make you miserable.

Do try to be peaceful.

6 Discussion

You could introduce the discussion topic by asking students:

'How far is it worth giving up daily pleasures in order to have success later?'

'Can you have everything? Is part of maturity accepting that you can't?'

7 Goal setting

In this exercise, students explore the value of setting goals. You can focus the exercise by giving further examples of immediate goals (telephone a friend, return library books), medium-term goals (complete school project, save up for new clothes) and long-term goals (train as a pilot, have a house of my own).

The exercise could open into an interesting discussion about when you should change your goals. You could ask: *'What would you say to someone whose goal was to become a ballet dancer/athlete? At 14 he/she is told he/she's too tall/ the wrong build to ever be successful.'*

8 Figurative meanings

There are many idioms in English. You could introduce the exercise by adapting a phrase from the reading passage:

'When Tina's friends travel abroad, she feels tied down.' You could ask *'Is she tied down by ropes or is it just a feeling?'*

Answers
1   wrestling
2   lifts
3   fighting
4   broke
5   battling
6   buried
7   crippled

Some other common expressions are:

a broken heart, an explosive argument, a stormy relationship.

It would be very interesting to elicit examples of figurative expressions in the students' own language(s).

TEACHING SUPPORT

'Figurative language' describes words or phrases which are not literal in meaning. Another word for figurative language is *metaphor*. If we tell someone, *'you're a star'* we are not suggesting that they are a ball of burning gas in the night sky, but that they are brilliant or special in some way. That is, they seem to shine. We use figurative language or metaphor to make a comparison between things or people and suggest that those things or people share a particular quality.

What we see in this exercise is metaphors in the form of verbs, e.g. *to bury yourself in your work, to fight the authorities.* Everyday language is often made up of such metaphorical words and phrases, but we don't notice because they have been part of our language for so long.

LEARNING SUPPORT

Allow students who require **support** to focus initially on just three examples (e.g. 1, 3, 5). They should use a dictionary to check the original, literal meaning and discuss with a partner what the figurative meaning is. What do these three examples have in common? All three verbs are associated with fighting, and express the idea of facing something difficult.

9 Homophones

Check your students' pronunciation of the homophones as it is important that they produce sounds which are exactly

13

the same. Sometimes students confuse minimal pairs, e.g. *still/steal, live/leave*, with homophones.

Answers

1 place

2 pain

3 peace

4 whole

5 allowed

6 pear

7 sight

8 There

9 four

10 sore

10 More homophones

Answers

1 steel

2 mail

3 you're

4 weak

5 our

6 bare

7 tale

8 sail

9 pour/pore

10 whale

The English language has a relatively wide variety of homophones. Again, it would be interesting to elicit examples from your students' own language(s).

C The price of greatness

1 Before you listen

TEACHING SUPPORT

See the Introduction for a general approach to helping students with Listening tasks.

The listening is an interview about the theories in a book *The Price of Greatness*. The speaker suggests that a disproportionate number of great thinkers have suffered from ill health or genetic disability, or come from lonely, stressful backgrounds. The speaker ends by suggesting that ordinary children can do very well through hard work.

The pre-listening exercise gets students thinking about someone they admire and exploring reasons for their views. Remind them, as always, to keep their notes as they will need them later.

(The photograph is of Nelson Mandela.)

2 Vocabulary check

Answers

1 E   2 H   3 G   4 A   5 C   6 D   7 F   8 B

3 Listening: Radio interview 🔊 CD 1, Track 2

The comprehension questions focus on the attitudes of the speaker and the interviewer. This is an area which is very challenging for IGCSE students as it requires an appreciation of difficult aspects of language, such as inference.

Let students hear the whole conversation through once to get the gist. After they have listened, you could ask some basic comprehension questions such as *'Does Steve think great thinkers had happy lives? Why/Why not?'*

Let them listen a second or third time, pausing the recording if necessary. When you check the comprehension, replay any parts of the conversation which students are confused by.

LEARNING SUPPORT

To **support** students who need extra help, provide them with a short list of easier, factual true/false questions for use on first listening, which will contribute to the understanding of the more difficult multiple choice questions later. For example: *The book is about sacrificing happiness to achieve great things.* (True); *Most gifted people had an easy childhood.* (False), etc. Break the listening into sections, and allow the students to confer and check understanding after each section. Then, before moving on to the multiple choice questions, give the students plenty of time to full understand the wording of the questions, which may itself be challenging. If students are still struggling after repeated listening, give them copies of the sections of the audioscript which contain the answers and allow them to follow this as they listen.

Answers

1 b   2 a   3 c   4 b

AUDIOSCRIPT

Listen to this radio interview and choose the best answer for each question.

INTERVIEWER: And time now for our interview of the day and my guest in the studio this afternoon is Steve Bowman. Steve's been reading an absolutely wonderful book, so he tells me, all about how you may have to sacrifice a lot of personal happiness if you genuinely want to achieve great things. Steve, what's the book called and can you please tell us what makes great achievers different from everyone else?

STEVE: Well, the main thing as I understand in this book, *The Price of Greatness* by Professor Ludwig, which is truly a fascinating study of great and original thinkers, Einstein, Picasso and so on, is that they have an enormous ... an enormous inner drive to succeed.

I: Hmmm. Far higher, you'd say, than the average person?

S: Much higher. And then there's the inborn talent. It's suggested in the book that you need a precise blend of brain chemicals which are inherited.

I: So parents do play a part?

S: Yes, indeed. But what is a lot more surprising is how much ... how much the environment plays in extraordinary achievement. Most people aren't aware of the setbacks these people suffered. Did you realise that a huge number of gifted people lost a parent before the age of fourteen? Others suffered from, you know ... a genetic disability of some kind. Or had a major illness like polio or TB before adulthood.

I: So Steinbeck wouldn't have become a great writer if he hadn't had pneumonia as a teenager?

S: That sort of idea, yes.

I: Ah, well, I ... I don't know. Surely a great many people got terrible illnesses, they lost a mum or dad – well especially if you're talking about the past – and

they didn't go on to split the atom (or) whatever.

S: It's the combination of many factors that's important. Obviously, many people have got ... got problems but are not going to be the next Nobel prizewinner. With great achievers, you can't just pick out one or two factors. It's a very complex web.

I: What other factors might you reasonably expect to find?

S: Clever but frustrated parents, erm, possibly brothers and sisters who they may have close but difficult relationships with, all these factors ...

I: But you would expect these ... well, these setbacks to be, er, very damaging to their future chances, wouldn't you? And you're saying they were not, in fact?

S: It seems that such children suffered from a feeling of ... well, a ... a feeling of inferiority, of not being good enough, which pushed them onwards to achieve more and more.

I: Hmmm. So as adults, many of them will have ended with a very unhappy emotional life though, won't they?

S: They've probably suffered from depression ... what Professor Ludwig calls a sense of psychological unease.

I: Well, Steve, you've told us about the very many drawbacks these people have. What does the budding genius seem to need?

S: Peace and quiet. They need to bury themselves in work. As children, they're loners and spend a lot of time by themselves.

I: And what might you tell parents who might ... well, you know ... might like to think they're bringing up the next Nobel prizewinner?

S: If you want your child to be well, you know, well adjusted, forget about greatness. If you want your child to be kind to others and what have you,

you're cutting down your child's chances to excel.

I: Do any of us want children growing up burdened with … well you've described it very well as psychological unease?

S: Yes, it … it may be that the … the sacrifice of personal happiness may indeed be the price of greatness. But, er, I wouldn't say that you ought to stop trying to achieve your potential. Er … think of it this way: you might have an ordinary kid, who, well, mightn't be the next superstar, the next Picasso, but everyone's got their own … their own individual potential. You've got to make the most of that.

I: So how can ordinary children fulfil themselves?

S: Studies have shown that ordinary children who are well balanced in their lives but achieve a lot – they play football for school leagues, or win prizes for chess, art, music or whatever – well, it's five per cent talent and the rest is hard work.

I: Ah ha! So you're saying you don't have to give up all enjoyment – it's important to keep a balance, isn't it?

S: That's right. You can still have time to do the things you want to do.

I: Thank you, Steve. It's good to end on that positive note.

4 Post-listening discussion

A Students could relate the question to examples of well-known achievers in their own culture(s).

B It will be very interesting to hear students' responses to the idea that ordinary children can reach a high standard of achievement mostly through hard work. Encourage them to explore how far other factors, apart from talent, can help achievement, e.g. a good teacher, financial support, parental encouragement.

5 Apostrophes (1)

This exercise is to be done deductively, as students will probably know something about the use of apostrophes. Encourage them to work together to work out why

apostrophes are used here (to show the omission of letters).

You could extend the exercise by writing on the board a few examples of sentences without contractions and asking students where the apostrophes would go if contractions were used, e.g.

He might have told us he would be late.

They were not happy with the results.

Pronunciation

Even when students are able to hear contractions, they frequently have difficulty incorporating them in their own speech. Remind them that using a non-contracted form (e.g. *She would not come*) conveys meaning accurately, but it sounds much less fluent than the use of a contracted form.

6 Apostrophes (2)

The aim of this exercise is to reflect the main problems IGCSE students have with the apostrophe. These are:

a using it whenever there is a plural, whether or not possession is signified

b failing to put the apostrophe where the missing letter or letters would be in a contraction

c confusing the position of the apostrophe when it is used to show possession. Remind students that if the noun is singular, 's is added: *my mother's garden*. If the noun is plural ending in s, an apostrophe is added *after* the s: *my parents' house*. But students are often confused by plural nouns which do *not* end in s; these need 's: *the people's leader, a children's home*.

You could extend the exercise by writing up a few phrases which show possession without apostrophes, e.g.

a field belonging to a farmer

a dining room for students

a library for children

a dress belonging to Mary.

Then ask students to substitute phrases which use apostrophes, e.g. *a students' dining room*.

7 Correcting sentences

Answers

1 The teachers listened to Carol's views.

2 They've bought a new car.

3   I went to my mother's office.

4   Please don't touch the babies' clothes.

5   It's hard to explain the programme's success.

6   She works in the women's ward of the hospital.

7   He's training to be a ladies' hairdresser.

8   You'll find her in the teachers' workroom – all the staff go there.

9   He might've become the next Einstein.

10   She couldn't understand why her cat had lost its appetite.

Monitor students' pronunciation of these sentences.

8 Speculating about a photograph

The aim of this exercise is to develop students' ability to describe people. They study a photograph of Alex (who is a composite character, not a real person), invented to develop the theme of finding happiness in your own way. Alex is a high-flying young entrepreneur who has found happiness through using his skills to help people start businesses in areas of high unemployment. Students may like to discuss the challenges and risk involved in investing in such enterprises and the benefits it could bring, not only to individuals but to families, communities and the local economy. They may like to contribute ideas about family businesses they know about and the difficulties they can face.

In addition to providing a physical description, students need to be able to describe character and give reasons for their opinions, so this is a good opportunity to widen their vocabulary and help them express opinions.

You can prompt them where necessary, e.g.

'Does he look as if he has had a hard life?'

'Does he look disappointed?'

'Does he look as if he could cope in a crisis? Why/Why not?'

9 Describing personal qualities

This exercise will help to develop students' powers of deductive reasoning. It builds on the skills they developed earlier, in Exercise 1.B.4, where they looked for practical examples of 'happiness principles'.

Answers

1 yes   2 yes   3 no   4 yes   5 yes

6 no   7 yes   8 yes   9 yes   10 no

You could discuss why answers are right or wrong and get students to supply evidence from the comments about Alex.

10 Discussion

The discussion could be extended to think about the qualities necessary for achievement. It would be nice for students to consider whether their particular heroes/heroines have these qualities. You could ask them for practical examples of the way the qualities are expressed.

11 Drafting a paragraph

Students should write a paragraph describing Alex. They can mention his appearance and describe his qualities.

Possible answer

A possible paragraph could run something like this:

> Alex looks relaxed and casual but he is very determined and hard-working. He has great optimism and belief in the resilience of people to overcome problems and make a business idea into a success. He wants to make the world a fairer place and to help others start their own businesses. He believes in himself and can tolerate criticism. Even if some business projects fail, he perseveres to do what he thinks is right. (*74 words*)

Encourage students to discuss their first draft with a partner. Remind them that rewriting is not a sign of failure, but simply part of the writing process.

D   Obstacles and challenges

1 Expressing fears and giving someone confidence

TEACHING SUPPORT

Before students begin this exercise, write the word *obstacle* on the board. Drill its pronunciation /ˈɒbstək(ə)l/ and then check that students understand the meaning of the word. An obstacle refers to anything that blocks someone's path and stops them from making progress. This could be an actual object, e.g. *The competitors have to get past six obstacles on the track in the fastest time.* Or it could be

17

something abstract, e.g. *My brother's lack of confidence in himself has been a real obstacle in his life. It's even stopped him from applying for certain jobs.*

Students study and practise the functional language in pairs. You could elicit from them the things they get anxious about.

You might like to elicit other phrases students may know to express fear, e.g. *I really dread …, I panic when I think about it.*

LEARNING SUPPORT

While more confident students can be **challenged** to expand their dialogues into mini conversations, students who require additional **support** could focus on one (or two) simpler dialogues. They could then swap partners with another pair so they have a further opportunity to practise the language.

TEACHING SUPPORT

See the Introduction for a general approach to helping students with Speaking tasks.

Practice

Students can practise expressing fears and giving reassurance in pairs. You could ask a pair of students who have done particularly well to perform an example to the whole class.

2 Pre-reading discussion

Students are going to read an article about a woman who was illiterate. She explains how her unhappy school days resulted in not learning to read. She disguised her problem, not even telling her husband, until the headteacher at her daughter's school asked her to take a job as a paid helper. The headteacher had recognised Monica's illiteracy and helped her to learn to read. Now Monica works as a 'parent-educator'; she involves parents in the education of their children.

3 Vocabulary check

Answers

bullied: when a person is frequently hurt physically or emotionally

illiterate: unable to read or write

volunteer: person who works without pay, often for a charity

4 Reading: Textual organisation

TEACHING SUPPORT

See the Introduction for a general approach to helping students with Reading tasks.

Before students start reading, you could ask them to predict something about the content of the article from the title.

LEARNING SUPPORT

For students who need more **support**, pre-teach vocabulary from the text or prepare a glossary for them to refer to. Items might include *to fool somebody, to dare to do something, to disguise, take over, unaware, struggles, pushy,* etc. Have them read, match and check the first three paragraphs only (to line 47) before completing the text. If possible, since this is a long text, it may be helpful for struggling readers to read the text at home ahead of the lesson but complete the activities in class.

Answers

A 7 **B** 2 **C** 1 **D** 5 **E** 3 **F** 6 **G** 4

5 Comprehension check

Students may reflect on the fact that illiteracy is a problem, even in richer countries. Encourage them to empathise with the embarrassment Monica felt and understand why says she could not 'join in the life other people were living'.

Answers

1 She disliked school because she felt like a failure / the other children made fun of her / she did not understand the lessons.

2 Monica hid the fact she couldn't read by saying she'd left her glasses at home, or she'd carry a book or newspaper around and pretend to read it.

3 i She was terrified.

   ii Students could infer that the headteacher noticed qualities such as empathy and natural intelligence that made her ideal for teaching.

4 The writer's attitude is positive, which is shown through numerous examples the author gives of

Monica's strength of character and the admiration she has earned from Sally

5   The third statement is incorrect.

6   **a**   120

     b   130

     c   April

     d   January, March, September

     e   November

6 Vocabulary: Odd one out

Answers

1   confident

2   angry

3   shy

7 Post-reading discussion

Monica took responsibility for changing herself from an insecure, illiterate woman to the person she is today. Her happiness seems to come from having satisfying work, being able to join in with ordinary life and from her daughter's success. Her 'achievements' are linked to her personal qualities. She is able to persevere to reach a goal, to be honest about herself, to give to others and to show warmth. In this sense, her happiness has come out of the person she is.

An interesting theme to draw out in discussion is '*How can someone with a low self-image gain self-esteem?*' You could link the responses to the example set by Monica.

International overview

Answers

1   17%

2   poverty, unemployment and ill-health.

3   Encourage any suggestions relating to a stronger economy, more international trade, and a healthier, better qualified and more fulfilled population.

4   The United Nations agencies have reliable figures on national literacy rates.

You could also discuss why more women than men are illiterate, eliciting ideas such as the fact that, in many countries, girls are expected to devote a lot of time to very basic household and family duties, e.g. fetching water and fuel to cook with, thus robbing them of time to go to school. Also, in some countries, schooling is very expensive and the opportunity is given to the male members of the household.

As always, encourage students to relate the information to the situation in their own countries. You could point out that in many of the world's affluent nations, it was the custom to give priority to boys' education until relatively recently.

8 Describing people

Sweet tells us that Monica's husband was a kind and thoughtful man. Sometimes, one adjective can provide just the right amount of information. The important thing is to choose the adjective which you think best describes someone or something.

The description of Sally's smile suggests that her relationship with her mother is a very close one. The writer conveys this to the reader by the use of the adjective *warm*, which suggests affection or kindness.

9 Using a wide range of adjectives

The aim of this exercise is to look at a variety of ways of describing people. Remind students to focus on both appearance and character. Elicit other examples of adjectives and adjective compounds.

> **TEACHING SUPPORT**
>
> See the Introduction for a general approach to helping students with new vocabulary.

> **LEARNING SUPPORT**
>
> To **support** students, offer some practice with forming compound adjectives to reinforce understanding. For example: a man with grey hair (*grey-haired*), a woman with a kind heart (*kind-hearted*), a bus driver with a bad temper (*bad-tempered*); someone who looks cross (*cross-looking*), someone who looks friendly (*friendly-looking*), someone who looks scary (*scary-looking*).

10 Adjective collocations/11 Positive and negative

Instead of working in pairs, students could be divided into four groups and each group assigned to one of the headings.

Answers

Appearance

slim ✓, plump ✗, well-dressed ✓, elegant ✓, scruffy ✗, overweight ✗, skinny ✗

Hair
wavy, straight, curly, frizzy ✖

Voice
deep, grating ✖, husky, quiet, high-pitched, gentle ✓

Character
shy, placid, ambitious, tolerant ✓, absent-minded, quiet, self-centred ✖, dreamy, mean ✖, altruistic ✓, generous ✓, considerate ✓, outgoing ✓, gentle ✓, argumentative ✖, bad-tempered ✖, domineering ✖, humorous ✓

Point out that the connotation of some words is subjective, e.g. *ambitious* will sound positive to some people and negative to others.

12 Negative prefixes

It's useful to compare the way opposites are formed in English with students' own language(s).

Answers
irresponsible
disloyal
immature
insecure
untrustworthy
unreliable
inefficient
unhappy
dishonest

13 Colour

Focusing on the role of colour in appearance will help make students' writing more vivid. You could ask them to link each other's colouring and clothes to images in the natural world.

Being creative
Students could read their sentences aloud to each other for fun and feedback.

14 Developing your writing style

The following sequence of exercises builds on the earlier work on adjective collocations. The exercises will help students structure more complex sentences and bring variety into their styles of writing.

Make sure students understand the meaning of the individual words in each quotation when they underline the clauses.

15 Conveying character traits

This exercise helps students understand how writers achieve their effects. Let them know that the extract describes an adult, not a child, before they begin to study it.

Analysing how a writer achieves his/her effects is very challenging. You will probably want to monitor students' analysis quite closely, prompt them with questions where necessary and give feedback on their work.

For example, through the description '*She was a tall, fragile-looking woman in a pretty blue hat that matched her eyes*' the writer conveys the impression that the woman is feminine. To help students understand this, you could ask '*Do you think she would be the type of woman who would be a tough businesswoman? Why/Why not?*'

You could ask '*What does the fact that she is wearing a pretty blue hat that matched her eyes suggest about her?*', eliciting that she is carefully dressed, perhaps in a slightly old-fashioned or traditional way. The choice of the word *pretty* suggests that the hat is attractive but not too bold. '*Is blue an exciting or a quiet, soothing colour? What does that tell us about her?*'

16 Writing your own description

> **TEACHING SUPPORT**
>
> See the Introduction for a general approach to helping students with Writing tasks.

Give students up to 20 minutes to write their descriptions. Encourage them to use what they have learnt in Unit 1, e.g. clauses with *which/that* and adjective collocations.

Feedback
Encourage students to give constructive feedback. They should say what they liked about a description, e.g. *I liked the way you said Simon puts his downloads into alphabetical order. That gives us a real sense of what he's like.* If they disliked something about a description, they should say how they think it could be improved, e.g. *You described Simon as 'trustworthy'. I'd have liked more information about why he is someone you can trust.* For example, '*I liked the way you showed that he is a methodical person by explaining that he keeps all his DVDs and books neatly, and in alphabetical order.*'

E Someone I admire

1 Example description

Students should study the description.

As always in the Student's Book, the example shows a range of things students could say, and aims to stimulate creativity. Although based on exam-type questions, these examples are *not* meant to be learned by heart to be reproduced in an exam.

The main topic of each paragraph is:

1 Simon's appearance and character traits
2 Why the writer admires Simon
3 Why Simon is a good friend
4 Conclusion

Comprehension check: suggested answers

1 He gives the impression of being studious, particular in his habits, and not concerned about his appearance.
2 He was unhappy at school because the other students said he was 'scruffy'.
3 Simon is determined because he was painfully shy but he overcame this through his own efforts.
4 The writer values Simon's friendship because he is trustworthy and straightforward and helped him face his fears.

Format

This exercise helps students to see how all the techniques are used in combination.

Beginnings and Endings

You may like to draw students' attention to the fact that the beginning is clear and to the point, and the final sentence sums up the writer's feelings very firmly so the reader is in no doubt of the writer's viewpoint.

2 Comparing two styles

The aim of this exercise is to show students how they can improve their writing style. It also shows the value of drafting work and taking advice. Encourage your students to see that the style of the first draft could be improved by the use of clauses and more vivid description.

3 Rewriting to improve style

In order to rewrite something, students first need to identify what needs to be improved. Read out the description and draw attention to the weakness of its style: the sentences are too short, which makes the description repetitive; the adjectives are too simple (*good, big, nice*) which means we are not given a memorable picture of the writer's friend.

Students could produce something like this:

My friend has large, sparkling green eyes and close-cropped blonde hair. She smiles often, showing her lovely white teeth. She is well-dressed with a style of her own. She enjoys studying other people and says she can judge their character from their clothes. She is a very hard-working student who gets high marks. She is kind, considerate and generous and never minds helping me with my homework.

4 Writing from notes

Many students will have heard of Lister and the theory of antisepsis from science classes. Lister was influenced by Pasteur's germ theory, which claimed that bacteria can cause disease, and that fermentation and rotting are caused by bacteria which live in the air. It would be nice to let students outline the main ideas before they tackle the rewriting from notes.

This is a good time to remind students that they can draw on knowledge from other areas of the curriculum to answer exam questions. However, they will have to make their knowledge fit properly into the context of the question. It would also be interesting here to ask about notable scientific advances made by scientists from the students' own culture(s).

It's worth highlighting '*anti*' as a prefix meaning 'to counteract or be opposite to'. Other examples to elicit could be: *antidote, antibody, antibiotic, anticlockwise, antiperspirant, antisocial.*

Example answer

I want to describe Joseph Lister. He was a surgeon who was born in 1827. In those days many patients died after operations because their wounds became badly infected. Lister wondered if (the) bacteria in the air which made meat decay also made wounds septic.

Lister decided to clean everything which touched (the) patients' wounds with carbolic acid. The carbolic acid destroyed all the germs/Carbolic acid destroys all germs. As a result of these precautions, patients recovered quickly after/from (their) operations. The rate of infection fell dramatically.

Lister developed safe, antiseptic operations, which was a major medical advance. He received many awards for his work. I admire him because he was dedicated and unselfish. He took great personal risks to make this discovery. Surgery used to be highly dangerous. People were terrified of the surgeon's knife. Lister changed all that. Modern surgery is a lifesaver.

Grammar spotlight

TEACHING SUPPORT

See the Introduction for a general approach to helping students with Grammar exercises.

Write the following sentences on the board and ask students to highlight which verb forms are wrong. Elicit or point out that 'knowing' and 'understanding' are incorrect because verbs which describe mental processes are rarely used in the continuous form. You could write examples of incorrect use on the board, e.g.

She is knowing several languages.

I am talking slowly but he is still not understanding me.

Answers

1 Josh is arguing with his friend Ken. He never normally argues with anyone.
2 You seem very quiet this morning.
3 Helping other people makes her happy.

TEACHING SUPPORT

If your students are advanced, or particularly enjoying the work, you may like to extend the exercise on the present continuous by exploring the ways that the present continuous form is also used to refer to the future e.g., *I'm seeing my friends tonight/We're playing tennis later today.*

LEARNING SUPPORT

Ask students who require extra **support** to explain to you the difference between the present simple and continuous, based on their existing knowledge, giving examples of each. If this is problematic, prompt them with contrasting examples (e.g. girl texting her mum: *I'm waiting outside the school. Please come and pick me up!* And girl complaining to her friend: *I wait for my mum outside school every day. She's always late!*). Provide a few practice sentences for students to complete with the correct form of the verb.

Exam-style questions

See the Overview of *Cambridge IGCSE English as a Second Language* section at the beginning of the Student's Book for the mark scheme and criteria for marking the writing questions.

Writing

2 Describing someone close to you – article

Example answer

The example shows one way students could respond effectively to the question. Remind students that when bullet points are given they should be covered to gain full marks, as in the example. The article recycles the vocabulary and expressions from the unit for describing people. In this case, a family member is described, but students are free to choose anyone they feel close to. The tone and register of the article sounds friendly and is suitable for the audience (a website aimed at teenagers).

My grandfather is a tall, humorous man with silver-grey, curly hair and a warm smile. Before he came to live with us, my twin brother and I used to argue all the time, but once my grandfather was living with us, we stopped. He often tells us funny stories about my mum when she was young, and we love hearing how naughty she was. He also takes us out to places we enjoy, such as the cinema and sports matches.

My grandfather is very practical. He taught me how to cut and measure wood and lets me use his tools. With his help, I recently made a coffee table, which I really like. I feel I have good practical skills now but only because my grandfather trained me, as I don't do subjects like design and technology at school.

Before my grandfather came, I used to get very upset if I did not achieve a goal, and also if my brother did better than me. My grandfather said that being a good person is what really matters, and to make that my goal. His words have helped me feel more peaceful and be more satisfied with what I do achieve. *(200 words)*

(Reading & Writing, Exercise 5: 16 marks (Extended).)

Listening 🔊 CD 1, Track 3

This multiple choice exercise reflects the themes of the unit. It should prepare students for what they might face in the actual exam. Students need to listen for genuine understanding and then identify the specific details which enable them to find the correct answer. They should read the statements carefully first, and then scan the options for the correct answer as they listen.

Encourage students to check their answers after the first listening, and to use the second listening to double check. As this is a challenging exercise, you may choose to let them listen more than twice.

Answers

1 b   **2** b   **3** a   **4** a   **5** a   **6** b   **7** a   **8** b

(Listening, Exercise 4: 8 marks (Core); 8 marks (Extended).)

AUDIOSCRIPT

You will hear Victor, a radio presenter, asking Carlos Gomez, a teenage blogger, some questions about his hobby as part of a radio feature on developing potential in young people. Listen to their conversation and choose the correct answer for each question. You will hear the interview twice.

PRESENTER:	Today we have an exciting guest, teenage blogger Carlos Gomez. Welcome to the show, Carlos.
CARLOS:	Thank you Victor. Pleased to be here.
P:	Our listeners would love to hear about your amazing blog, *boyzownzone*, which is one of the most successful in the blogosphere. What do you blog about?
C:	Anything! Well, that is not strictly true. I'm very selective about what I blog about. A blog – it says a lot about you as a person.
P:	That's a good point. I suppose blogging gives everyone the opportunity to give their opinions and well, just be yourself. And there are certainly some amazing blogs on the internet.
C:	There are some fabulous blogs for teenagers, but they are mainly for teenage girls. If I'm honest the motive for doing my blog in the first place was that

23

I thought it was something I could achieve. I said to myself, 'Carlos come on, start your own blog. It can't be all that hard.' I wanted to achieve a blog that would be interesting to read.

P: So you blog about your daily life, what you are doing at the moment, with a focus on activities boys like?

C: That is absolutely correct. I love blogging about scientific inventions … that is one of my favourite things. I used to focus on teenage boy inventors but now I write about anyone who deserves recognition even if many people haven't heard of them or their work.

P: You have sections dedicated to different topics: music, art, football. It is not all about inventions.

C: And don't forget my book review section! I am a reading fanatic and have reviewed some amazing books. People say boys only want to watch action movies or play on the Playstation but now I gets loads of hits from boys about books I recommend. I also get comments from little kids, mums, dads and grandparents who want to buy books for their grandchildren. One lady asked her local bookseller for one of the books I had recommended, and he said that the book became his bestselling book overnight.

P: Sounds like you have made reading cool. That is not bad.

C: I got a brilliant post from a boy who said that he used to be anti-reading unless it was social media, and he wasn't very interested in that. He used to play computer games all the time. Then he started reading 'The Dark in their Eyes' which is the horror series I blog about. I guarantee these books are as thrilling as any action movie. He says he is now a reading addict, just as I am. His friends can't believe it! He's a total bookworm!

P: I hear you are interested in the *Wonderworld* series of comic books. They have very unusual drawings, don't they?

C: *Wonderworld* is laugh-out-loud funny. Comic books with a difference! My family say the illustrations are strange and they would prefer pictures of flowers or sunsets, but that kind of art leaves me unimpressed. I look up to those artists who create the artwork – they are so talented. If I ever win the lottery, I am going to buy the original artworks and put them on my bedroom wall. The *Wonderworld* books are expensive but they are definitely worth it. I persuaded my school library to buy a set of *Wonderworld* and now almost everyone at school is on the waiting list!

P: How do you find time for all this?

C: Blogging makes me happy and is a priority. Some bloggers communicate almost constantly but, although I love sharing my news, I think quite carefully before I update my blog. However, people visit my site almost daily so I do not want to let them down by not updating. I post up a page when I get a free evening or when there is a quiet lunchtime at school.

P: Any tips for would-be bloggers who might be listening now?

C: Just go for it. Don't let your spelling or anything hold you back. People don't judge you. My grammar and spelling used to be rubbish but blogging has made my literacy better. What matters most is the people who are going to read your blog so think about what they would like. Using appealing pictures makes a big difference to the blog as well.

P: What are your future goals?

C: If I have a future goal, it is to meet one of the wonderfully talented people I have blogged about. Just to get a post from one of them would be a dream come true.

P: Thank you Carlos. We have had lots of texts coming in from listeners while we have been talking. Here is one from . . .

Wider Practice

1   Students could further develop their skills for describing clothing. Fashion websites, catalogues and magazines are a rich source of pictures to stimulate descriptive writing. Students may enjoy looking through them and choosing outfits for each other. They could write descriptions of the outfits using clothes vocabulary. It's good to elicit relevant vocabulary, e.g. *short-sleeved, made of leather*, before this exercise.

2   Tell students to imagine that they have the chance to refurbish a common room or classroom. They are to choose the colours, fabrics and furnishings. Encourage them to study manufacturers' paint charts, fabric catalogues or websites if they are available where you teach. They could write up the article for the school website.

3   Magazines, TV and radio programmes, and videos uploaded to video-sharing sites often run interviews with well-known people in which they describe key stages in their personal development. This can make an interesting follow-up to the work on happiness and life's challenges, especially if it is a personality students can identify with.

Students could be set this work as a project to research in their own language and present a translation to the class, if English-speaking TV, radio, etc. are not easily available.

4   To help students develop their ability to link character with appearance, you could bring into the class some photographs of people cut from magazines, etc. Alternatively, you could freeze a frame of a character on a video clip or DVD.

You could then ask students to study all the details of the person's appearance: facial expression, body language, clothing, shoes, accessories, hairstyle, etc. You could ask questions like:

'What kind of person is he/she? What clues do we have from his/her appearance?'

'What is he/she thinking?'

'What do you think his/her home life is like?'

'What kind of job do you think he/she does?'

Encourage students to be as speculative as possible, as there are no right answers. Students could follow up this exercise with some creative writing in which they build a situation around the character.

5   If students were intrigued by the fact that Alex Garcia became a multimillionaire by the age of 21, they may like to find out more about teenage millionaires who have made use of the internet or modern technology to build successful businesses. They could develop the project in interesting ways, support their findings with facts and statistics and present it to the class.

Unit 2
You and your community

Overview

The main aim of this unit is to develop students' ability to give information about themselves, their families and the areas they live in. In an exam, life at home and personal interests are usually put into the context of a specific community. At the end of the unit students will practise writing a welcome email to an exchange student from another country.

Theme and skills

The theme of the unit is home and community life. In addition to personal description, students are required to comment on local community issues in the role of a responsible citizen. Through discussion, reading, listening and role play the following issues are raised:

- how best to give information about ourselves and our lives in conversation.

- how we form impressions of individuals and their background

- how we can describe a favourite place in a way which makes our listeners enthusiastic too

- how to present ourselves positively in writing

- how we engage with the needs of our community in our role as citizens.

Students study a feature called 'Home Town' and a magazine article on improvements to a community hospital. They listen to a discussion about whether to convert a disused warehouse into a study centre or youth club.

Language work

This aspect of the course challenges students to communicate effectively. In order to create a memorable picture of who they are, students require not only a wide vocabulary, but also an understanding of how the language they use shapes the impression they make on others. The unit provides students with analysis and practice of presenting themselves both orally and in writing. It also develops their reading strategies, and helps them find the right tone and register in their writing.

Students' understanding of spelling is improved through studying the rules for doubling the consonant in one- and two-syllable words. Vocabulary development focuses on words for describing places and people, loan words from other languages, and colloquial language in context.

The *Grammar spotlight* looks at the use of the gerund and infinitive after various verbs, as encountered in texts in the unit.

A Home town

1 Interview / 2 Group A / 3 Group B

The aim of this role-play interview is to get students talking about their home lives. This exercise is based on an exam-style exercise in which the interviewer would be an examiner.

The questions aim to be challenging. Questions of the *'Where do you live?'* / *'How many brothers and sisters have you got?'* type have been avoided. However, it's worth letting them know that questions of this type are used in the warm-up phase of the exam.

Put students into two groups: 'journalists' and 'interviewees'. Go over the content areas and language points, making sure that students know what to do.

With the journalists group, you may choose to drill the question forms briefly and help students decide which of the prompts to include on their list. Elicit ideas of possible answers they might get in the interview and other prompts they'd like to use.

The functional language includes dealing with personal questions, being flexible/adapting questions and showing you need thinking time. It addresses the comments made by examiners (and by interviewers in general) about the difficulties of understanding how an interviewee is feeling.

It's helpful to drill the functional language with students and to check their understanding, especially in relation to dealing with personal questions.

Students will probably need examples of how they can adapt questions. You should offer prompts, such as *'I'm afraid I don't know much about my parents, but I can talk about my sister, who I live with now'* or *'I can't tell you much about a community project which improved neighbourhood facilities, but I can tell you about a project I was involved in to get a coffee bar at school.'* Obviously, the adaptation has to be sensibly related to the original question asked by the interviewer/ examiner.

It's useful to remind students that an oral examiner is likely to be looking for the ability to sustain a conversation with facts, examples and stories.

LEARNING SUPPORT

Have the 'journalists' choose three or four points from those listed and plan one question for each in written form first. Encourage them to ask a follow-up question for each, to elicit more information from the interviewee; offer them the following prompts to give them ideas: *Why …? What …? How …? Do you / Did you …?*

If students are unclear about 'open questions', offer them the following examples and ask them which may be more effective in getting information from their interviewee: *Do you like your neighbourhood? Or What do you like about your neighbourhood?*

Have the 'interviewees' prepare two or three words or phrases as prompts for themselves about each of the topics suggested in Exercise 3 (the street you live in, etc.). They should check any unknown vocabulary in a dictionary.

Set up the role play by asking students to interview you before they interview each other: this will provide them with a model to follow. You could do two short interviews about your home life. In the first, be the perfect interviewee. In the second, point out that the questions are too personal and ask for more time to think.

TEACHING SUPPORT

Role plays aren't real conversations, but a kind of show. Encourage students to see themselves as actors playing a particular part: that of a journalist doing an interview, and that of a person being interviewed for a publication. Such an approach might help students deal with nerves both in class and in the Speaking exam.

See the Introduction for a general approach to helping students with Reading tasks.

4 Honest feedback

It is helpful to analyse students' interviews to see how successful they were. Give students feedback based on your view of how well they performed in the role-play. Focus on the areas you think need the most improvement. The following are examples of what often goes wrong in interviews. Read them out in turn. Ask students to identify the problem in each case (the problem is given in brackets) and to think of solutions to those problems.

I would have talked for longer if you hadn't been yawning/ shuffling papers. (body language)

I would have felt more comfortable in the interview if you hadn't kept asking me about pets when I had told you we didn't have any. (flexibility)

I would have been able to give better answers if you'd let me think about the question a bit longer. (allowing time for answers)

Most of your answers were just one or two words. It was very hard to get the conversation going fluently. I needed detail in your answers to be able to choose the follow-up questions. (communication)

I had to keep asking you to repeat what you said because I couldn't understand you the first time. (pronunciation)

You kept using the wrong words or missing words out. I couldn't always understand what you meant. (vocabulary)

Students are asked to make a note of what they want to remember for next time, e.g. *Next time I'll think more about my body language / try to give more complete answers / try to give examples / use more open questions / listen more carefully / work at developing my vocabulary.*

5 Reading

The text is about Chris Brown, a young British scientist who is adjusting to life in the American city of Seattle. By using Chris's words, the writer gives us greater insight into Chris's life and experiences.

Answers

a 1   **b** 3   **c** 5   **d** 2   **e** 6   **f** 4

6 Discussion

Straight after the first reading, ask students what they thought of the journalist's interview skills. You can ask: *'Do you think the writer has been successful in getting Chris to talk freely about himself? How do you think he or she did this?'*

7 Detailed comprehension

> **LEARNING SUPPORT**
>
> In order to answer the questions, students will need to skim the text to get a general sense of its meaning as well as scan it to find specific information. Ask students to briefly explain to you the difference between skimming and scanning, to check their understanding. If necessary, write the following definitions and get students to identify which is which.
>
> *Looking through a text carefully to find out particular information*
>
> *Reading a text quite quickly to get the general idea.*

Answers

1 He explored the countryside on his bike. He went to Ireland on his own.

2 Suitable ideas include: Chris is confident, relaxed, open-minded, tolerant, patient, likes to think the best of people.

3 **a** He is close to them but is able to live his own life.

4 **b** The mix of indoor and outdoor activities suits him well.

5 **a** Numerous examples of his positive tone include 'so much I love about America' / 'I have inspiring colleagues' / 'even better career opportunities' / 'great city for the arts'.

6 7735 km

    a West
    b Atlantic
    c Washington, Idaho and Oregon
    d West

7 **A** There are five possible points for students to find.

- work at a cutting-edge cancer research centre
- inspiring colleagues
- colleagues who mentored him
- exciting career prospects
- more research opportunities.

B The paragraph could go along these lines.

Chris was able to work at a cutting-edge cancer research centre where he met inspiring colleagues. His colleagues have also mentored him. In addition, he has many exciting career prospects and there are more research opportunities ahead.

Vocabulary: answers

a pharmaceuticals
b carefree
c dens
d ferry
e angler
f cutting-edge
g homesick
h persevered
i mentored
j the outdoors

8 Describing Chris

thoughtful, academic, open-minded, resilient, courageous, sociable, persistent, appreciative, adventurous, curious

9 Describing Chris's family

The adjectives in the box can all be used to describe Chris's family and friends. Encourage students to use a dictionary to check the meaning of any words they don't know. They can then work in pairs to match the adjectives that have a similar meaning. Once students have completed the matching exercise, ask them to find the information in the text which lets us know that Chris' family and friends are supportive, fun-loving, hospitable, etc. Give students the following example to help them: *We know Chris's family are supportive because he says that when he was feeling low, his parents encouraged him to keep going and not to give up.*

Answers

close-knit – supportive

active – dynamic

hospitable – welcoming

down-to-earth – ordinary

fun-loving – lively

To **support** students who are struggling, have them look up the meaning of only one word from each pair (*supportive, active, hospitable, down-to-earth, fun-loving*). Then check their understanding by having them match the words with one of the following: someone who has a lot of energy and does a lot of sport; someone who is always having fun; someone who is friendly and welcoming to visitors; someone who deals with problems in a practical and sensible way; someone who helps and encourages you.

10 Colloquial words and phrases

It is a good idea to ask students about the advantages of using colloquial words (they sound friendly; they help you seem more fluent if you use them in conversation) and the disadvantages (they don't always have a very precise meaning; it's hard to know how you can use them; it can be difficult to know when a word is colloquial or slang).

Answers

1 C   2 D   3 B   4 A

Drill the pronunciation of *colloquial* /kəˈləʊkwɪəl/ and make sure that students understand the meaning of the word. Colloquial language is the informal sort used in everyday conversation. Although it is sometimes confused with slang, there is a simple difference between the two. Slang refers to very informal words and phrases that tend to be used by a specific group of people. For example, someone tweeting 'YOLO' may only be understood by those who are familiar with internet acronyms ('YOLO' is an abbreviation of 'You Only Live Once').

By contrast, colloquial language tends to be used quite widely and simply represents a more informal way of saying something. For example, '*My Arabic course is really difficult, but it's early days.*' is much less formal than '*My Arabic course is really difficult, but as it's only just started it is too soon to make a judgement as to whether or not I will find it any easier later on.*'

See the Introduction for a general approach to helping students with new vocabulary.

11 Translation

Check with students which colloquial words they like using in their own language(s) and ask them to suggest some equivalents for the words in the passage.

12 Discussion

Encourage students to make links in the discussion between home and family life and the kind of person you eventually turn out to be. You may like to consider cultural attitudes to family duties and responsibilities. You could ask '*How much do children owe their parents?*' It's also interesting to hear students' ideas on the support and inspiration they can receive from outside the family circle.

As students will be considering cultural ideas about families later in the unit, this is an opportunity to check '*How far does Chris's family conform to your notion of a typical British family?*' Try to establish exactly how and why students think they are similar or different.

This could lead on to an interesting discussion about the supposed characteristics of different nationalities (Are all people from the Caribbean warm and jolly?, Are all English people reserved?, etc.) and how we come to form ideas about what people from other countries are like (e.g. historical reasons, media, folklore, lack of direct knowledge and contact).

13 Idioms

Write *idioms* on the board and elicit the meaning of the word. An idiom is a phrase whose meaning can't be worked out from the individual words, e.g. *When the tornado came, we drove **hell for leather** away from the town.* 'Hell for leather' simply means 'very fast'. When learning idioms, students need to be cautious. Idioms can go out of fashion and don't always sound natural in conversation. A classic example of an idiomatic expression that students of English as a second language all seem to learn, but which native speakers don't use is *It was raining cats and dogs.* The three introduced in the exercise, however, are all used quite frequently.

Answers

1 You have more obligations to someone when there is a blood relationship.

2 People related to you by blood. The expression is usually used by parents referring to their children.

3 We were able to keep the home we lived in.

B Favourite places

1 Discussion

The discussion focuses students' thoughts on the new topics.

The aim of the following sequence of exercises is to encourage descriptive writing of a favourite place, giving reasons for the choice. The place the students choose to write about has to be in their area, be real not imaginary, and be somewhere they are genuinely enthusiastic about – not just a place they think they should like. Encourage students to produce an original description which offers insight into a place that means a lot to them, and to give reasons for having chosen that place.

One of the challenges for students will be working out what exactly is appealing about a familiar place and explaining its effect on their mood. It doesn't matter how ordinary the place is (a local park, a nearby patch of woods). Remind them this is a personal piece of writing, not a tourist brochure description – although it could be adapted for this later.

2 Reading and vocabulary

You'll probably want to spend some time working on this preparatory exercise. It involves reading a personal description of a market, and deciding which categories the adjectives and descriptive phrases belong to. You should check with students whether the market appeals to them and ask why/why not, to give them practice in explaining their reasons.

3 Writing

Before they begin to write a draft description of their own favourite place, encourage students to do the visualisation exercise which will help them recall the place in detail and the feelings it evokes.

The actual writing might be best done for homework. Emphasise that using a dictionary will be essential.

TEACHING SUPPORT

The section on descriptive language introduces phrases which tend to be used in articles on travel and tourism. However, there is a balance to be struck in descriptive writing, between saying too much and saying too little. Encourage students to think carefully about the language they use. They should not include phrases such as *off the beaten track* in a description simply for the sake of it. What matters is not how many phrases a student uses in a description, but whether the phrases they choose capture exactly what they want to convey. As a way of practising this, **challenge** some students to use the descriptive phrases in Exercise 3 to describe some places they know well.

LEARNING SUPPORT

Some students may benefit from a basic frame for writing their description. Offer the following, encouraging students to go back and expand their description after the first draft.

One of my favourite places is …

When I'm there, I can see …

I can hear the sounds of …

I can smell …

This place makes me feel …

4 Reading aloud

It is a good idea to keep the written pieces anonymous, for the sake of more self-conscious students. Encourage students to respond warmly to the descriptions they hear, giving reasons why they would enjoy the place too. This will foster the spirit which makes all the difference to group dynamics.

5 Showing enthusiasm 🔊 CD 1, Track 4

Remind students that appropriate stress and intonation are vital if you are to convince your listener you are genuinely enthusiastic. Point out that the voice jumps to a higher pitch at the beginning of the stressed words and then falls.

Grammar notes

Point out to students that they are using

what + noun or noun phrase:

What a great place! I think my friends and I would love the atmosphere there!

What fun! My younger brothers and sisters would love it!

or **how** + adjective:

How exciting! It would be a fascinating place for my friends and me to go at weekends.

How relaxing! It'd be a wonderful place for me to unwind after studying all day.

AUDIOSCRIPT

As in the Student's Book.

6 Order of adjectives

Remind students that numbers usually go before adjectives, e.g. *two large eggs*.

Commas are generally used between longer adjectives and in longer sequences, especially where a slight pause would be made in speech.

As three adjectives before the noun are usually enough, students practise putting this number of adjectives into order.

> **LEARNING SUPPORT**
>
> Order of adjectives is a distinct feature of English that students don't always find easy to get used to. Once they have read and understood the rules, elicit some example descriptions of objects in the room, and put these descriptions on the board, e.g. *Juana's got a beautiful new silk scarf*. Alternatively, before students do the exercise, write some descriptions on the board, but make sure the adjectives are in the wrong order, e.g. *I live in a three-bedroomed French charming apartment*. (*charming, three-bedroomed, French* is the correct order). Ask students to correct the word order, justifying their answer with reference to the rules.

Answers

1   I've lost a red canvas sports bag.
2   We stayed in a beautiful, three-bedroomed Swedish house.
3   The new boss is a friendly, middle-aged Egyptian woman.

4   I want to buy a good-quality black leather jacket.
5   I've bought a warm woollen winter coat.
6   Thieves stole a priceless, oriental silver teapot.
7   Kieran got a smart, inexpensive, grey cover for her new tablet.

7 Developing your writing style

Clauses are used to give information in descriptions. They sound more natural than using a long sequence of adjectives before the noun.

> **TEACHING SUPPORT**
>
> If students require extra **support**, ask them to underline the adjectives or adjective phrases, crossing out words that won't be needed (e.g. ~~It was an~~ unusual ~~box~~.). Ask them whether any changes need to be made to create the adjectives, prompting the use of a dictionary as necessary (e.g. *wood to wooden*). Once they have done this, they may find it helpful to write the separate parts of the description on slips of paper so they can move them around to find the best order.
>
> See the Introduction for a general approach to helping students with Writing tasks.

Practice: answers

1   He gave her an unusual Russian box made of wood with a picture of a famous story on the lid. (*or* … *an unusual Russian wooden box*)
2   She was wearing a brown wool suit which looked too warm for the weather.
3   It's a white, Japanese, portable television with 100 channels.
4   It's a heavy, French, copper frying pan with a lid.
5   Someone's taken my blue ceramic coffee mug with my name on it.
6   He has lost a polyester school coat with/which has his name on the inside.
7   Rosanna decided to wear a long green-and-white silk dress which she had bought in America.

C Improving your neighbourhood

The listening exercise is based on a typical IGCSE scenario: a disused warehouse is going to be converted. Should

31

it be turned into a study centre or a youth club? Why? A dialogue takes place between two officials. Pamela has looked through the letters about the conversion from local teenagers and is in favour of a study centre. John, her colleague, prefers the idea of a youth club.

1 Discussion

Prepare students by asking them to talk about any community initiatives they may have taken part in, and let them explain the difficulties they faced and their feelings (frustration, pride, etc.). If it's more appropriate, you could make this discussion more school-based, and ask them if they have been involved in making improvements at school (e.g. getting a common room).

Extend the discussion to consider the improvements they would like to see in their own neighbourhood.

2 Before you listen: Vocabulary check

Answers

maintenance: keeping something in good condition

budget: a spending plan; to make such a plan

facilities: buildings or services provided for a particular purpose

voluntary: (working) without pay

wear and tear: the effect of repeated use

premises: a piece of land and its buildings

drain on resources: using up too much money

3 Listening for gist 🔊 CD 1, Track 5

> **TEACHING SUPPORT**
>
> See the Introduction for a general approach to helping students with Listening tasks.
>
> As always, it's a good idea to listen once for the main ideas and to check basic understanding. Replay the recording, pausing in places if necessary.

Answers

1 She wants a study centre.

2 He wants a youth club.

3 'When you put it like that, maybe …'

AUDIOSCRIPT

Listen to the conversation for general meaning first, and find answers to the three questions.

PAMELA: Right, John, I've put all the letters we received with unsuitable or impractical ideas over there for you to look through later if you like. Two ideas really stood out. The idea of converting the warehouse into a study centre for after-school studies was very popular. Also very popular was the request for a social club, a sort of youth club.

JOHN: What do you want to go for?

P: I'm all in favour of converting it into a study centre. It would be very cheap to run because it wouldn't need much maintenance. Students could come after school and at weekends to do homework or research school projects. As a lot of them are sharing bedrooms at home, they have nowhere suitable to study.

J: But Pamela, do you really think it's a good idea to develop it as a study centre? After all, we already have an excellent public library, only five minutes away. What's wrong with that?

P: But it's always crowded! The staff are rushed off their feet with all they have to do and they aren't very helpful to students.

J: A study centre sounds all right in theory, but in practice it's not going to solve the very real problem of the lack of leisure facilities for teenagers.

P: I take your point, John, but qualifications are very important if they're to do well in the future. Isn't it up to us to help them?

J: Oh, talking about the future is all very well, but what about the present? Teenagers who aren't interested in studying don't want a study centre. Having a youth club would be fun for everyone. They all deserve a place where they can unwind after a long day at school or work.

P: Well, I'm not absolutely convinced. I think parents would prefer a study centre much more than they want a rowdy and undisciplined youth club.

J: We can't know what parents want because they haven't been asked. I don't think young people will be rowdy. Most of them are well behaved. Just think of how hard local teenagers work to raise money for disabled people in the town.

P: Well, I think it's rather unrealistic to expect no noise or litter or wear and tear. In my view, a youth club is going to be expensive to maintain. It'll be a drain on resources.

J: Well, I accept that a youth club will be more expensive to maintain than a study centre. We could reduce maintenance costs and control misbehaviour by having a supervisor in charge.

P: Can we afford a supervisor?

J: I've had a look at the budget and it would stretch to paying a small wage for the first year of the club's operation. After that we'd have to review it. Even consider voluntary help.

P: Hmmm. Not many people want to work for nothing.

J: And we shouldn't forget that the premises are next to a sports field, so there's no worry about a lot of noise late at night. (Well,) it's not as if it's in a residential street.

P: That's true, but you never know, do you? I still say a study centre is the better bet.

J: Well, look at it this way: what's worse – a youth club or the situation of young people hanging around the streets at night? Do you remember that awful case in the papers recently?

P: Oh, that was a tragedy!

J: It was said those teenagers would be alive today if they'd had a decent place to spend their free time.

P: Yes, I remember that.

J: I know we both feel the safety of young people comes first.

P: I agree with you there.

J: A well-run youth club could put many people's minds at rest.

P: Hmmm. When you put it like that, maybe a youth club isn't such a bad idea after all.

J: So you're willing to give it a try?

P: Only if a proper supervisor is taken on.

J: Oh great! I'll let the Social Committee know. Well, let's keep our fingers crossed they give the idea the go-ahead.

4 Detailed listening 🔊 CD 1, Track 5

Let students listen again for detail and to find the answers to the multiple-choice exercise.

LEARNING SUPPORT

Pair students who will find this task challenging. One from each pair should pre-read and listen out for the answers about Pamela, while the other should focus on John. They can compare answers after listening and swap roles for a further listening.

Answers

1 b 2 a 3 c 4 a 5 b 6 a 7 c 8 b

5 Follow-up

Let students discuss their feelings freely. How they feel will naturally depend a lot on their own cultural background and the opportunities they have around them.

Inference

The answer is c. (John does not directly say the library is 'well-resourced and efficient', but telling Pamela the library is 'excellent' makes c a reasonable inference).

More about inference

Answer c. (John tries to persuade Pamela, rather than give orders, and she is confident about rejecting his views without an apology or embarrassment which suggests they are on equal terms.)

33

Idioms

The idioms *I'm digging my heels* in and *I'm sticking to my guns* could be applied equally to John or Pamela, as neither wants to give in.

6 Persuading: Stress and intonation 🔊

CD 1, Track 5

This additional listening to the dialogue focuses on the intonation of informal persuasion. The phrases have a generally falling pattern. Before starting the exercise, it may be interesting to find out from students which phrases they now use when they want to change someone's mind.

Make sure students can complete the phrases appropriately, e.g.

*Do you **really** think it's a good idea to encourage teenagers to stay out at night?*

*That's all very well, **but** other things are more important.*

*That's true, **but** not everyone will enjoy it.*

Monitor their stress and intonation.

7 Role play: Spend, spend, spend

TEACHING SUPPORT

See the Introduction for a general approach to helping students with Speaking and Reading tasks.

LEARNING SUPPORT

Elicit from students language they can use to express their opinion strongly (e.g. *I really think that we should …, I am very keen to …, I think it would be a great idea to …*). Allow them to practise this for their own role before they begin the role play. Additionally, give them time to read through the other three role descriptions and to prepare one argument against each of these proposals, looking up any vocabulary that they may need.

Role plays are a good opportunity to practise functions and intonation in a more spontaneous context. Here students imagine they are part of a family of four (mum, dad, two teenage children) that has won $20,000 in a competition. Each student aims to persuade the others

that his/her ideas are the best way of spending the money for the benefit of the whole family.

Students could recycle some of the language they heard in the listening, e.g. *I'm all in favour of …* It's good to remind them, however, that role plays work best when they use all the language resources at their command without being too self-conscious. Emphasise the fact that the need to communicate is more important than accurate grammar and vocabulary in a role-play exercise.

Divide students into groups of four. Allow them a few minutes to prepare before starting, and clarify any misunderstandings.

D Making a difference

1 Pre-reading discussion

The text focuses on the determination of one woman, Dolores, a former nurse, to make a hospital stay more pleasant for children, teenagers and their families. She has done a lot of charity fundraising so that her local hospital can afford a wide range of additional, non-medical facilities.

It will be interesting to see how students respond to the idea that going into hospital should be a pleasant and comforting experience. However, this might be a sensitive topic if a student has had to go into hospital for treatment or has experienced serious illness in the family. If so, the discussion can be kept fairly objective. It is wise not to single out any particular student, but to let them make the contributions they would like to make.

2 Reading for gist

Answers

Dolores has been successful in improving the experience of young people and their parents in her local hospital.

3 Vocabulary

Answers

1 F   2 G   3 C   4 E   5 D   6 H   7 A   8 B   9 I

A ward is a room in a hospital with beds for patients.

Liaison means exchanging information and ideas.

4 Post-reading discussion

The aim of this exercise is to equip students to use clues in the style of the writing to identify an author's main aim.

Encourage them to back up their choices with examples from the text.

Answers

Tone: **b**

Main aim: **c**

Structure: **a**

Style: neutral

5 Comprehension check

Answers

1 She didn't answer the phones / she didn't master the computer / she was often away from her desk.

2 Dolores felt frustrated that children could not have what they asked for / could not have ice cream outside meal times. She knew families could benefit from meeting each other but, because of confidentiality, she could not pass on anyone's details.

3 The children now have an outdoor play area / the corridor to the children's ward has been redecorated / the corridor now has mosaics / there is a common room designed for teenagers (with trendy furniture / computers / internet access / snacks and drinks).

4 Parents now have access to refreshments in an improved kitchen. They can support each other through family liaison groups.

5 They have organised street parties / sponsored walks / sky-dives / car washes / picnics / concerts.

6 Students should aim for a description along these lines:

Dolores is understanding of the needs of sick children for comfort and to feel relaxed in hospital. Her attitude is positive, practical, understanding and down-to-earth. People want to donate money to the charity because they see she has these qualities and they also want to help sick children. Furthermore, she can also demonstrate how the money is being spent through factual evidence of improvements. (63 words)

You could finish the exercise by encouraging students to speculate and develop their ability to use inference. You could ask what they think Dolores herself has gained from her efforts. (For example, possibly more confidence in herself and a greater sense of purpose.)

6 Further discussion

The discussion could explore ideas along the following lines.

A Students can enjoy comparing the role of friends, who are more commonly associated with fun and socialising, with the support their family might give them.

B It will be interesting to explore the idea of 'general well-being' and whether it is more, or less, significant than medical care, advanced medical techniques, medication and access to surgery. Perhaps a desire for comfort in illness could be contrasted with a need for the most up-to-date treatment, especially in serious illness.

C The concept of raising funds for charity through personal or community effort rather than by simply donating a sum of money is more familiar in some cultures than in others. It is well worth exploring the advantages and disadvantages of both approaches.

D How health care should be funded is a controversial issue, so it will be interesting to hear what students think.

7 Colloquial language in context

This exercise will further develop students' grasp of colloquial language. They need to try to identify the meaning of the colloquial expressions in context rather than find exactly similar expressions.

Answers

1 I was no good at all/performed extremely badly at/in the job.

2 I got ready to do some hard work and made it happen.

3 The money does not disappear into a general fund, where it would be hard to track.

35

4   The corridor has been attractively redecorated.

5   The children need their parents, or grandparents, to be people they can always depend on.

Extension ideas

You could ask students to prepare a radio interview with one student acting as Dolores and the other as a radio/TV journalist who questions her about her fundraising and suggests it is not worthwhile. 'Dolores' has to fight her corner and defend her methods and results. Students could then perform the interview.

You could consider asking students to imagine they have visited a friend in the hospital where Dolores has made improvements. Ask them to describe the impressions they had of the visit. They could write this in the form of an email or a diary entry.

8 Spelling: Doubling consonants when adding suffixes

Doubling the consonant in one-syllable and multi-syllable words presents lots of problems for students and is a very common source of errors. Studying the rules and patterns will deepen students' awareness of language as an orderly system, and is an ideal opportunity to expand their understanding of how affixation alters word meaning and function.

Unfortunately, the rules are complex, but if they are presented to students in the context of developing a broader grasp of overall language patterns, students should quickly appreciate the value of the exercise. Encourage them to be on the lookout for links between spelling, grammar and word stress. Probably the easiest and most dependable rule for students to remember is: one vowel + one consonant = double consonant.

Practice: answers

1   ringing

2   hottest

3   stopped

4   enjoyed

5   saddest

6   shopping

7   chatting

8   walking

9   sending

10 cheaper

11 waiting

12 asking

13 looking

14 swimming

9 Adding suffixes to multi-syllable words

Practice: answers

1   regretted

2   permitted

3   occurred

4   reasoned

5   committed

6   happened

7   explained, beginning

8   preferred

10 Look, say, cover, write, check

Students undoubtedly benefit from using a visual strategy to strengthen their recall of spellings. Extra practice with this trustworthy method particularly supports students who do not have a strong visual memory and those who find it difficult to recognise patterns in language.

11 Words from different languages

If students have access to etymological dictionaries, they can investigate the origins of many common English words. It is interesting to discuss how words came into the language (for example through colonisation, settlers bringing new words, or French and Viking invaders). There are many interesting stories behind words. For example, *kindergarten* literally means 'children's garden' in German. The idea comes from the 19th century philosophy of a man who thought that young children were like tender plants which need nurturing to grow.

Other examples to investigate are *zero* (Arabic), *bandit* (Italian), *boomerang* (Australia/aboriginal), *yacht* (Dutch) and *slogan* (a Scottish war cry).

Answers

Arabic:	sofa
Aztec:	chocolate
Chinese:	tea
French:	cuisine

Greek:	athlete
Hindi:	bungalow
Italian:	opera
Japanese:	karate
Latin:	villa
Norwegian:	ski
Persian:	caravan
Spanish:	patio

E Welcoming an exchange visitor

This sequence of exercises focuses on achieving an appropriate tone and register when welcoming an exchange visitor to one's home. Achieving a suitable tone is basic to effective communication but a difficult skill to acquire. The exercises will give students a range of techniques.

1 Reassuring your guest

It's a good idea to check first that students understand the concept of an exchange visit. Students of foreign languages, for example, often take turns staying with each other's families. It's an inexpensive way to have a holiday in a foreign country and to find out more about the culture and practise the language. This topic presents an excellent opportunity to share cultural information about how guests are normally treated.

A good starting point before students make their notes is to ask them to see the exchange visit from the point of view of their guest. Elicit the fact that the guest will probably be a bit anxious, and then discuss ways of making him/her feel at home. Encourage students to think of the most attractive aspects of their home and surroundings, eliciting a few specific examples, before they write their own notes.

Beginnings and endings

Beginning and ending emails is not as straightforward as it might seem. It is easy to to make the mistake of writing either too formally or too informally. Phrases A–F in the exercise are common ways of beginning and ending an email. They are all appropriate for emails between teenagers, even ones who do not know each other that well. Students should work alone to complete the sentences

using the words in the box. They can then compare their answers with a partner before you check answers with the class. As as an additional activity, you may like to ask students which of the phrases sounds the least formal to them. The answers are A, D and F because all have a more conversational tone which suggests that the writer of the email knows whoever he or she is writing to quite well.

Answers

a get
b for
c to
d it
e forward
f forget

2 Example email

The example email aims to show a straightforward way of describing one's home and neighbourhood. One of the biggest challenges for IGCSE students is getting the tone and register right. An email of this type should sound welcoming and the plans/places described should sound inviting.

The format exercise asks students to work out exactly how this effect is achieved. You could point out that the email gets to grips with the topic quickly, which students often fail to do.

3 Finding a suitable tone

TEACHING SUPPORT

Before students begin the exercise, check their understanding of register and tone. Register refers to the vocabulary, grammar and level of formality we use depending on the people we are communicating with or the situation we are in. For example, we might say *'Good morning, Mr. Brown'* to an elderly neighbour, but *'Hi'* to our parents. Tone refers to the mood or attitude conveyed in speech or writing. For example, a text message which reads *'Happy birthday.'* is different in tone to one which reads, *'Happy birthday!!!!'*. Make sure that students understand why register and tone are important – if we get them wrong, we might upset or offend someone.

Rewriting

When students have done the pairwork, they can consolidate their learning by rewriting a few sentences with a more appropriate tone. They can have fun choosing sentences and altering the tone and register.

4 Correcting mistakes

The second and penultimate sentences of the email are too formal. Students need to rewrite them. They also need to organise the email into three paragraphs and a separate closing sentence.

Example answer

Hi William,

I'm back! I just wanted to write you a quick email to say thank you so much. I had a great time staying with you and your family last week. You were all so kind to me. I've got so many good memories of the trip. Everyone was so friendly – your family, the neighbours, all the students at the college. Tell your mum she is the best cook in the world! Can she come and live with us here?

I really liked your town, by the way. I think you are lucky to live there. I had such a good time there – we did so many interesting things! I'll send you some photos of our camping trip in my next email.

You know, you *must* come and stay with us soon! Do you remember I told you that our house is near a lake? Well, Dad's just fixed the boat, which means we can go out on the lake on it, if you like! The beaches here are great and now the summer is on the way we'll able to go swimming all the time. I know how much you love that. Whenever the weather is not so good, we can go to some of the big malls in the centre of town. Tourists love them! What do you think? Will you come and stay with us?

I can't wait to hear from you. Email soon!

Love,

Jacob

5 Sentence completion

This exercise gives students further practice in presenting their home environment positively. You may like to extend it by asking them to write a couple of sentences about their home town using the same pattern, e.g. *Although there is a lot of traffic where we live, we are within walking distance of the shops, cafés and leisure centre.*

Reassurance

It will be interesting for students to compare how people give reassurance in their language with how it is done in English.

6 Surprise party: Tone and register

Students revise and reinforce their understanding of tone and register. The best answer is **3**; the others sound aggressive and abrupt in writing.

7 Reordering

Students find problem solving fun. This is an ideal exercise to do in pairs, or groups of three.

Answers

The order of the email is as follows, although some variation is possible:

1 n   2 i   3 e   4 k   5 a   6 o   7 f   8 c   9 j

10 h   11 b   12 l   13 m   14 d   15 g

8 Writing

Students now have an opportunity to put into practice the skills they have developed in the unit.

International overview

Reasonable suggestions for why people may have stopped using a local or native language could include: preference given to a more dominant language (which may be perceived as superior), the spread of global media, the growth of tourism, the tendency among some communities to be educated outside the home country, and international business.

Answers

1   Chad, Tanzania and Cameroon.
2   Depending on their background, students may be surprised at Africa's linguistic richness and diversity.
3   Students' responses could include: government initiatives to support teaching the native language in schools, using the native language throughout the media, making sure oral languages are written down and recordings of them are made, and production of dictionaries.

You could discuss the idea that some people believe the emphasis on English language acquisition in many countries takes attention away from local languages, their history and literature. You could ask students which languages other than English they think are desirable to learn, and why. Experts believe that the way people feel about speaking more than one language depends on the attitudes other people have to those languages.

Many experts believe that bilingualism helps general intellectual development. You could ask students whether they share this view, and why.

Grammar spotlight

TEACHING SUPPORT

See the Introduction for a general approach to helping students with Grammar exercises.

Answers

A   My parents always encouraged me to give it time, not to give up.
B   I loved exploring the countryside. / I've always liked fishing.

E   Seeing her work spread nationwide is Dolores's dream. / Coping with illness is a challenge.

Verbs whose meanings change depending on whether they are followed by either the gerund or the infinitive need attention. Focus, then, on Part C of the *Grammar Spotlight*. Once students have read it and completed the exercise, test them on it. For example, tell them you're going away at the weekend. Ask: *'Have you got to remember to lock the door or remember locking the door?'* (Answer: *to lock*). Which of the two sentences with '*stop*' and '*talk*' suggests that the neighbour might be talkative? (Answer: *Her neighbour didn't stop talking*).

If students struggle to understand how the meaning of the other verbs listed is changed, give them the following examples to look at:

1   Forget
a   'I'll **never forget arriving** in Seville for the first time: what a beautiful city!' (This means I will always remember it.)
b   'I **forgot to do** my homework yesterday. Miss Brand was not very pleased with me.' (This means that I didn't remember to do it.)

2   Need
a   'Dad said he **needed to wash** the dishes.' (This means it was necessary for him to do it.)
b   'Dad said the dishes **need washing**.' (This means that the dishes needed to be washed by someone, but not by the speaker's father.)

3   Try
a   'Is it still not working? **Try turning** it off.' (This means turn it off as an experiment to see if it works.)
b   'My computer's still not working. I **tried to fix** it last night but I was just too tired to concentrate.' (This means that the person made a great effort do fix it.)

4   Go on
a   'The teacher **went on to talk** about the history of Ancient Egypt.' (This means that the teacher stopped talking about one thing and started talking about something else.)
b   'The teacher **went on talking** about the history of Ancient Egypt.' because he wanted to make sure he covered all the important points. (This means that the teacher continued talking without a break).

LEARNING SUPPORT

Support students who struggle with this grammatical topic by encouraging them to make up sentences using the different forms. For example, provide a list of sentence starters for them to complete, such as the following: *My parents don't allow me …; I need someone to help me …; You should never risk …; As a young child, I remember …; Something I really can't stand is …; When I am in a hurry, I sometimes forget …* Students could work with a partner to complete the sentences orally, checking that their partner has used the correct form.

Exam-style questions

See the Overview of *Cambridge IGCSE English as a Second Language* section at the beginning of the Student's Book for the mark scheme and criteria for marking the writing questions.

Writing

4 Community day – article

The example answer shows how students could approach the question. Encourage students to use their imagination to project into the situation of a community day to help the elderly, so they can describe their feelings and the events that took place convincingly. Remind students to show some awareness of the audience (school students), as shown in the example answer.

Example answer

I was nervous when I saw the old people coming into our school hall to learn how to use computers. I thought the elderly people might not trust me to help them.

My first customer was Mrs Rose, who wanted to learn about email, as her grandson has moved to Colombia and she wanted to keep in touch.

We experimented by writing an email to her grandson and he replied immediately, with, 'Wow, grandma, you are online!'. Then we both started laughing.

I helped some other people with social media, and how to shop online.

Everyone thanked me, which made me feel very proud.

From helping with the Community Day, I now understand I can use those skills to help other people enjoy their lives. If we have another Community Day, I suggest more of us get involved, as you get lots out of helping others. (149 words).

(Reading & Writing, Exercise 5: 12 marks (Core).)

Listening 🔊 CD 1, Track 6

This exercise is similar in style to the gap filling exercise in Question 5 of the listening paper. Students should enjoy listening to Neeta, a teenager living in Australia, describe what she likes about the community, Riverside, where she lives. Neeta describes a close knit, supportive environment where neighbours care about each other. It will be interesting to hear students' views of that sort of community. While it has clear benefits, some students may dislike that sort of community atmosphere and feel it leads to a lack of individual freedom and the privacy to do 'your own thing.' It will be most intriguing to hear their opinions.

The exercise recycles ideas from the unit (welcoming newcomers, fundraising, family life, enjoyable activities to do, interesting local places to visit) and the related language and vocabulary for these topics. Examples of the gerund and the infinitive can be reinforced, if it seems useful for your group. Students, for example, will hear Neeta say that when her grandmother meets her friends, '…they never stop laughing and remembering the old days,' and you can ask them what that means. You could draw their attention to the infinitive form, 'they never stop to laugh and remember the old days,' and ask if the meaning is the same or different and why.

Remember that in the real exam students always listen twice. Remind them that they should fill the gaps with **one** or **two** words only, and the completed text should make sense and be understandable to someone who has not heard the original recording. Spelling should also be correct, but a minor spelling mistake may not matter as long as the meaning is clear and the misspelling does not make another word.

Answers

a   South India
b   daily newspaper
c   washed
d   outdoors
e   medical equipment

f   since/from school

g   green velvet

h   safe/secure/security

(Listening, Exercise 2: 8 marks (Core); 8 marks (Extended).)

AUDIOSCRIPT

You will hear Neeta, a student, talk on a radio programme about the community where she lives. Listen to the talk and complete the notes below. Write one or two words or a number in each gap. You will hear the talk twice.

PRESENTER: In today's programme we're talking to Neeta, a student who is here to tell our listeners all about Riverside. Welcome, Neeta.

NEETA: Thank you. I'm thrilled to be here tonight. I've never been on radio before. Well, where shall I start? Towards the beginning of the last century, my ancestors came to Australia from South India and I was born and brought up in Riverside, in the north of our city. I absolutely love living in Riverside because of the fabulous community atmosphere we have here.

Riverside might not be the richest area but is it's so friendly. There are lots of small shops where people are always stopping to chat. If I go shopping, even if it's only to buy a daily newspaper or a loaf of bread, it takes a long time because I always meet someone I know and they want to catch up on all my news. When I get home, my grandmother always asks who I met when I was out, what they said, even what clothes they were wearing! She's lived in Riverside all her life, and so did her parents.

It's a close-knit community here and we look out for each other. Recently, my little brother fell off his bike and cut his knee badly. One of my neighbours comforted him and washed the blood off his knee. You'll always find someone to help you in Riverside, no matter what you need.

Apart from the lovely warm atmosphere, we have so many brilliant facilities and clubs, and what's more, you can walk to them! We are a very active family. I go to an art group, my brother loves the outdoors and he is in a hiking club. Dad is in an angling club which meets at weekends to fish in our beautiful river. Mum is a member of a choir which gives concerts to raise funds for our community hospital. The funds are used by the hospital to buy medical equipment and now you recover much more quickly if you do need hospital treatment.

There are lots of activities for elderly people too. My grandmother likes to keep fit and goes to a weekly Tai Chi class in the park. Afterwards, she has tea with her friends in our local cafe, *The Jade Garden,* and they never stop laughing and remembering the old days when they were all at school together.

It's a fact that people in Riverside sometimes have to move away from the neighbourhood, but we shouldn't forget that this brings opportunity. We have lovely families from all over the world who have moved into the area and they bring fresh energy and ideas for businesses. As a result we have a wide range of restaurants, shops and services. One lady from Bangkok started a dressmaking service, for example. My parents have just celebrated their twenty-fifth wedding anniversary and needed new outfits for the celebration. The owner made a green velvet dress for mum. For my dad, she made a white silk shirt with silver buttons. She stayed up late to get them finished in time. My parents said they have never felt so well dressed!

So don't tell me community life is dead! Here in Riverside, knowing that we belong gives us a feeling of security, of being in a safe place and we can put down permanent roots if we want to. Riverside does that for me, definitely!

Reading

In the multiple matching exercise, four people share their thoughts on a place that is special to them. The exercise reflects the unit's themes and recycles the vocabulary and grammar practised in the unit. Encourage students to read the rubric and scan the questions so they get a general idea of what the text might be about. Then they should read the texts for general meaning. When they have finished reading, they should tackle the first question. In this particular exercise, students are asked to decide which person occasionally buys things. Scanning the text again, they will see that both Anh, Person A, and Hayley, Person C, mention buying, so these two possibilities are close. Person B and Person D do not mention commerce so these two people can be eliminated. Students then need to compare Anh and Hayley even more carefully to see which one occasionally buys things, as only one answer will be right. Although Anh sells, she does not buy, only customers buy. The correct answer therefore is Hayley, Person C, because although the paintings for sale are too expensive for her to buy, she occasionally buys an artistic card.

Students can then tackle the next question and repeat the process and so on. Students' knowledge of vocabulary and topic will be crucial in helping them distinguish between ideas which are similar but not the same. When students have finished the first 'round' of reading and matching, they should return to any 'problematic' matches and refine their choice by checking the detail of the question against the detail of the text.

To finish the exercise, you may like to discuss the underlying idea conveyed in the views expressed that it is not the specific place that make the people feel at ease, but their feelings about it. It would be interesting to find out what students think of that idea, and which of the places they find most appealing.

Answers

1 Person C 2 Person B 3 Person A 4 Person C
5 Person D 6 Person A 7 Person C 8 Person B
9 Person C 10 Person D

(Reading & Writing, Exercise 2: 10 marks (Extended).)

Wider practice

1   If you have access to English-language TV, you could record an interview from a chat show. These contain superb real-life examples of functions, e.g. avoiding awkward questions, expressing regrets, praising, commiserating, offering congratulations. Pause the recording in places to let students home in on a particular function. Alternatively, you could look for interviews on a video-sharing site. Try to find a personality students like.

2   For more work on confidence building, students could interview local people to find out their feelings about the neighbourhood and its facilities. Retired people often have a little more time and can tell students how life in the area has changed. Community officials could be interviewed about how the work they do benefits groups in the community. Interviews which are carried out in the first language can be translated into English for reporting back in class.

3   Short role plays can give further practice in use of register and functional language. The following are some possibilities:

You have to decline an invitation to your friend's party. What do you say?

You have been invited to stay for a week with people you don't know very well. You want to know the house rules. What do you say?

Your friend wants you to babysit but you want to go to bed early that night. What do you say?

4   Language has a fascinating history. Students could research a project on one of its many aspects. For example, the history and development of handwriting is rewarding to investigate. They could find out more about the stories behind the world's many scripts and present an informative talk to the class.

5   If students have joined online groups they could give a short talk about them to the class, outlining the benefits and drawbacks.

Sport, fitness and health

Overview

This unit deals with note-making and summarising. These skills are likely to be tested in the reading and writing components of an exam.

Summarising

The challenges of summarising for students are:

- reshaping the text in their own words while preserving its original meaning
- recognising what is relevant to the summary question and what is irrelevant
- connecting the summary grammatically
- keeping to a word limit.

A good summary should demonstrate communicative competence – students need to show that they have genuinely understood the text and can give its main points. Slight grammar and vocabulary errors are of no great importance as long as they do not affect the meaning. It is important, however, to keep to the specified word length (about 70 words for Core level and no longer than 120 words at Extended level).

Many students tend to start writing the summary without going through the essential sequence of steps. The unit emphasises using textual clues, predicting content and the writer's intention, and recalling information.

Students often find doing summaries on their own a struggle. Pairwork is used in the exercises at each stage to check accuracy and for mutual support.

Note-making

A good note-making answer will be clear, understandable and easily followed by someone who has not seen the original passage. Headings and bullet points are there to guide students, and one separate point should be found for each bullet. Unlike in the summary question, students are not instructed to keep to a word limit, nor do they have to use their own words. However, the notes should be brief and concise. Most importantly, copying out large chunks of text should be avoided.

Note-making from a text is an easier task than summarising. In this unit, it is treated as one of the stages in producing an effective summary. Students are asked to make notes from a text and then join the notes into a connected summary. Incidentally, this is excellent practice for the note-making and summary exercises in Paper 1 and directly supports the way the tasks are structured in the latest Cambridge syllabus.

Paper 2 uses different texts for note-making and summary writing. However, this unit practises the essential skills at a challenging level for the benefit of Extended-level students.

Please also note that the unit practises the skills of identifying and extracting key information which students need for reading comprehension tasks.

Theme

The theme of sport and its role in education runs throughout the unit. In addition, there is a discussion and summary passage on the importance of a healthy lifestyle in keeping us fit. These are popular topics, which students should be able to identify with.

The unit raises the following issues for discussion:

- Is competitive sport a good idea for young children?
- Can sport be used as a tool for helping disaffected teenagers feel better about themselves?
- Are fitness programmes useful and can they genuinely help us change lifestyle habits?

Language work

Specific language exercises focus on ways of writing more concisely, e.g. using compound nouns and noun phrases, finding an exact word instead of a phrase and avoiding unnecessary repetition. There is also work on analysing headlines. Headlines are short cuts into the meaning of a text. While difficult, they are well worth trying to understand.

Spelling focuses on a common problem: whether to drop or retain the final -e when adding a suffix.

The *Grammar spotlight* focuses on the use of the passive.

A Is sport always fun?

1 Note-making and summaries: Sharing ideas

Encourage an open discussion about what students like or dislike about summarising and what they find difficult. It's nice to point out, if you can, the strengths they are already demonstrating in their approach to summarising. Lots of IGCSE students find the summary question difficult and spend exam time on the comprehension questions or on the essays.

You could consolidate this exercise by asking students to make a list of very specific points they need to improve and ways they could help themselves, e.g. using textual clues, underlining the text.

You could begin by asking students what the main differences are between notes and summary writing, eliciting the idea that phrases and abbreviations can be used in note-making, whereas sentences in a summary should be grammatically constructed. Headings and numbered or bullet points can be used in both. Ask them if they use coloured pens or highlighters when they want to mark the main points of a text.

2 Discussion / 3 Quiz

The discussion and quiz set the scene for the topical work in the subsequent exercises. Bring the class together after the quiz to share their views. Hopefully, responses will be diverse and provide an opportunity for students who are pro- or anti-sport to understand each other's viewpoints. It would be a good idea to check key vocabulary now, as the concepts run throughout the chosen texts, e.g. *self-discipline, coordination*.

4 Is sport always fun?/5 Pre-reading discussion

Encourage students to describe sports day at school. They could say what races they enjoy entering and which they do not like. If they do not have a sports day, they could say if they would like such an event at their school.

6 Predicting content

Point out that predicting the content of a text is a way of preparing for reading tasks in an exam. Students should think about what information they would expect a text to include based on such things as the summary of it included in the rubric, its title, the photograph accompanying it and so on.

7 Developing reading skills

This text is a bit shorter than many exam-style texts set for summary writing. Students should find the content interesting and it will provide practice in following the development of an argument.

The original headline has been removed from the text to provide a question later.

Before they read the text, you could tell students they'll be 'tested' on its content. Although this is a rather artificial approach to reading comprehension, it will encourage maximum concentration on the detail.

8 Comprehension check
Answers
1   stomach pains, being sick, difficulty sleeping
2   at a large village primary school
3   They fall down on the track.
4   immense pity
5   very enthusiastic
6   an afternoon of team games and a few races for those who want them

Finding the main ideas

Students should be able to do this exercise quickly and practise their scan-reading skills at the same time.

Answers
A 4 **B** 3 **C** 5 **D** 2 **E** 1

9 Checking predictions

It's interesting to relate students' pre-reading predictions with the actual content of the text. You could ask: *'Do you think predicting the content of the text makes it easier to understand, even if your predictions are proved wrong?'*

10 Choosing a headline

Selecting a headline for the article will help students consider the whole of the writer's argument. Detailed work on headline formation comes later in the unit. You could ask *'Which headline tell us about the writer's attitude to sports day?'*

'Mum slams sports day' would be a good choice. 'To slam' something means 'to criticise it severely'.

You could conclude this stage of comprehension by asking students if they sympathise with the writer's view.

You could ask: *'Isn't competition an essential ingredient in modern society? Isn't it best that children get used to the idea of winning and losing early on?'* By presenting the issue in this way, you could lead students to think about the wider implications of competition. You could also contrast the competitive ethos with a more cooperative economic ethos based on sharing and being supportive, reflected in the writer's notions of 'team games'.

11 Note-making practice

Introduce the exercise by telling students of the need to approach note-making methodically. Many may feel the exercise is 'easy', especially in view of the preparatory work they have done, and often tend to treat notes relatively casually. It's worth pointing out the difference between writing notes for your own benefit and writing them for others. Organised and clearly-presented material is important in exam-style answers.

Answers
Reasons for having a sports day
- competition is character-building
- taking part is important, not winning
- school tradition

The negative effects of sports day
Any two of:
- stomachache / being sick / not sleeping the night before
- children who are overweight / not good at sport are upset/embarrassed
- children who fall over in front of everyone are shamed

Sports day: possible improvements
- team games
- a few races (for those who want them)

Underlining relevant parts of the text

After students have underlined the relevant parts of the text, do insist they work with a partner to compare notes and clarify any differences. In pairwork it can sometimes useful to pair students of differing abilities but this should not become a rule.

Making notes and checking your work

Students should try to present their notes in their own words as far as possible. Exam note-making exercises don't usually specify 'in your own words'. In practice, however, students do need to use some of their own words

because, like the summary, the note-making question tends to be slanted in a particular way, e.g. asking students to advise, evaluate, compare and contrast, give the history of, outline the advantages and disadvantages of.

For the exam-style summary question, students always have to write in their own words where they can. Evidence suggests that many IGCSE students move straight from underlining the text at the reading stage to writing the finished draft. If your students do this, they may fall into the trap of 'lifting' (copying) from the text. Such answers fail to demonstrate the comprehension of the material which is vital for success.

12 Comparing two summaries

The example summary versions present very common mistakes which reflect the problems IGCSE students have, e.g. inappropriate linking, failure to use own words, introducing ideas/opinions of one's own. Introducing one's own opinions is a particular problem for IGCSE students when the text is opinion-based. Make sure students do discriminate between the writer's opinion and the 'own ideas' of the example versions.

After students have worked alone or in pairs to compare and contrast the two summary versions, it's nice to draw them together as a class. This is an opportunity to address any queries they have so far with summary writing or note-making.

Answers
1 Summary 1
2 Summary 2
3 Summary 1. *Moreover* is wrong. A contrast word or phrase is needed, e.g. *On the other hand, nevertheless, however. Despite* should be *Even.*
4 Each summary introduces, at the end, an opinion which is not mentioned by the writer.
5 Summary 2, because it uses the student's own words.

B Enjoying sport safely

1 Compound nouns

Compound nouns (noun + noun combinations) are common in English and are increasing in number as more new ideas and things are invented. In this exercise, students are asked to identify some commonly used compound nouns from a possible list.

Answers

The words which commonly follow *sports* are: *bag, car, centre, club, drink, equipment, instructor, man, person, woman*. Note that, unlike the other compounds, *sportsman, sportsperson* and *sportswoman* are written as one word.

Sports drink is a compound which has been introduced following the invention of a special drink for sport. You can use this example to talk about the relative flexibility of English.

Practice: answers

swimming + costume, hat, pool, team, trunks

football + match, players, shorts, team, boots, field, shirt

hockey + match, players, stick, team, boots, field

fitness + programme, centre

skating + costume, programme, rink, team, centre

leisure + programme, centre, shirt

cricket + match, bat, team, field (Note: a cricket player is called a cricketer.)

Elicit examples of other compounds students already know and write them on the board. Point out that common compounds consisting of two short words are usually written together, e.g. *postman, toothpaste, timetable*. Hyphenated compounds, e.g. *dry-cleaner's,* are becoming increasingly uncommon.

Compounds usually have the stress on the first syllable. Some compound nouns can be reversible, with different meanings, e.g. *racehorse, horse race*, which is a special feature of English thought not to be found in other languages.

2 Pre-listening discussion

The listening exercise asks students to listen to a recorded announcement about a sports centre and complete a diary. The term 'sports centre' has a culturally specific meaning, so it's wise to check with students that they understand that all kinds of facilities (swimming, squash, aerobics, weight training, etc.) are usually offered under one roof.

3 Listening to a recorded announcement

◀) CD 1, Track 7

Before students listen, point out some features of recorded announcements. As someone is reading from a script, and needs to make sure that listeners hear the most important information, the delivery of announcements tends to be slower, with more emphasis given to key words. To illustrate the point, write the following sentence on the board: *Players can book the tennis court between 4 and 5 pm*. Say that sentence to the class, but read it quickly, and do not put any emphasis on the times at the end of the sentence. Then read the sentence as an announcer would, more slowly, giving heavy emphasis to *tennis courts, 4* and *5*. Ask students to say which version was clearer and why, then get them to practise reading the sentence as if they were delivering it for a recorded message.

The first part of the exercise builds on the work on compound nouns. First, let students listen for general meaning and to complete the compound nouns on the list. Then they should listen again to fill in the diary.

Replay the recording as often as you wish.

Answers

1 open-air swimming pool
2 coin-return locker system
3 changing rooms
4 badminton court
5 table tennis
6 cheap-rate tickets
7 sports centre members
8 application form
9 reception desk
10 keep-fit classes

Sports centre diary: answers

i Need 50p coin for lockers
ii Sports centre closed
iii Bring own badminton racket
iv Ask supervisor for free bats and balls
v Gym open 2–4 p.m.
vi Must wear indoor shoes

vii Collect application form from reception desk

viii Senior citizens' keep-fit classes

Membership of the sports centre costs £12 for adults and £6 for junior members.

AUDIOSCRIPT

You are going to hear some recorded information about facilities available at a sports centre. Listen first for general meaning and try to complete the list of compound nouns, putting one word in each space.

On Monday we have swimming in the open-air swimming pool from 9 a.m. to 11 a.m. Please make sure you bring a 50p coin with you as a coin-return locker system has recently been installed in the changing rooms. On Monday afternoon the sports centre is closed. On Tuesday morning the badminton court is available from 10 a.m. to 11.30. Players must use their own badminton rackets. On Tuesday afternoon we are open for schools only. Table tennis is available on Wednesday morning from 9 till 11.30. The bats and balls for the game are supplied free of charge by making a request to the supervisor. The gym is open on Wednesday afternoon from 2 till 4 p.m. It is essential that indoor shoes are worn. Membership of the sports centre is £12 for adults and £6 for junior members. Please note that cheap-rate tickets are available to sports centre members only. If you wish to become a member, please pick up an application form from the reception desk which is open on Thursday mornings. On Thursday afternoons, keep-fit classes especially for senior citizens are held. Please enquire at reception.

4 Marking the main stress 🔊 CD 1, Track 8

Stressing words correctly is an important part of conveying meaning. In this exercise, the main stress is marked on words which the SPEAKER wishes to emphasise, to correct any misunderstanding. Give students a few examples before they listen, e.g.

A: *Did you forget your football shorts?*

B: *No, I forgot my **boots**.*

A: *What did you learn from the coach?*

B: *I learned **ev**erything from the coach.*

Ask students to identify where the main stress falls. Ask them *'What is the SPEAKER trying to show by emphasising this word?'*

Now let students listen two or three times to the recorded dialogue and then have them practise by reading aloud in pairs.

AUDIOSCRIPT

As in the Student's Book.

Practice: answers

The key words which should be stressed are: *never, no one, everybody, any.*

5 Analysing headlines

Headlines are a fascinating area of English, with a style and grammar of their own. For brevity and dramatic effect they use short words which are uncommon in ordinary language, e.g. *wed* instead of *marry*, or words with unusual meanings, e.g. *bid* for *attempt*, *slam* for *criticise*.

Being more aware of headlines will help students deal with summarising newspaper articles. The exercises in the Student's Book can give only a 'taste' of newspaper-speak. However, you may like to refer students to *Practical English Usage* by Michael Swan, which has a comprehensive list of headline vocabulary with clear definitions.

You could introduce the topic by bringing in a few headlines from English newspapers to read aloud to the class. This would be especially useful if you could compare the headlines for the same story in different newspapers. If no suitable real headlines are available, write some on the board, e.g. JUDGE SLAMS UNREPENTANT BIRD WOMAN, and encourage students to break them down by approaching them in reverse order.

Ask them if *bird woman* is a regular compound noun or made up for the purpose, and what it could mean (a woman who cares for birds). *Slams* is newspaper-speak for criticises. *Unrepentant* indicates that the woman has been criticised before and has not followed the judge's orders.

Elicit from students the reasons why newspapers adopt this style. Answers could include: to save space, to be dramatic, to be eye-catching, to be humorous.

Let students complete the exercise in pairs and then check their answers in the whole group.

Answers

The key words in the report are: *female student, injured, collision, bus, rejected, compensation.*

The job of a headline is to reduce a story to the words which make that story intelligible. These four words do that in this case. *Crash* tells us what happened. *Woman* tell us who it happened to. *Rejects* tells us what the woman has done. *Deal* tells us what she has rejected.

The compound noun is *Crash Woman*. This has been invented.

The present simple makes a story sound more immediate.

Crash and *deal* have been used because they are shorter.

The headline can be understood without the articles, which means they can be cut and space can be saved.

6 Expanding headlines

The language of headlines provides a real challenge. Students should work on this exercise in pairs or in small groups. You will need to provide support while students do this exercise, helping guide them to the right answers.

Answers

1   Reading the phrase backwards, helps us to think of the meaning: *There is hope for the baby who is in a coma.*

2   *To operate* expresses the future. This is an abbreviation of *going to operate*. Abbreviations of this type are very common in newspaper headlines because they save space.

3   The colon is used to introduce the second part of the headline, which explains the *hope* mentioned in the first part by revealing that a surgeon is going to operate on the baby.

4   There is hope for the baby who is a coma because an American surgeon is going to operate on him/her.

5   *Train blaze* is used because it shorter than *big fire on train*. In addition, it's more dramatic.

6   Only the past participle part of the passive is used. We are given *found* rather than *has been found*.

7   Inverted commas in headlines tell us that something is a quote or that nobody is certain yet about the truth of something. The inverted commas around 'unhurt' suggest that a journalist has been told this but has not yet been able to check whether it is true or not.

8   A child has been rescued with only minor injuries from a fire on a train.

Do some work with the class on the first headline before you ask them to complete items 1–8. This would be of particular benefit to students who need more **support**. Put COMA BABY HOPE on the board and then ask questions about it: *'Why does the headline call the baby a "coma baby"?'* (Answer: To tell us that the baby is in a coma. A similar example would be CAR CRASH DOG BACK HOME, which tells us that the dog was involved in an accident.) *'What does the word 'hope' suggest?'* (Answer: That something has happened or is going to happen to make people believe that the baby will come out of the coma.) *'Do we know what is going to happen?'* (Answer: Yes, we do. The second part of the headline tells us that the baby is going to be operated on.) Once you have gone through these questions, refer students to items 1–8 and ask them to work on the exercise.

7 Noun or verb?

This exercise gives more practice with the vocabulary of headlines.

Answers

The missing word for each pair of sentences is as follows:

1   aid

2   head

3   arm

4   vow

5   cut

6   jail

You could extend the exercise by discussing the way the stress shifts in some words depending on whether they are used as a noun or a verb, e.g. *record, reject, produce.*

8 Comparing languages

Why not ask students to bring in examples of headlines in their own language to compare with headlines in English?

9 Discussion

If students are slow in producing ideas about reasons for injuries, you could suggest:

- not warming up
- not using the right technique

- not following the rules
- failure to wear protective clothing.

10 Rewording

As a step towards summary writing, students are asked to put single sentences into their own words. It is interesting to discuss which words can be changed and which words (e.g. technical terms) need to stay the same.

There is no set formula for the alterations. Using active instead of the passive forms is one possible option. You need to encourage students to make the most of all their language resources and to ask themselves *'Which words in this sentence is it possible to change? Have the changes in structure and vocabulary altered the meaning significantly?'*

As students study the example, ask them:

'Is the meaning the same as the original?' (Yes, it is close enough to be perfectly acceptable as a summary.)

'Is it more concise?' (Yes. 'Should' and 'do' are more concise than 'would be well advised' and 'carry out'.)

'Which words haven't been changed and why?' ('weight training' and 'gym' can't really be changed because there are no concise synonyms.)

When students have completed the exercise, ask for examples of rewording to compare and contrast among the whole group.

To support students who find writing summaries difficult, you may wish to cut down the number of sentences in the exercise, or you can pool ideas and write the best answers on the board.

sentence on the board. (See item 1 in the Answers above.) It might be a good idea to use this approach and do the rest of the exercise as a whole-class activity, particularly for the benefit of students who need more **support**.

Possible answers

1 Many severe injuries cause bleeding and discomfort.
2 For the first day, ice should not be used for more than ten minutes at a time.
3 Never put ice straight onto the skin because it may cause burns.
4 The best treatment for the initial swelling and pain is rest.
5 However, you should start gently moving the injured part as soon as possible.
6 If possible, ask a physiotherapist to supervise any exercise.
7 Medication from your doctor may help to reduce the pain and swelling of your injury.

11 Writing a short summary

This exercise is not too demanding and you could set it as a timed exercise for your more able students. With a group of students who require more support, it will help to build up their confidence. When students have finished, you could ask for help from the whole group in building up a complete version on the board. Draw their attention to the fact that the list of examples of protective equipment should be left out.

Possible answer

You can avoid sports injuries by using a rational and well-organised approach to training. Do not attempt to train when you are tired, as fatigue can lead to injuries. Ensure that you use good techniques and that you wear protective equipment if necessary, and suitable footwear.

12 Expressing warnings

In this exercise, students practise warning each other about the risks of various sporting activities. You could **challenge** some students to read the model dialogues aloud to the class. Check understanding of the more specialised vocabulary items, such as *run aground*.

Support some students by asking them to choose three of the dialogues to focus on. When they have practised each dialogue until they are confident, Students A and B should swap roles for further reinforcement.

Practice

Monitor the mini-conversations to ensure that students are incorporating appropriate warning language. As always, pairs of students who have performed well could be asked to present good dialogues to the rest of the group to round off the exercise.

Additional situations could be:

- canoeing: make sure you wear a helmet
- skating: watch out for thin ice
- swimming: look out for dangerous currents.

C Motivation through sport

1 Pre-reading discussion

Introduce the topic by explaining that a sports project is being used to help students who have dropped out of school regain their self-esteem and motivation to achieve. You could explore the topic by asking why some young people drop out of school (family problems, financial situation, peer group pressure, lack of confidence, etc.) and what are the consequences of lack of education (unemployment or dead-end work, boredom, nothing to look forward to, poverty, difficulty engaging with the community and in taking part in meaningful activities, etc.). As students are developing the skills of identifying key points, you could write down their ideas on the board in the form of 'spider' diagrams with the words '*reasons for school drop-out*' and '*lack of education means …*' in the centre. It will be interesting to hear students' views and whether they take a sympathetic view of such young people and how far they believe they have only themselves to blame.

2 Predicting content

If students are slow in coming up with ideas, you could suggest other points to see how they react, e.g.

- attitudes of the participants
- how long the project is
- where the project is based
- comments from the coaches
- how successful the project has been overall.

3 Vocabulary check

Answers

1 B   2 D   3 A   4 E   5 C

4 Developing reading skills

The text reflects exams in difficulty and the type of ideas. Remind students of the value of combining fast and slow speeds for maximum reading efficiency. Remind students that they can read more efficiently by spending more time focusing on the complex parts of a text and less on those that they find easier to understand.

See the Introduction for a general approach to helping students with Reading tasks.

For students who find reading texts particularly challenging, break the text into sections. Allow them just enough time to skim read a particular section, then ask them for a quick summary of what they have just read. Repeat with the next section.

5 True/false comprehension

As always, the true/false comprehension will enable you to check what students have understood and assimilated from the reading text. You might like to set a time limit for the work, allocating a suitable time limit for the ability levels in your group.

Answers

1 false   2 false   3 false   4 true   5 true   6 true
7 false   8 true   9 true

6 Checking predictions

Students can't really be told often enough that predicting content is a great way into a quick understanding of a text. This exercise gives them further practice.

7 Writing a headline

Ask students '*What headline would give the reader a good idea of what this text is about?*' Encourage them to apply what they have learned about headlines (strings of nouns, few grammar elements, short words, dramatic effects, use of present tenses). Above all, it is important that the headline is short and punchy. Students could read out their headlines and comment on each other's.

8 Post-reading discussion

1 Teenagers sometimes use diaries (and some write online blogs) so it will be interesting to see what they think of the idea of diary keeping in this context. Any ideas suggesting that the diary is safe way to channel participants' confused or conflicting feelings would be insightful.

   You could ask any students who say they keep a diary (or write a blog) to talk about how it helps them.

2 To finish the reading exercise, you could ask students what they think would help 'graduates' of the project to maintain positive attitudes into the future. Elicit ideas such as follow-up support to check that young people are pursuing their goals, and setting up a network to keep everyone in touch through email and social media contact.

9 Making notes

Encourage students to find a clear point for each bullet. They could exchange their notes and check that their partner has approached the task methodically.

Answers
Aims of the project
- to help 16–25-year-olds from disadvantaged backgrounds
- to teach organisational skills through sport
- to teach communication skills through sport

What participants learn
- the basic skills of various sports
- how to teach/coach others in the same skills

- communication skills/how to get along with people of different backgrounds/nationalities
- self-discipline

Reasons the project is popular
- they learn new skills
- they have new experiences/experience being abroad
- they meet other nationalities and share ideas and beliefs/compare cultures
- they meet different people with similar problems

10 Correcting a connected summary

The connected summary contains names and other details which are redundant and should usually be avoided in summaries.

11 Rewriting a summary

Example answer

> The aim of the project is to encourage young people who have not been successful at school to improve their ability to communicate with other people and to develop their organisational skills. Participants are taught a range of skills for a variety of sports and are then expected to coach each other. From these activities, the young people learn self-discipline, cooperation and how to manage others on their team, even when they behave in a troublesome way. The participants enjoy being abroad, sharing ideas and beliefs, learning new skills and discovering that they are not alone with their problems. *(99 words)*

12 Expressions of measurement

Practice: answers

1 She uses a fifty-minute fitness video.
2 He made a six-inch cut.
3 Ali got a thousand-dollar contract.
4 They ordered a six-course meal.
5 I need a one-pound coin for the locker.
6 It's a ten-minute drive to work.
7 Tanya gave birth to a seven-pound baby.
8 I'd like a two-kilogram bag of sugar.

Other examples to discuss are: *a two-litre bottle of milk, a fifteen-minute wait, a three-day course.*

51

With a fairly able group, you could extend the exercise by explaining that the plural -*s* is retained when we use 'worth', with the addition of an apostrophe, e.g.

I paid a lot of money for five minutes' worth of help.

He bought six dollars' worth of tokens to use in the machine.

13 Vocabulary: Using fewer words
Answers
1   challenge
2   overcome
3   ignore
4   obvious
5   abroad

14 Redundant words
This exercise will increase students' awareness of a key difference between speech and writing. If possible, play a recording of about one or two minutes of unedited, completely natural conversation. Ask students to write down exactly what they hear. It's very interesting to analyse the way people really speak, especially with regard to redundancy.

If you aren't able to do this, you could write on the board as an example:

When writing a summary it helps to start by using small steps to begin with.

Ask students which words are repeating the same idea *(start/begin with)*. You could then ask why we tend to repeat ourselves in spoken language, eliciting that redundancy in speech is a form of emphasis. We repeat ourselves to make sure that someone has heard and understood what we have said.

Answers
1   first/begin to
2   's feet
3   old; which are so valuable it is impossible to say how much they are worth
4   unexpected
5   very
6   to cut with

7   saying the same words over and over again
8   unhealthily

International overview
Answers
1   10 000 hours
2   108 hours
3   Japan
4   Finland

D Health, diet and fitness

1 Pre-reading discussion
Students consider a new topic by looking at the way a sedentary job, 'empty' calories and poor work-life balance can affect health and fitness.

2 Predicting content
The pre-reading tasks, as always, encourage students to use clues to predict the content of the text, the target audience and the writer's intention.

3 Vocabulary check
Answers
nibble: eat in small bites

sluggish: lacking in energy

snack on: eat between meals

packed lunches: cold food such as sandwiches prepared at home to take to work or school

(Students might like to know that *nibbles* is also a noun meaning snack foods like crisps and nuts, to accompany drinks.)

4 Reading
The reading pointers will help guide students through Shalimar's story. You could check them through afterwards and ask students to identify examples of the points in the text.

It will be interesting to see how students react to the story of someone who reaps considerable health benefits from small lifestyle changes. Let them discuss the topic freely. They may enjoy considering whether Shalimar would have developed bad habits if she had stayed in her family home instead of living independently.

5 Post-reading discussion

Discuss with the students the idea that her mother took a risk and plucked up the courage to confront Shalimar because Shalimar might have reacted angrily – it was not predictable.

Health experts are now more inclined to encourage people to make small changes, as Shalimar does, that fit in with their lifestyle, as research shows these changes are more likely to be maintained and will build up to a big difference over time. Students are asked to consider whether this approach is wise, or whether it would be motivating enough, because results might be slow. There are no 'right' answers.

6 Writing a summary

There are no comprehension questions after the passage. This reflects the way exam summary questions are set. However, you may want to check that students have grasped the main points they should include in the summary.

Example answer

Before Shalimar went on the fitness programme, her lifestyle was very unhealthy because she was not doing any exercise or eating regular meals. She devoted herself to developing her gaming business and she worked long hours, surviving on snack food and sipping fizzy drinks. She had no energy, and after work she would feel too exhausted to cook and did not sleep well. Since starting the programme, she has taken proper meal breaks, has become more active, and more creative. She feels the fitness programme was appropriate because it helped her to make easy and sensible changes in her habits. (100 words)

You may wish to copy and circulate the example answer for students to compare with their own versions.

7 Vocabulary: Phrasal verbs

You could introduce this exercise by eliciting some phrasal verbs that students know. Students can then work in pairs or small group to decide the meaning of each of the phrasal verbs in the box, using the context of the article to help them.

Answers

1   start up
2   plunge in
3   give up
4   plucked up
5   conjure up
6   made up

Challenge students and reinforce understanding of the phrasal verbs by asking students to try to write a sentence of their own using some or all of them. Check that they have used the phrasal verbs correctly. You could prompt with questions: do you have a bad habit that you would like to give up? If you could start up a new business, what might it be? Give an example of when you had to pluck up courage to do something.

8 Spelling: Adding suffixes to words with a final *-e*

This exercise gives students practice in a very tricky area of spelling. Drawing analogies is one of the best ways of building up knowledge of spelling and vocabulary. Encourage students to make intelligent guesses about why the final *-e* is kept or dropped when a suffix is added. It's an opportunity to make the most of their understanding of word formation.

Keeping or dropping the *-e* basically depends on whether a vowel or consonant suffix is added: consonant suffixes keep the *-e*; vowel suffixes drop it. As you might expect, however, there are numerous exceptions, which is one of the reasons students find this spelling rule rather treacherous.

English is said to have one of the most inconsistent spelling systems of any language, due to its wide variety of language influences over history. It's a fascinating subject, which you may like to explore a little further with your students.

Students often feel that the problematic spelling is compensated by a relatively uncomplicated grammar and the flexibility it allows in word formation, e.g. turning nouns into verb, adjectives and adverbs.

Practice: answers

education

having

exciting

creativity

movements

introduction

motivation

stimulating

participating

encouragement

achieving

celebration

stylish

diversity

imaginative

You might like to develop the exercise by exploring some of the possibilities in the other lexical items, e.g. *festive* and *festivity(ies)* linked to *festival*.

9 Word building

Answers

1   timing, timely
2   concentrating, concentration
3   refining, refinement
4   exercising
5   welcoming
6   involving, involvement
7   aching
8   stately, statement
9   uniquely, uniqueness
10   awareness

10 Look, say, cover, write, check

As usual, a visual strategy will reinforce learning.

Grammar spotlight

TEACHING SUPPORT

See the Introduction for a general approach to helping students with Grammar exercises.

The *Grammar spotlight* picks out ways of using passive constructions, using examples drawn from texts in the unit. As always, the examples are selected to show students that they have been handling these structures confidently and the spotlight enables them to consolidate this knowledge.

You may like to give some examples of active structures on the board and encourage students to change them into the passive, e.g.

Last year's champion presented the prizes.

*The prizes **were presented** by last year's champion.*

A doctor examined my bruised leg.

*My bruised leg **was examined** by a doctor.*

When discussing the organisation of a passive sentence which has two objects, direct and indirect, you could write an example on the board first to elicit that the preference is to start with the indirect object. This is considered better style, e.g.

A tennis racket was given to Santos by the sports assistant.

***Santos was given** a tennis racket by the sports assistant.*

LEARNING SUPPORT

For less confident students, check understanding of why we use the passive form. Give them **support** with the following examples and elicit from them why the active form would not be possible/appropriate here: *The actor was awarded an Oscar for his role in the film. Some of the best chocolate is produced in Switzerland.* (Answer: Sometimes we do not know who carried out the action or it is not important in the context.)

Where students are uncomfortable with using the passive where the active form has two objects, look at a practice example together, e.g. *The bank lent Maria $2,000 to start up her own business.* Elicit from students who the main focus is in the sentence (Maria) and ask them to change the verb to make it passive: *Maria was lent $2,000 by the bank to start up her own business.* Discuss whether 'by the bank' is important information or whether the sentence makes as much sense without it (this probably depends on the context). Give students further examples to practise with.

Answers

A It is time that sports *were banned* from the school curriculum. (Exercise 3.A.10)

It is essential that protests *are made* about the unfair ways young children *are treated* … (Exercise 3.A.10)

Participants *are taught* a range of skills … and then they *are expected* to coach each other. (Exercise 3.C.10)

B The youngsters are given diaries to record their thoughts and experiences. (Exercise 3.C.4)

As always, if students need more help understanding and applying the passive structure, they should be encouraged to do further practice.

Exam-style questions

See the Overview of *Cambridge IGCSE English as a Second Language* section at the beginning of the Student's Book for the mark scheme and criteria for marking the writing questions.

Notes and summary writing

1 Sleep – summary
The following example shows the good summary style that is required at Extended level, including good spelling, punctuation and vocabulary, and good use of linking words and some use of own words.

Example answer

> Teenagers need more sleep than adults because their brains are still growing. The brain grows and is repaired during slow wave sleep. Teenagers need 40% of their sleeping time in slow wave sleep. In contrast, adults need to spend only 4% of time in slow wave sleep. Lack of sleep interferes with the brain taking sugar effectively from the bloodstream which makes teenagers slower to learn. It makes it harder to reach goals and avoid harmful behaviour. Slow wave sleep is also needed to move new words learned earlier from the short term to the long term memory. *(98 words)*

(Reading & Writing, Exercise 4: 16 marks (Extended).)

Students doing the Extended paper should select up to eight ideas from the text in order to write their summary. The following shows an example of the sort of content that a student might select from the text about the sleeping habits of teenagers.

Why young people need more sleep than adults

1 They require slow wave sleep for 40% of sleeping time.

2 Slow wave sleep is when the brain carries out the healing and repair functions.

3 Teenagers need enough overall sleep to get 40% of sleep in slow wave.

Negative effects of lack of sleep

1   Teenagers perform less well on tests of mental agility.
2   The brain cannot extract sugar effectively from the bloodstream.
3   A lack of sugar means the brain is less alert.
4   It is more difficult for teenagers to fulfil a goal.
5   Teenagers display more impulsive/foolish behaviour.
6   Teenagers cannot retain information/new vocabulary or learn a new language effectively
7   Emotional experiences are not processed by the brain.

The answer is marked for reading (content) (eight marks) and writing (eight marks) making a total of 16 marks available. The best answers should show up to eight relevant content points based on their notes for answering question 2. To gain the writing marks available, students need to use some of their own vocabulary and do some reorganisation of sentence structure, and use the correct spelling and grammar. The word limit of 120 should be observed. If you are using this as a mock exam, count the words and do not credit anything written after the maximum word limit.

2 Fear of swimming–note making

The example note-making answer shows all the correct points in the 'Fear of Swimming' text that students might identify. For full marks, Extended students should find up to nine points. Students should aim to cover all the headings given and put at least one correct point under each heading. Encourage them to write the notes briefly. Small mistakes in their writing are not important as long as the meaning is still clear.

Example answer

Why some children fear learning to swim

- Fear of water is a natural response
- Pools cold **and** noisy
- People splashing **and** shouting

Ways of overcoming a fear of swimming

- Choose a smallish /quiet /warm/ pool (any two required)
- Have fun in the water/enjoy it (any one)
- Get used to going underwater
- Take it slowly
- Avoid group lessons/have one to one tuition (one point)

- Build up confidence **and** skills
- Pour water over the head gently/blow bubbles (one point)
- Wear goggles

How some adults were put off learning to swim

- Being ducked/splashed
- Being pushed around by a pole
- Having a rope tied around their waist

(Reading & Writing, Exercise 3: 9 marks (Extended).)

3 Raw food diet – summary

Encourage students to apply the method for summarising a text. They should try to use some of their own words and to organise and link ideas coherently. Their answers should cover both the advantages and disadvantages. There are six marks available for the relevant content points and six marks for language, making a total of 12 marks. Each relevant content point is worth one mark. The example answer shows the full range of content points possible but students only need to find up to six of these points. Specialised words such as calcium do not need to be paraphrased.

Example answer

A raw food diet has advantages. Firstly, food is eaten fresh so it contains more vitamins than processed food. Also raw food takes longer to chew and to be absorbed by the body. This makes it more filling so we do not overeat. However, if we eat too much fruit on the diet, we can get tooth decay from high sugar levels. Furthermore, we might lack calcium, iron and zinc. Finally, the diet is not based on scientific evidence. (79 words)

(Reading & Writing, Exercise 4: 12 marks (Core).)

Listening CD 1, Track 9

This exercise sums up the sport themes in the unit, so you may like to let students listen more than twice. Remind them that they should listen for authentic understanding, rather than simply matching words on the recording with words in the statements. If they do this, they might choose an incorrect answer, so it is useful to draw attention to the way paraphrasing is used.

You may like to pause the recording when checking the answers in order to focus on a particular expression or individual word. Encourage students to discuss why this particular word or phrase is important in making the right answer correct. You may also like to explore the fact that there is no evidence on the recording for statement E.

Answers

SPEAKER 1	G
SPEAKER 2	D
SPEAKER 3	C
SPEAKER 4	F
SPEAKER 5	B
SPEAKER 6	A

(Statement E is not needed.)

(Listening, Exercise 3: 6 marks (Core); 6 marks (Extended).)

AUDIOSCRIPT

You will hear six people talking about sport. For each of the SPEAKERs 1 to 6, choose from the list A to G which opinion each SPEAKER expresses. Write the letter in the box. Use each letter only once. There is one extra letter which you do not need to use.

SPEAKER 1

My favourite football star, George Razak, is only 17, the same age as me, but he is amazing. I have watched him mature in the last 12 months and now he plays a great all-round game and is improving at a spectacular rate. He's won all his matches this season. Young sports stars show so much determination to succeed and get ahead, no matter what the effort. They make me more aware of my potential and desire to achieve. My friends say the same. We are inspired to put more into everything we do. We feel we can win if we try hard enough.

SPEAKER 2

To get to the top of my game as a professional tennis player, I have needed to be quite single minded. I got interested in tennis around the age of ten I suppose, and my dad used to drive me to my coaching sessions and to play in matches. I spent hours and hours on it every week of my childhood and as a teenager, building up strength and stamina. But no one can develop skills and potential without putting in the time. It would have been no good at all if I had waited until I was an adult before going into tennis. I would not be where I am today, if I had done that.

SPEAKER 3

I just love sport. There's so much excitement. On a Saturday morning we play matches, and I can't wait to get out on to the sports field with my team. We all run around, trying to get the ball, trying to win. Sure, we're focused on concentrating on our technique, but we all care about winning too. Winning is great! That's what sport is about. I have never heard anyone say they want to lose a game.

SPEAKER 4

My grandson is ten years old and I get so much pleasure seeing him and the other young kids run out into the playground when school is over for the day. They kick a ball and some can run like the wind too. When I was my grandson's age we had hours of sports lessons every week – we called it PE, and if you ask me, it's what's lacking these days. 'Put more sport into the school timetable' is what I say. When you are young, you need exercise and fresh air, not to sit still in a classroom all day, every day.

SPEAKER 5

I understand what people mean when they say sport is a lesson for life. At school, we are often told that losing a game is good because it can help us cope with disappointment in everyday life. But I don't think life is just about losing and disappointment, it's about fun too. Sport is brilliant for me, I love it, and I think we should be encouraged to see it as fun and an amusement, not as something serious. Sports lessons in the school curriculum can reflect that.

SPEAKER 6

Teenagers are giving up sport at school and say they don't care who wins or loses. If you ask me, that attitude isn't going to help them at all. Kids need to do sport at school and experience winning or losing because it's such a great way to learn what life will be like later on. Dealing with disappointment and accepting luck isn't always on your side are important lessons best learned when you're young. Teenagers need to understand this before they leave school and get a job. There will be setbacks sometimes, and they will have to cope in a grown-up way – taking responsibility for their actions.

Wider Practice

1 Summarising is hard, but remind students it gets easier with practice! You could help them develop their ability to summarise by asking them to choose topics they have a strong interest in: TV programmes, information from blogs and chat rooms, live talks they have attended, radio broadcasts, as well as extracts from books, websites or the printed media. Their summaries could be presented to the class orally.

2 You could develop the sport theme further by asking students to research a sports personality of their choice and present a profile. Or they could research a topical issue in sport and fitness, e.g. sport sponsorship, women in sport, sports injuries, how to get fit for sport. Students may be interested in doing a project on the history of a particular sport.

3 Students might enjoy visiting their local sports centre or swimming pool and finding out about its day-to-day operations, its role in the community, the facilities it offers, etc.

4 Students may enjoy keeping a class diary or online blog in which they record their ideas for new sports or fitness activities they would like to see offered in the curriculum, or describe recent sporting and fitness challenges they have encountered or any other interesting aspects of their shared sports, fitness or health experience.

Unit 4
Our impact on the planet

Overview

This unit focuses on transport and environmental concerns, including carbon footprint and climate change, which are all popular IGCSE topics. Students are expected to have a broad, general understanding of these topics so they can discuss them intelligently. Detailed scientific or geographical knowledge is not tested or required.

The main aim of the unit is to help students produce a well-reasoned article, email or report for the school magazine, local newspaper or headteacher/school management committee. Students should be aiming to develop the ability to give reasons clearly. Students are usually given a stimulus, e.g. *'A new airport is planned for your area. Is this a good idea? What do you think?'* They can choose to agree with the proposal, disagree with it or be impartial. They are not asked to be 'for' or 'against' in a very rigid way. They might also be asked to write a report on a school visit for the headteacher, for example, saying whether they thought the visit was worthwhile or not and why.

The most important thing in students' answers is coherence. They should be able to develop the theme clearly, structure their ideas soundly and offer some examples and explanation. They need to present the argument in a fairly formal style for a newspaper or report and a slightly more informal style for the school magazine, and they should show some awareness of their audience. The reading items include a factual article on the arrival of the first railways in the 19th century, a leaflet advertising a sponsored cycle ride to raise funds for the environment and a student magazine article about climate change. The exam-style reading comprehension is based on a multiple matching format similar to those found in the reading and writing component of exams.

For listening development, students listen for specific information in a discussion on the results of a school survey carried out to determine the patterns of car usage among school pupils. There is also an exam-style listening exercise based on the style of questions found in the listening component, recycling the vocabulary and themes of the unit.

The discussion areas, as always, focus on encouraging students to think of relevant ideas and express opinions. This is even more important in an argument essay, as students can't produce a convincing argument if they can't think of ideas in the first place!

Language work

The language work focuses on developing reasoning skills. Students extend their understanding of the functions of linking words. Logical sequencing skills are also extended.

Spelling and pronunciation are developed by highlighting the contrast between hard and soft *g* sounds. Functional skills practise listening to and asking for a favour. Vocabulary development focuses on ways of walking, euphemisms and words often confused.

The *Grammar spotlight* looks at ways of expressing the future, using examples students have encountered in the unit.

A Transport then and now

1 Pre-reading discussion

A The discussion focuses students' thoughts on transport and safety in their country. As always, it is helpful to encourage them to share their experiences of what they have noticed about the popular modes of transport.

B The discussion leads into students' experiences of train travel, which could vary considerably.

Brainstorming

Students are asked to think about how life changed when the first railways came in the 19th century. Travel was often a rare occurrence as people tended to stay in the area where they were born. Students are encouraged to use their imagination to consider how people who had been used to going by horse-drawn carriages, carts or stagecoaches might have felt about the concept of a fast-moving vehicle with an engine. It is not expected that students will have historical knowledge, so the brainstorming exercise is designed to be fun and inclusive.

Some ideas to elicit are:

- People were worried that the trains were very dangerous.
- They were curious about how the engines worked. (They were powered by steam.)
- They wondered where you got on a train/what a railway station might be.
- They wondered how the train stayed on its tracks or what would make it stop.
- People might have thought trains were dirty and noisy.
- They might have wondered how crashes could be avoided.

2 Vocabulary check

Answers

passenger: a person who travels in a vehicle or other form of transport, other than the driver, pilot or crew

suspicions: concerns that something is wrong

rigorously: very carefully/strictly

immobilised: stopped from being able to move

novelty: an enjoyable new thing or experience

3 Reading

TEACHING SUPPORT

See the Introduction for a general approach to helping students with Reading tasks.

You might like to let students read the article through once as a whole-class exercise for general understanding, pausing in places to ask some gist questions, and to check further vocabulary items which might be unfamiliar (e.g. near misses, generated).

The follow-up reading task encourages students to scan the text to spot specific details in it. This is also very good training for multiple matching exercises found in exam reading and writing components.

LEARNING SUPPORT

Where students need **support**, tell them in which paragraph they will find the answers. As follows:
1 para 3; 2 para 3; 3 para 4; 4 para 5; 5 para 7; 6 para 8.

Answers

1 medical professionals
2 farmers
3 well known/respected public figures
4 (trained) railway engineers
5 people from small towns and villages
6 labourers

4 Making notes

Students can complete the notes individually, as this makes excellent practice for note-making exam questions. They can then check their answers with a partner. The pros and cons of the standardised clock would also make an interesting discussion.

Answers
Fears of effects on rural life

- destroy beauty of countryside
- destroy gentle pace of life
- destroy crops
- scare farm animals

Safety Improvements

- standardised clock
- strict regulations controlling building of tracks, bridges, tunnels
- safety checks on trains/unsafe trains immobilised

Impact on employment

- people could travel to a wider range of jobs
- railway construction generated new employment

5 Post-reading task

1 Encourage students to give a personal opinion as there is no right answer.
2 Possible answers include:
- There are regulations controlling the building and maintenance of the railways.
- There is a standardised clock.
- Unsafe trains are not used.
- Engines are checked and replaced if necessary.
- Newspapers dramatise events to grab attention.

3   It will be interesting to see if students feel the article helps develop a balanced perspective on the dangers of plane travel.

To finish, students might like to know some further information about the impact of trains, such as the fact that they enabled frequent postal deliveries. People also had more opportunity to vary their diet as perishable food, such as fish, could be transported quickly from other regions.

6 Language study: Logical reasoning

Logical reasoning is important in formal written arguments. Interesting compositions are sometimes spoiled by inadequate reasoning techniques.

Answers

A   The words expressing reasoning are *because* and *As a result*. *Because* could be replaced with *as*; *As a result* could be replaced with *Consequently*.

B   *If … then* is a conditional construction: one thing depends on another. 'Then' is often not explicitly stated. A comma is often used after the 'if' clause.

You could elicit other sentences with this structure, e.g. *If the company closes, (then) jobs will be lost. If you pass the exam, you can go to university.*

C   *Furthermore* is an alternative to *In addition*. Both are similar to *and* but are more formal and more suitable as introductory expressions in writing.

7 Completing a text

This exercise enables students to practise using some of the linking devices and structures they have studied earlier.

Answers

Because / as / since, In addition / Furthermore / Moreover, As a result / Consequently, as / because / since

It would be interesting to round off this section by asking students *'In what way has the article changed your views about people's fears today about various forms of travel?'*

8 Spelling and pronunciation: The letter *g*
🔊 CD 1, Track 10

Recognition

The aim of this exercise is to increase students' awareness of spelling/pronunciation patterns. Note that *gu* pronounced /gw/ is a relatively unusual

sound and is often linked with words of Spanish origin, e.g. *guacamole, guava. Fire extinguisher* is the only example in the text.

Recognition: answers

1 s   2 g   3 s   4 g   5 s   6 g   7 s   8 s
9 g   10 s   11 g   12 s

AUDIOSCRIPT
As in the Student's Book.

Other examples in the text you may like to elicit are: *wagons* (*line 7*), *eager* (*line 30*), *luggage* (*line 34*) and *strange* (*line 2*), *carriages* (*line 6*), *gentle* (*line 21*), *registered* (*line 33*), *generated* (*line 67*).

Practice

You could ask students to contrast these sounds with voiceless sounds in English such as /s/ and /p/, where they can feel there is no vibration in the vocal cords. You might like to ask them to say *sssss* and let it gradually become *zzzz* (a voiced sound).

It would be interesting to contrast voiced and voiceless sounds in English with sounds in students' own language(s), to compare those which are voiced and those which are not.

9 Spelling patterns

Students scan the word list they have just practised and circle the significant spelling features. The soft *g* rule is a fairly trustworthy spelling rule, so it is worth teaching.

Remembering the spelling pattern for soft *g* words will help students spell a wider variety of words and provide some tools for decoding pronunciation. You could follow up this exercise by asking them to make intelligent guesses as to the pronunciation of more unusual words you write on the board, e.g. *pageant, ginger, gibberish, Egyptian, geography.*

10 Vocabulary

This exercise checks the meaning of words students met in the earlier exercise. Physically writing out the words will help students remember the spelling patterns.

Answers

1   apology

2   oxygen

3   engineer

4   passengers

5   challenge

6   guarantee

7   regulations

8   figure

9   rigorously

Words 1–5 contain soft *g* sounds; 6–9 contain hard *g* sounds.

11 Odd word out

This exercise introduces some additional common words containing hard and soft *g* sounds.

Answers

A   regard (it has a hard *g* sound)

B   pigeon (it has a soft *g*)

12 Look, say, cover, write, check

You could ask students to identify why these words pose spelling difficulties, eliciting ideas such as: *'Privilege is often misspelt with a d'; 'ou is a difficult pattern'; 'ie words are often misspelt'; 'the e in the middle of vegetable is silent and is often left out.'*

You could round off this section on spelling by getting students to compose some fun sentences containing as many of the target sounds as possible. They then dictate the sentences to each other, e.g. *Egyptian giraffes eat ginger.*

13 Before you listen

The pre-listening discussion helps focus students' thoughts on the transport they use in their daily lives. You could encourage them to think about alternative methods of transport and ask *'If you had a completely free choice of transport, what would you choose and why?'*

Vocabulary check: answers

Get a lift from someone is a common idiomatic phrase meaning to ask someone to drive you free of charge in his/her car. You could contrast this with *take a taxi*.

Acid rain is rain that is polluted with chemicals and causes damage to rivers, ecosystems, etc.

Asthma is a common chest disease which causes breathing difficulties and has been linked to car exhaust fumes.

14 Listening for gist / 15 Listening and note taking 🔊 CD 1, Track 11

> **TEACHING SUPPORT**
>
> See the Introduction for a general approach to helping students with Listening tasks.

As always, allow students to listen first for general meaning and then for specific information. Many of the notes paraphrase what is said on the recording rather than using the same words. This is typical in exams, which often aim to test genuine comprehension and avoid 'direct matching' activities.

> **LEARNING SUPPORT**
>
> Where students need **support**, pair them with another student. They should both read all the questions, but Student A should focus on writing the answers to the odd-numbered questions, and Student B to the even-numbered. They should then check answers together, and listen again to focus on those questions that neither is sure about.

Answers

1   11–20

2   50 car trips a week

3   80%

4   **a** is on a bus route

5   **b** too inconvenient

6   too dangerous/not safe enough

7   **b** health concerns/effects on health

8   the family needs a new car/parents buy a new car

AUDIOSCRIPT

You are going to listen to a discussion between two friends, Paolo and Linda, on the results of a survey. The survey was carried out to determine patterns of car usage by pupils in their school. Listen to the discussion first for general meaning.

PAOLO: Anyway, we've got the results of the survey now.

LINDA: Right, well, I can note the main points that come up and then fill in the chart. The school magazine is the best place to publicise the findings, don't you think?

P: Yes. Erm, well, you know, it's interesting to see the extent of car usage. Usually pupils are making between 11 and 20 trips by car a week. Mostly they're, you know … it's what you'd expect, getting lifts from their parents. A small percentage, 5%, make over 50 car trips in a week. The results really aren't encouraging.

L: Gosh, 50 car trips a week! That is a lot, isn't it? They must have a good social life! And understanding parents who don't mind being a taxi service! What was the response like to the question about whether there was an alternative to the journeys they make by car?

P: Well, a whopping 80% said they would get a lift even if they didn't really have to. They could easily have walked to where they wanted to go, but it seems they prefer to get lifts from their mum or dad. I think often it's just laziness.

L: Yes, although having said that, I do think a lot of pupils at this school do seem to walk to school.

P: 40% said they walked to school regularly but then, well, 33% said they always come by car, which is not so good.

L: I wonder why, when the school is on a bus route and there's a train station only five minutes' walk away?

P: Erm, well, from the survey it seems that coming to school by bus or train is either too expensive, or too inconvenient. Their homes aren't near a bus stop or train station – it's just not available where they live.

L: What did that 33% who come by car say about coming to school under their own steam – walking or cycling, for instance?

P: A lot of them said their parents wouldn't allow them to walk or cycle because it's just not safe enough. The roads are really dangerous for cycling, and some pupils live over eight miles away, so walking to and from school would just take too long. You can't really expect them to undertake that kind of trek every day.

L: What about wanting a car when they leave school?

P: Well, that was pretty encouraging from the point of view of protecting the environment. A third of those who responded were against having their own car when they were adults. One of the main reasons they gave was concern over the environment. They're worried about car exhaust fumes contributing to acid rain and affecting the wildlife. And they're also worried about, well, the health issue in general. They think car fumes can cause asthma.

L: Well, it's good to know they're not all desperate to become car owners themselves. But what about all those kids constantly being driven around in their parents' cars?

P: Well, one thing was mentioned. When the family needs a new car, a lot of children said they discussed what kind of car would be best with their parents. Er, they said they tried to, you know, persuade their mum and dad to buy a small, fuel-efficient model because that's better for the environment.

16 Post-listening discussion
It will be interesting to hear students' views on whether car usage should be restricted. If your students live in areas which are congested and polluted, they may be more inclined to recommend formal controls on the use of cars, such as road tolls, fines for being the sole occupant of a car, and limits to using the car at certain times of the day. On the other hand, if they live in areas of low population and open spaces, they may see no need for restrictions at all.

17 Euphemisms
Asking students to offer examples of euphemisms in their first language(s) would be interesting and also a good way of checking that they have understood the concept.

Matching: answers
1 H **2** B **3** E **4** F **5** G **6** A **7** D **8** C

63

18 Asking for a favour

You might like to ask a couple of students to read the dialogue aloud first to highlight the appropriate intonation patterns.

You could ask *'Does Joe sound tentative or does he sound demanding when he asks a favour? Which approach is more suitable for the situation?'*

Elicit or teach the meaning of the adjective 'tentative'. If someone sounds tentative when they ask a question, it means they are unsure of what they are doing and do it without confidence.

Remind students that *Would you mind* … is followed by a gerund (*waiting/giving,* etc.). You could also ask them to identify the more formal/less formal expressions, e.g. *put you out/be a nuisance* are more colloquial than *not too inconvenient.*

After they have practised the conversations in pairs, you could offer more prompts, e.g. *wanting to borrow money, needing help to carry a heavy load.* Or you could ask students to develop conversations around situations of their own.

B Nature under threat

This section develops the theme of transport and environmental issues by focusing on cycling.

1 Pre-reading discussion

This activity could be done effectively in small groups as an alternative to pairs.

Students sometimes say they don't like brainstorming because it gives less motivated pupils the chance to let other people do the work for them. You might think it worth raising this issue in class and making it clear that finding the 'points' for a set topic is a shared responsibility. You can name selected students to be responsible for the feedback from their groups to the rest of the class. You can also name an individual before the start of the activity to act as 'teacher' and write up the points on the board. If you choose different students each time, you can make sure that everyone contributes.

Setting a time limit helps keep students on task and makes the activity more tightly structured.

Some further possible advantages of cycling are: It's enjoyable / good exercise / cheap / quiet (an environmental benefit).

Some further disadvantages: You are exposed to rain and cold / bicycles can easily be stolen / they can't easily be taken with you in a car or on a train / you can't carry much with you on a bike / you need to be fit to cycle / cycling is dangerous on busy roads, during bad weather and at night / it's tiring.

2 Predicting content

As always, encourage students to be 'detectives' and to try to pick up as many clues as possible from the pictures in the leaflet, e.g. the group riding together suggests it is an activity for the whole family, the pictures of attractive locations suggest the route will be scenic. (The places mentioned are in the south of England, near London. Windsor Castle is one of the homes of the British royal family.)

Before students start reading, you may need to explain that Friends of the Earth is an environmental pressure group. They organise campaigns to raise public awareness of environmental threats. Anyone who sympathises can join and work for them as a volunteer in their spare time. It would be interesting to hear from students about similar organisations in other cultures.

Explain that in a sponsored walk or cycle ride, a sponsor usually promises to give a certain amount of money for each mile/kilometre completed by the person he/she is sponsoring.

3 Reading for gist

> **TEACHING SUPPORT**
>
> See the Introduction for a general approach to helping students with Reading tasks.

> **LEARNING SUPPORT**
>
> Where students need **support**, ask them to predict why an organisation called Friends of the Earth might be organising a sponsored bike ride. Make a brief list of any suggestions, then tell students to read the first column of text to see if any of these are mentioned there.

Answers

The three reasons the bike ride is being held are:

1   for enjoyment
2   to raise awareness of the threats to the environment of road-widening schemes (the M3, M4 and M25 are motorways near London)
3   to raise funds for FoE's long-term transport campaign

4 True/false comprehension: skim reading

Encourage students to scan the text to 'spot' the answers. Multiple matching questions in exam reading components do not usually follow the order of information in the text, so the ability to scan as well as skim read and read for detailed meaning is a key skill. In other parts of reading exams, questions do not often follow the order of the text, but students should take care to read any information given in captions or individual boxes, if it is provided, as well as in the main body of the text.

Answers

1   false
2   false
3   true
4   false
5   false
6   true
7   true
8   false
9   true
10 false

5 Post-reading discussion

It will be interesting to hear students' experiences of doing something for charity.

As road building is a very sensitive topic in the UK (but not necessarily in all other countries), and it features as a topic for the next section, you might wish to finish the exercise with a question-and-answer session about the problems of road-building schemes.

You could ask the following questions: *'Why are new roads a problem?'* eliciting/prompting:

Roads take up a lot of space. In small, densely populated countries, such as the UK, valuable countryside may have to be destroyed to make way for new roads. Cars burn petrol which produces fumes. If directly breathed in, these fumes can damage people's lungs.

'How did pressure groups such as Friends of the Earth get involved?' eliciting/prompting:

In Britain, as in many other countries, people are given the chance to object to proposed new roads. There is usually a planning inquiry. In practice, the inquiry has almost always decided in favour of a new road, so people lost faith in the system and found other ways to protest. Protests might include setting up camp in the path of the new road and refusing to move. As a result, the roads cost more to build and sometimes the project is abandoned. People have joined Friends of the Earth (and similar organisations) to raise public awareness about road building.

'What are the alternatives to new roads?' eliciting/ prompting:

65

Many people argue that we need better public transport and better traffic management schemes, not more new roads.

6 Reordering an article

Students could work together in pairs or small groups to put the sentences into a logical sequence. Encourage them to copy out the article when they have finished, to help them understand the flow of a piece of writing and think about where new paragraphs should begin.

Answer

Cycling is an enjoyable, efficient and liberating mode of transport which has many benefits. **g** In the first place, cycling is cheap because second-hand bikes are not expensive. **k** You can also save money by carrying out simple repairs yourself. **b** In addition, owning a bike frees you from dependence on your parents to take you to places. **l** It also removes the frustrations of waiting around for a bus to turn up.

Although cycling has many advantages, there are some drawbacks too. Cycling can be dangerous on busy roads and you can be seriously hurt if you are knocked off your bike by a motorist. **a** Cycling at night is particularly dangerous, especially along dark country roads as a motorist may not see you until it is too late. **j** Moreover, many roads are polluted by traffic fumes which makes cycling unpleasant and unhealthy.

However, some of these problems can be eliminated if you take sensible precautions such as using lights at night and wearing reflector strips. **h** Attending a cycling training scheme also enables you to cycle more safely and may help you identify the less polluted routes.

In conclusion, although there are certainly some drawbacks, I feel that the personal enjoyment and freedom you get from cycling outweigh the disadvantages.

It is important for students to think about how they address the reader in their writing. The writer of the article in Exercise 6 addresses the reader directly by using the word *you*, e.g. 'owning a bike frees you from dependence on your parents'. A writer may also choose to use *we/our/us* to suggest that he or she shares values and assumptions with his or her readers, e.g. *We all enjoy riding bikes. Our bikes are a way to explore the world around us.*

You could remind students that pronouns like *we/our* can be used to imply a set of shared values and assumptions between writer and audience. You could present a sentence like this:

We deserve special consideration from our families when we're in the middle of our IGCSE exams and ask 'Who does the writer think will read this article? Who is he/she writing for – old people, small children, sportsmen, or students of the writer's age and background?'

LEARNING SUPPORT

This could be a whole-class activity, guiding students to an understanding of how one sentence connects to another in a logical sequence. For instance, you could show how the phrase *in the first place* alerts us to the fact that sentence **g** follows on from sentence **f** at the beginning of the article. Make sure that students make use of the phrases in italics for these are the clues showing how one sentence links to another. A good example of how this works are sentences **e** and **a**. Sentence **e** contains the word *dangerous* and sentence **a** *particularly dangerous*, which alerts us to the fact that there may be a link between them.

Students who find the task difficult will benefit from being able to manipulate the sections of text either electronically or on slips of paper. It may be helpful to point out that the title of the article provides a clue, and ask students to group the sections which refer to 'pros' and those that refer to 'cons'.

7 What makes a good argument essay?

The aim of this exercise is to get students to reflect on what makes a good essay. It should have a formal style, flow, be easy to follow, and be persuasive. It should give equal weight to both sides of the issue. Remind students that they should offer their own opinion in the final paragraph of their essay – they shouldn't leave the reader in any doubt as to what they think about the subject they have written about.

8 Presenting contrasting ideas in the same paragraph

An alternative style to that of 'The pros and cons of cycling' is to present the contrasting ideas in the same paragraph, or even in the same sentence. This exercise provides a starting point into this style.

Answers

Nevertheless

Although I recognise … cycling, in my opinion it is essential …

I recognise … cycling. In my opinion, however, it is essential …

I recognise … cycling, but/yet in my opinion it is essential …

In spite of the fact that … cycling, in my opinion it is essential …

9 Presenting more contrasting ideas

Encourage students to work in pairs to complete the sentences in a logical way. Why not ask them to compare their answers with the rest of the group?

10 Language study: Linking words

There is a wide variety of expressions of similar meaning which carry out the functions listed in the headings. Students will certainly be aware of some of them, and the aim of this exercise is to extend their knowledge by introducing a wider variety of linking words.

Possible answers

LISTING: First of all, Secondly, Thirdly, In the first place, Lastly, Finally, Last but not least

ADDITION: also, moreover, furthermore, as well as, added to that, and, in addition

CONTRAST: but, however, on the other hand, although, even though, whilst, despite/in spite of (the fact that)

REASONING: because, as, since, for this reason

OPINION: We think, In my view, To my mind, I feel, I believe, As far as I am concerned

EMPHASIS: above all, surely, in particular, especially, particularly, undoubtedly, there is no doubt

CONSEQUENCE: so, consequently, as a result, therefore

SUMMING UP: On balance, To sum up, In conclusion

Other headings to elicit are:

EXAMPLE: for example, for instance, such as, like

CLARIFYING: that is to say, in other words, namely

11 Brainstorming / 12 Text completion

The text completion exercise focuses on the environmental benefits of trees. You may like to ask students to look up information about the functions of trees in a reference book. Alternatively, they may well have discussed topics such as global warming in their science or environmental studies lessons. This topic gives them a good opportunity to explain what they already know.

Encourage them to think of some advantages and disadvantages of the proposal.

Answers

1   Although
2   In the first place
3   also
4   Furthermore
5   because
6   yet
7   In addition
8   also
9   In my opinion
10 On the other hand

13 Discussion

The email is appropriately formal. This is shown by the absence of colloquial language and by the formality of expressions such as *In the first place*, *Furthermore*.

The writer shows an awareness of his audience by saying that he would be interested in what other readers think.

Roland's argument is convincing because he gives clear reasons for his views, e.g. the wood is a habitat for wildlife., the air is cleaner because of the trees, and they help to make a noisy urban area quieter. He also writes that the wood is a beautiful place.

14 Words often confused

The words in this exercise are regularly confused by IGCSE candidates.

Answers

1	**a**	council	**b**	counsel
2	**a**	effect	**b**	affect
3	**a**	there, their	**b**	they're
4	**a**	lose	**b**	loose

5	**a** alternate	**b** alternative
6	**a** lightning	**b** lightening
7	**a** practise	**b** practice
8	**a** past	**b** passed

C A new motorway for Rosville?

1 Pre-reading discussion

Use the pictures to focus students' thoughts and stimulate an interesting discussion on the advantages and disadvantages of motorways (major roads, which may be known as highways, freeways or expressways in various parts of the world).

Brainstorming
Advantages

- They can be fast and efficient.
- They link towns effectively, making business communications easier.
- Building them provides jobs.
- They reduce traffic on local minor roads.
- They can be safer than narrow, winding roads.

Disadvantages

- They destroy countryside – need a lot of land.
- They are expensive to build and maintain.
- They pollute the atmosphere.
- They are noisy.
- They can encourage people to drive too fast.
- Serious accidents can happen on a motorway.
- Traffic jams can build up during roadworks or in the rush hour.
- They can encourage car use, especially for long journeys.

2 Reading an example text

Students need to study the example text carefully. The style is suitable for a formal email to a newspaper.

3 Comprehension check

As usual, the comprehension check will make sure that all students are in no doubt about the factual content of the email.

Answers

1   a newspaper
2   boost to business through improved communications; easier, faster and safer commuting; reduced pollution through tree planting; lorries will bypass town centre
3   It's convincing because there are specific reasons and examples given.

Vocabulary: answers

a   recession
b   boost
c   communications
d   commuting
e   bypass

4 Analysing the text

These questions focus on the overall structure of the email and reinforce the linking words students have been learning.

You may like to add a little more to earlier discussions about the importance of first and last paragraphs. Perhaps students feel they have no right to persuade someone one way or another, or perhaps they aren't interested in the topic they have been asked to write about. Remind them that they need to be clear about what they think, and that they will get good marks for sounding persuasive in their compositions.

Answers

1   *delighted, because*
    The opening paragraph grabs attention because it focuses immediately and clearly on the topic and uses emotive language such as *delighted.*
2   *above all* and *not only … also* are used for emphasis.
3   The opposing point of view is the concern over air pollution from the motorway. *On the contrary* is used to introduce a contrasting opinion.
4   *Finally* is used to show that the argument is being rounded off.
5   The last paragraph uses emphatic expressions like *There is no doubt* and *really*, which make the writer's views clear.

5 Putting forward an opposing viewpoint

In this exercise, students read an outline of an email to the local newspaper which is in response to the email from the Rosville Business Group. As always, check that they understand the factual content of the email before they move on to the next exercise.

6 Redrafting

Example answer

Some sentences have been restructured for emphasis in this campaigning email and to improve the flow, but don't worry if your students are unable to do this. The main aim is to add the linking words and paragraphs. Exclamation marks have been added for emphasis.

Dear Editor,

We were horrified to hear of the plans for a new motorway for Rosville and we are sure our feelings are shared by many of your readers.

Firstly, we believe the scheme would destroy the environment and damage wildlife. Secondly, the motorway itself will cost a great deal of money to build. Using this money to improve the rail network would not only help local businesses but city commuters would benefit too.

The idea that the motorway will be more efficient is completely unfounded. The new road will soon attract heavy traffic and become heavily congested. Furthermore, the suggestion that planting trees alongside the motorway will help eliminate pollution is ludicrous. Trees can never make up for the destruction of wild flowers and wildlife!

Finally, many of us cycle or walk across the road to get to school or work. The new road will split the area into two, making this impossible.

Please, people of Rosville, don't stand by and watch your environment being destroyed! Support the Rosville Nature Society campaign by writing now to your local councillor.

Yours faithfully,

The Rosville Nature Society

Students could, finally, read out their emails to the rest of the class and compare the efficacy of different linking words.

The Nature Society email is, like the Business Group email, one-sided. Both emails build up an argument in one direction only, so lots of linking words like *furthermore, moreover* are needed rather than several contrast expressions such as *however, on the other hand*. It would be useful to compare the effect of writing a one-sided argument with one that gives a more equal weight to both sides (such as 'The pros and cons of cycling' in the Student's Book, Unit 4, B Nature under threat). You could elicit the fact that a one-sided argument tends to be more emotive.

7 Relating to your target audience

This exercise uses skimming and scanning reading techniques and consolidates earlier work on showing audience awareness in your writing. It provides some more examples of typical audience-awareness statements. Once students understand the concept, they usually don't have too much difficulty with putting the idea into practice in their own writing.

Answers

A   music and video sharing site for internet users
B   school magazine for school pupils
C   letter to the local newspaper for the general public
D   e-newsletter for elderly people
E   formal report for the headteacher

8 Writing a report for the headteacher on a new facility

TEACHING SUPPORT

See the Introduction for a general approach to helping students with Writing tasks.

Before students write their reports, discuss the pros and cons of the proposed school facility with them. This will help them focus their thoughts. You could also elicit the expression *I recommend/would recommend* as it is one that they can use in the final part of their report.

The tone of the report is important. It should sound respectful as it is for the headteacher, but should also be direct and honest about the positive and negative points – this is expected in a report. There is no need to express thanks to the headteacher, but, if appropriate, the positive aspects can be strongly emphasised.

69

TEACHING SUPPORT

To **support** some students with the structure of this semi-formal report, provide a pre-prepared writing frame, or elicit the language from the students. The opening paragraph: *I am writing because* … Listing the positive points of your argument: *Firstly, …* ; *In addition, …; Furthermore, …* Presenting any negative points: *However, …; The only thing that could be improved is* … The finishing paragraph: *In conclusion, I believe …; I would recommend … but I suggest that …*

Example answer
A possible answer could be along the following lines.

I have been asked by our headteacher, Mr Anil, to write a report on the new covered area from the students' point of view.

Firstly, the covered area gives us protection when the sun is very hot. Some students have become concerned about sun damage, especially those who have studied climate change and the greenhouse effect in science lessons. In addition, we have had stormy, unpredictable weather recently and the students say they are thankful that they can go under cover in wet weather.

The small tables that are provided are helpful when we want to eat our lunch or do some homework. Furthermore, students are mixing outside their normal friendship circles because a wide range of students from different ages and classes come to enjoy the protection of the shaded area. It is also peaceful in this part of the grounds as it is further away from the traffic on main roads. We can all enjoy nature and hear birdsong. We go back to our lessons feeling refreshed and in just the right mood to study.

In conclusion, I believe this is a successful facility and very popular with students. I would recommend a similar facility for the younger children, and suggest this is situated in the part of the playground nearest to the water fountains, as young children get very thirsty when they are playing.

9 Writing a report on a proposal for the benefit of elderly people
Allow up to 30 minutes for the writing task, or set it as homework.

Example answer
A possible answer could go like this:

Report for the council of the proposed development at Antalya Place
The council has asked for a report representing the views of the residents of Antalya Place about the proposal; to dig up the paved area and create a flower garden for elderly people.

First, there could be many benefits to the proposal. A flower garden would be attractive and brighten up a drab area. Also, the flowers and plants would be a habitat for a wide variety of insects. In addition, old people in the area say they are often a bit lonely and they have no meeting place, so the garden would be a pleasant place for them to relax in. Furthermore, the trees would provide welcome shade, reduce pollution and noise levels and give some protection on windy days.

However, many young people live in flats and have nowhere else where they can play ball games. Also, local teams won't be successful if they cannot practise, so team confidence will sink. At present teenagers use the area to meet friends, enjoy picnics and watch matches. If young people lose this area, they will be very disappointed and even resentful.

In conclusion, I believe the fairest solution is for the council to divide the area into two. One part could become the flower garden for the elderly but there would still be enough space left for young people to socialise and play ball games. All the residents would benefit.

Maryam Al-Fyed

10 Understanding a typical exam-style stimulus

Go through the prompts to make sure students understand each one. You could ask them to link the prompts to direct personal experiences they have had, e.g. *Have they noticed litter being dropped by visitors near rivers they visit? Does it matter? Why/Why not? If there was a sudden influx of tourists wanting to fish in a local river, would it cause problems? Why/How?* Students should be encouraged, as always, to remember that a report should sound formal and be as objective as possible. Opinions should be supported with clear reasons.

11 Redrafting an exam-style answer

The positive points of the answer are that it is clear and easy to read and there are no language mistakes. Its weaknesses are that it does not flow well due to a lack of linking words. There is also too much copying from the prompts without adding any original thoughts. The ending is confused. It should be clear what the writer believes. The final sentence is not suitable for a report.

Example answer

An answer which selects from the prompts and develops them could read as follows. It would be useful to highlight some of the key elements for students.

> **Should our river be developed for boating?**
>
> The council are proposing to develop the local river for tourism and have asked for a report outlining the possible advantages and drawbacks. I'd like to consider the advantages and disadvantages of the proposed river development.
>
> In the first place, the river is in a lovely part of the countryside. People who live and work in the noisy, crowded city are able to come and benefit from the peaceful atmosphere of the countryside. Moreover, if people come to the area they will spend money, which will give a boost to our local economy and many jobs will be created.
>
> On the other hand, engine oil and litter from the boats will pollute the water. The blades from boats tear up plants which feed on pollution. This will eventually make the water dirty and stagnant. In addition, if too much fishing goes on, many species will die out. The sensitive ecology of our river will be ruined.

> To sum up, I think it would be wrong to develop the river. Although we need to progress and become more modern, I think this can happen without sacrificing our wonderful river.

D Global warming

1 Vocabulary check

This exercise brings together some useful expressions connected with global warming.

Answers

global warming, greenhouse gases, carbon footprint, climate change, carbon emissions

International overview

Throughout the unit, students have been exposed to the idea of human and technological developments having an impact on the planet, and have been considering solutions. They have explored the way that progress and the needs of a changing world create a dilemma – is it better for us to move forward no matter what, or should we take greater account of the harm we are doing and make changes before it is too late? The *International overview* provides some factual background information to support these ideas. The section then extends the topic by incorporating a popular and controversial issue – climate change. Experts are not always in agreement about the causes of global warming and whether it leads to climate change. Nevertheless, it is worth helping students to feel confident with the general ideas and possible solutions. A detailed technical knowledge is not required. You may like to encourage students to find out the individual carbon footprint of their own countries. In the UK it is about 10 000 kg of carbon dioxide per person per year.

Answers

1   Home (coal, oil and gas consumption) contributes the most to the footprint. Financial services and public transport contribute the least.

2   Statements a, b and d are true.

2 Pre-reading discussion

Students should enjoy the pre-reading discussion, which may well link to their cross-curricular studies in science and geography. It is ideal for pairwork.

A The incorrect statement is 3. (Nuclear energy does not produce greenhouse gases.)

B A discussion about the possible benefits and disadvantages of climate change should be fruitful. Sometimes people like to imagine life would be better with warmer winters or less intensely hot summers. However, experts warn us that climate change is generally worrying as a country's economy and way of life is linked to the traditional climate, and change will be disruptive to agriculture etc.

C The incorrect idea is installing more air conditioning to achieve a more even temperature. Cooling just one main room at home would be more beneficial to the environment, as less energy is consumed.

It will be intriguing to find out whether students feel able to make changes in their lifestyles, and to what extent a reduction in energy use at home is motivated by saving money.

3 Reading for gist

Students should enjoy reading and discussing Deepak's article. It provides them with thought-provoking information about some of the problems and solutions to climate change.

Answers

intrigued: very interested, curious

resourceful: good at working out solutions to practical problems

ingenuity: cleverness, inventiveness

4 Comprehension check

Answers

1 The extent to which his choices contribute to his carbon footprint
2 Built strong shelters for their animals, learned veterinary skills
3 To grow floating vegetable gardens
4 They can now produce rice which grows in salty water.
5 Make one small change every day to their carbon footprint
6 Attend the club meeting at Thursday lunchtime

5 Tone and register

The informal tone and register elements are underlined below. Students are likely to recognise at least some of the informal elements, which include the use of

contractions, colloquial expressions, rhetorical questions and exclamation marks. They are likely to understand it is an appropriate tone and register for talking to your peers.

Although I <u>don't</u> usually write to the school magazine, I have recently joined a school club, Friends of the Planet. I thought you might be intrigued to know more about what we do.

The club members have been researching facts on global warming and putting them on our school blog. <u>Do you know that</u> by flying in a plane for an hour we produce the same carbon emissions as a Bangladeshi citizen produces in a whole year? Earlier this year, <u>my whole family flew to America for a wedding so we definitely increased our carbon footprint.</u> Being in the club has made me think more about the environmental impact of our lifestyle choices.

We have found out <u>lots of</u> other important things at the club too, such as ways people in different parts of the world are coping with climate change.

In the Andes in Peru, for example, farmers have had to cope with much more severe winters. The bitterly cold weather had been killing the alpaca, a domesticated animal which provides milk, cheese, meat and wool. The farmers could have given up, but they learned how to build strong shelters for the animals and developed veterinary skills. As a result, the communities are surviving and are even more resourceful than before.

In another part of the world, Bangladeshi farmers have found their own ways to overcome a problem of a different sort: widespread flooding. Using wooden rafts, the farmers developed vegetable gardens which float on water. <u>Isn't that an amazing idea? And it works!</u>

Finally, I want to tell you about Sri Lanka. Sea levels around the coast are rising due to climate change, and, consequently, the rice paddies were being contaminated by salt. It was extremely worrying because rice is the farmers' main crop. However, they experimented with different types of rice and found a strain of rice which can flourish in salty water! <u>How is that for ingenuity!</u>

In the club, we decided that, if other people can make changes, so can we. Therefore, we are going to make one small change every day to our carbon footprint. We will be doing <u>things like</u> using our bikes, recycling rubbish and turning off electrical appliances when we leave the room. It <u>might not sound like much,</u> but we think it will eventually make a real difference.

Would you like to reduce your carbon footprint? <u>Then join us at the club to find out how!</u> We meet at lunchtime on Thursday in Room 12. <u>See you there!</u>

Grammar spotlight

The *Grammar spotlight* looks at specific ways to express the future, using examples drawn from previous texts and written information in the unit. The examples are selected to show students that they have been handling these structures confidently and the spotlight enables them to consolidate this knowledge.

Answers

A   The funds raised from Bike to the Future *will help* sustain our campaign …

C   … *we'll give* you a free Bike to the Future T-shirt.

D   Therefore *we are going to* make one small change every day to our carbon footprint.

Exam-style questions

See the Overview of *Cambridge IGCSE English as a Second Language* section at the beginning of the Student's Book for the mark scheme and criteria for marking the writing questions.

Listening 🔊 CD 1, Track 12

Students will listen to four short recordings which recycle the environmental themes and language from the unit.

The listening passages reflect the style of Exercises 1–4 in exams. In exam conditions, of course, students will hear the recording twice, but obviously, in the classroom, they can hear the recordings as often as you think is appropriate. Specific items students find difficult can be targeted for replay and double checked. Students should focus on accuracy and use key words in the answer. They should focus on content words which contain meaning, not small grammatical items such as prepositions and articles. They can write up to three words.

Answers

1   a   (in) (a) school/ school hall

   b   soap (and) towel

2   a   B12

   b   Past (the) library / turn left/ turn right (any two)

3   a   Breathe Deep

   b   Make/give (a) donation

4   a   metal workshop/make/making (a) necklace

   b   50 minutes

(Listening, Exercise 1: 8 marks (Core); 8 marks (Extended).)

AUDIOSCRIPT

You will hear four short recordings. Answer each question on the line provided. Write no more than three words for each detail. You will hear each recording twice.

QUESTION 1

TEACHER:	Good afternoon. Now I think everyone has finished their lunch and is here in the school hall, so I'll begin giving you your instructions for our trip tomorrow. We are going to be camping in an extremely environmentally sensitive area. We must keep to the cycle paths at all times and bring all our rubbish home with us, and that includes all tins and bottles. Yes, Anil, how can I help?
ANIL:	Can we bring insect spray to keep mosquitoes and other bugs away?
TEACHER:	I am afraid not. It is usually perfumed and no perfume is allowed. All you are allowed to bring is soap and a towel. Hot showers won't be available. We have to collect the water for washing from the local river.

QUESTION 2

STUDENT: Er, sorry to bother you, but I wonder if you can you help me? I have just enrolled for an environmental studies evening class. This is my first time here and I was told by reception to go to B12 but there is no-one in that room.

TEACHER: I'm sorry. We have had to reorganise our teaching timetable at the last minute. B12 is going to be used later on by the technology group so everyone on your course needs to go to A16. Go past the library and turn left. Almost immediately you should turn sharp right for A16. You can't miss it.

STUDENT: Thanks a million. I've been going round in circles. I'm glad I allowed myself a bit of extra time to get there.

QUESTION 3

We are a travelling theatre group and I am here on local radio tonight to say we have just written a fabulous play, 'Breathe Deep'. The play has an amazing environmental message. We know the planet might be in trouble but our play shows how we can love and protect it. We are going to be in the town square at seven tomorrow evening. You don't have to pay to watch the play but you can make a donation and we will use the funds to continue taking our play to towns and cities all over the country.

QUESTION 4

Welcome everyone to the 'Greener Future' environmental centre. First let me tell you about the work of the centre. It was set up by a local businessman who owned a soft drinks factory. He wanted to make sure the glass bottles he used would not damage the environment so he built a recycling workshop near the factory. That was quite a few years ago now and the workshop has grown into an educational centre. We've got a guide who will show you around the various rooms. At the end of the visit, I am sure you will enjoy shopping in the gift shop where you can purchase a small gift made from recycled material. I also really recommend that you visit the metal workshop. You will have a chance to make a necklace so do allow enough time – it takes about 50 minutes to make the necklace and paint it. Now, does anyone have any questions before Andrew, your guide, starts the tour?

Reading

In the multiple matching exercise, four young people explain why caring for the environment is so important to them. The exercise reflects the unit's themes (nature under threat, pollution, global warming, climate change) and recycles the vocabulary and grammar practised in the unit. Encourage students to apply the logical, step by step method they have practised in the exam-style multiple matching reading exercise in Unit 2.

Remind students to:

- read the rubric carefully for context

- scan the questions to get a general idea of what the texts are likely to be about

- read for general meaning

- match speaker to statement through a process of careful checking and elimination.

It is important students are patient and proceed logically, when answers appear 'close', students should take extra care to identify the most correct one. If a question is problematic (it seems to match with more than one person) students can pencil in their answer(s) and refine their selection at the end.

For example, the first question asks students to decide which person says nature can be harmed but never destroyed. While all the speakers are concerned about environmental damage, only one speaker, C, mentions the regenerative power of nature: 'Whatever we do to harm nature, I sense it will still be with us, renewing and regenerating the world. '

Answers

a	C
b	D
c	B
d	D
e	A
f	D
g	C
h	C
i	A [Extended]
j	B [Extended]

(Reading & Writing, Exercise 2: 8 marks (Core), 10 marks (Extended).)

Writing

In Paper 2 (Extended), **two** prompts are provided for the writing in Exercise 6. If you think your students need them, you may like to elicit two additional prompts from the students themselves. Or you could provide additional prompts along the following lines.

'It will be great to travel abroad so easily.'

'The airport will disturb our peaceful way of life.'

'We felt we had gained an important skill for ourselves.'

'The vegetables were not as good as those in the supermarket.'

'We should all try to save energy and avoid waste.'

'New jobs and businesses should be our priority.'

'Very young people are safe drivers – they take more care.'

'Young people do not appreciate how dangerous a car can be.'

5 Visit to environmental centre – report

Technical knowledge of an environmental centre is not expected; any reasonable description of a centre which carries out some kind of work that helps the environment would be enough. Students should aim to express their reasons clearly and back up their opinions with some examples. The report should sound formal or semi-formal. As always, they can use the comments given but they are free to make up their own ideas. Below are two additional prompts which you may like to provide if you think your students need them:

'We learned how to recycle rubbish at home properly.'

'There was so much noise we couldn't hear our guide.'

Example answer

> ### Visit to the environmental centre
>
> Our visit to the environmental centre was very interesting. First, we watched a film about recycling and then listened to a long talk about climate change.
>
> After that we were taken on a tour of the workshops. It was fascinating to see how things you think are worthless are carefully collected, sorted and recycled into useful items. We saw old car tyres

> being made into shoes and tried some of them on. Mr Barway even bought a pair for his son as they were so comfortable. We were told that the money goes to support charities that clean up our rivers and beaches.
>
> Finally, we made some recycled items ourselves. I made a photograph frame from wood for my mum and other people made necklaces from glass beads and old plastic bags. The items we made were lovely, and knowing we were helping the environment made them even more special.
>
> We all enjoyed the visit, though the talk was hard to understand, so perhaps future groups could miss that and spend more time making recycled items. On the train home, we all agreed we would try to recycle more, as it is easier than we thought. (196 words)

(Reading & Writing, Exercise 6: 16 marks (Extended).)

Wider practice

1. Inviting a member of a nature conservation or pressure group to class to talk about their aims and projects could be an inspiring experience for students, who sometimes feel overwhelmed by the thought of environmental problems. It's especially good if students can hear about a successful environmental campaign.

2. Watching a nature documentary online, on TV or DVD can lead to an increased understanding of ecological issues, which students can make use of in their work in class.

3. In order to provide extra report writing practice, students can write reports on real places they have visited, experiences they have had or products they have bought, so they get enough practice in developing a calm, measured tone, rather than an emotional one. They could send those reports to real people: companies/owners of businesses welcome market research of this kind.

4. Getting and keeping informed of current topics in the news can be challenging. Encourage your students to open their eyes and ears to what is around them. Their local environment may provide lots of stimulus

for argument and discussion on matters such as local measures to reduce the carbon footprint, saving energy and reducing waste, or the value of building a future for everyone as opposed to living in the moment without thought for tomorrow.

5   There may be nothing better than going out to a forest or lake to study nature. Nature Conservation Areas, Country Parks, National Parks and so on often have group leaders who are specially trained to teach school parties. They can teach students about ecology, the history of trees, and so on. A joint visit organised with science and environmental teachers might be especially interesting.

6   As a change from brainstorming ideas for a topic, why not try brainwriting? Each student writes an idea about the topic on a slip of paper. No names are used. The slips of paper are collected and each anonymous idea is discussed in turn in the group.

Unit 5
Entertainment

Overview

The main aim of this unit is to develop students' ability to produce a review, suitable for a student audience, of a film, novel or live performance. Students learn how to review something both orally and in writing, with the emphasis being on expressing personal opinions clearly.

Although most students enjoy watching films and many read for pleasure, they will find that producing a concise review is harder than it looks. Conveying exactly why you found a particular film or book so compelling, is challenging.

In their reviews, IGCSE students need to demonstrate analytical skills and an appropriate use of language. They also need to be able to highlight the aspects of a particular work that make it effective, offering examples so as to make things as clear as possible for the reader.

Theme

The unit is thematically linked by discussions relating to the role of entertainment in our lives. Obviously 'entertainment' involves more than films, music and books. Try to encourage students to contribute information about any form of entertainment they enjoy, including online entertainment and computer games. This makes the work more stimulating and better prepares students for the way in which the Speaking Test is conducted. A discussion which starts with a review of a novel, for example, could easily progress to questions about the problems parents have encouraging their children to read, and whether electronic books encourage more young people to read.

The theme includes:

- what it feels like to perform or be otherwise involved in a work of entertainment
- the consequences of the trend towards home-based entertainment
- the impact of the internet
- working in the film/animation industry.

Unit organisation

The exercises are organised so that the first half of the unit (approximately) deals with films/live performances and leads up to an oral presentation about a film. The second half mainly develops book reviewing skills. You'll need to bear in mind that students should gradually build on what they've learnt as they progress through the unit from film and live performance reviewing to book reviewing.

Language work

The language work focuses on strategies to help students develop analytical skills. These include developing awareness of important aspects such as characterisation, plot, etc., and providing the means to discuss them. Specific language exercises include using adjectives and collocations, and the structures *so … that* and *such … that* to express personal responses to films.

Spelling and pronunciation focus on the letters *c* and *ch*.

The *Grammar spotlight* focuses on *will* for prediction, and superlative adjectives, both of which are useful structures in reviews.

A Talking about entertainment

1 Introduction and discussion

A   This introductory exercise helps students to explore the role of entertainment in their lives. Encourage them to discuss how their preferences for music, for example, vary according to mood and circumstances, e.g. they may like loud music at parties but prefer gentle music while they are studying. Some students may want the escapism of TV soap operas, computer games or chat shows to help them unwind after a hard day, but at other times prefer serious documentaries or factual programmes.

B You could also discuss the special excitement generated by live entertainment. Students who have been to live shows could say what they thought of them. If students have taken part in a live performance, allow them to describe the part they played, what they enjoyed about it and any problems they had.

C If students have uploaded a video to a video-sharing site, they can describe what they did and why, and whether users of the site posted comments on their video.

D Finally, ask students to say whether they would enjoy a job in the entertainment business. They could explain what personal experience, skills or qualities they think such a job would need and how these might be acquired.

The subsequent exercises are based on reviews of films, plays and novels. However, the skills are generic and you can adapt them to include reviews of computer games and online entertainment, including participation in online fantasy games. The same skills are also relevant to music concerts, poetry and drama evenings, live song and dance, and so on. Help students to understand that similar vocabulary and structures can be used to review the quality of the performance, the atmosphere, personal responses, costumes, music, special effects, and so on. Students who do well in their studies have the ability to adapt their knowledge and experience to fit a particular question. This is very important when they are asked to present new angles on familiar topics.

2 Film vocabulary

This exercise, which checks film vocabulary, would be ideal to set as homework to prepare students for the work of the unit. It's essential that they can use relevant vocabulary when describing a film. The exercise checks specialised nouns and a few verbs; subsequent vocabulary exercises will emphasise adjectives. You may like to point out that *genre* is of French origin.

Answers

1   Oscar
2   performance
3   heroine
4   played by
5   role
6   plot
7   scene
8   cast
9   characters
10 directed by
11 box office
12 film
13 genre

3 Film quiz

This film quiz ranges from personal feelings to more topical issues. It provides a starting point for thinking about what makes films enjoyable.

4 Pairwork: Asking for information

The paired conversation focuses on helpful phrases to ask for and follow up information.

After the pairwork, you may like to follow up on any points about which students feel strongly. It may simply be a case of asking students to describe their favourite actors, or the discussion may become more topical. For example, they may feel that more films should be made locally or that there is too much crime shown in films today.

LEARNING SUPPORT

To provide extra stretch and improve class discussion skills, consider drilling the phrases provided before the students use them in pair work. Some students can be **challenged** by being reminded of the value of actively incorporating these phrases into classroom talk.

5 Following a model discussion about films 🔊 CD 1, Track 13

In this exercise, students read and listen to a conversation at the same time. The conversation is about two films: a futuristic thriller 'The Way to the Sea' and a high school drama 'You after Me'. The aim of the exercise is to show students the ways films can be analysed. They should follow the discussion in their books as they listen, as they are not really practising listening skills. If you prefer, they could read the dialogue aloud in class. The dialogue is constructed so that the aspects of films (character, plot, etc.) which the students need to use in reviewing films are shown as clearly as possible. Unlike the recorded exercises in other units, the dialogue is not aiming to reflect 'natural' conversation.

Before they listen, ask students what they think the films will be about. Ask students to focus, while they listen and read, on the teacher's questions and the way in which she follows up the students' responses.

AUDIOSCRIPT
As in the Student's Book.

6 Aspects of films
Ask students to tick the aspects of the films that were mentioned by Navid and Marta. All the boxes should be ticked, except soundtrack. To reinforce learning, you could go through the list and check that the students understand how the vocabulary is actually used by the speakers by asking:

'Did Marta mention genre when she spoke about "You after Me"?'

'How did she describe it?'

'What other kinds of genre do you know (horror, westerns, etc.)?'

'Did Navid talk about the hero of "The Way to the Sea."?'

'What did he say about him?'

Encourage students to find the answers in the dialogue in their books. The answers could be noted on the board, so they all have the same record.

You could round off the discussion by asking students which aspects of film reviewing would be useful for discussing a novel. (They all would be, except for the special effects and soundtrack aspects of films.)

7 Tenses
The plot of a film, play or book is usually described in the present tense. (Marta and Navid describe their reactions to the film in the past tense because they are now looking back at how they felt at the time.) In practice, native speakers often mix the tenses when they describe films or books. It is of no great importance, as long as the meaning is clear and there is consistency.

8 Comprehension
Answers
The incorrect statement for Navid is **c**. The incorrect statement for Marta is **g**.

Navid and Marta convey the qualities of each film because their reasons and examples are clear and exact. Students tend to generalise quite a lot in their answers, and the dialogue shows the importance of being analytical and succinct.

In Marta's opinion, destructive behaviour can be shown on screen so long as the underlying message is that it can be overcome by good. This is a controversial view. You may like to ask *'Does this view justify any kind of evil being shown on the screen? Where would you draw the line?'*

9 Language study: *So … that* and *such … that*
This structural review exercise practises ways of expressing personal responses. Expressing personal responses to a film (or book) is something many students find hard to do well. As an example, you may like to write on the board this sentence, which is taken from a student's essay:

What with all the exciting music and sound of the guns, I thought I was inside the television.

Ask students how the sentence needs to be changed to become unambiguous, eliciting, for example:

The music and sound of the guns was so exciting that I was completely carried away/totally absorbed in what would happen next.

or

The film contained such exciting music and sounds from the guns that I felt as if/it made me feel as if it was really happening.

or

The exciting music and sound of the guns made me feel as if I was actually part of the action.

Practice: answers
1   I was *so* keen to see the concert *that* I was …
2   She was *so* disappointed not to get the role of the princess *that* she …
3   The film took *such* a long time to make *that* the director …
4   It was *such* a fascinating story *that* the film company …

10 Involving your listener
Students should not have difficulty with the sentence completions. You may want to ask them to continue by originating some sentences of their own.

B Recommendations and reviews

1 Discussion

The discussion aims to explore how technology is shaping our leisure time by providing more and more ways we can be entertained without leaving our sofas.

The discussion is based on a way of life where streaming and the consumption of films, DVDs and CDs is very high. If you don't feel that this is very appropriate for your students, you might like to focus more on the pleasures of going out to places of entertainment.

After students have completed the exercise, you could build up notes on the board eliciting their ideas.

Advantages

- It can be cheaper.
- It's safe, comfortable and secure at home.
- You can watch a film on a DVD or online several times over but only see a film at the cinema, or attend a concert, on one occasion.

Disadvantages

- Films are made for a wide screen and can be disappointing on a small screen.
- Home entertainment feels less exciting than going out to a place of entertainment.
- It's a more diluted, less concentrated experience.

Dangers

- Theatre and cinema audiences are declining in some countries, which may result in a shrinkage of the industries.
- Places of entertainment close down, which can make town centres seem empty.
- The dangers of city centres become exaggerated as people have less experience of going out, particularly at night.

- People become overweight and unfit as their leisure activities become more sedentary.

2 Choosing a film / 3 A wider vocabulary

Using adjectives effectively is particularly important in reviewing. It is one of the main ways in which ideas in the film and opinions of it are conveyed.

The dialogue raises questions about habitual ways of talking about films ('that was good') which fail, in fact, to reveal much about them. Before students read the dialogue, you may like to write *The film was good* on the board. Elicit from students adjectives which convey information more precisely, e.g. thrilling, terrifying, fascinating.

Students should enjoy reading the dialogue aloud, and substituting more precise adjectives for *nice* and *good* in Section B, Exercise 2.

4 Collocations

If you share the students' first language, it may be helpful to make cross-cultural comparisons about which words can 'go with' other words. Or, in a multilingual class, you may like to encourage students who share a mother tongue to make these comparisons in their language groups and produce examples for the rest of the class.

LEARNING SUPPORT

This is a higher-level exercise, so you may want to reduce the adjective word list for mixed-ability groups or split the class into smaller groups and give each group a section heading to work on.

Suggested answers

PLOT: impressive, magnificent, stunning, superb, enjoyable, satisfying, memorable, violent, amusing, hilarious, witty, quirky, sad, poignant, dramatic, gripping, breathtaking, mysterious, thought-provoking, engaging, mesmerising, convincing

CHARACTERS: impressive, memorable, tough, violent, amusing, hilarious, witty, stylish, quirky, sad, engaging, mesmerising, convincing, appealing, likeable, attractive

COSTUMES: impressive, striking, magnificent, stunning, superb, memorable, hilarious, stylish, attractive

SETTING: impressive, magnificent, stunning, superb, memorable, dramatic, breathtaking, mysterious, attractive

SPECIAL EFFECTS: impressive, magnificent, stunning, superb, enjoyable, memorable, amusing, hilarious, dramatic, gripping, mesmerising, convincing

PERFORMANCE: impressive, magnificent, stunning, superb, enjoyable, satisfying, memorable, amusing, hilarious, witty, stylish, dramatic, gripping, breathtaking, thought-provoking, engaging, mesmerising, convincing

5 Understanding the style of short reviews

This exercise helps students analyse some of the techniques used by professional film critics. The examples are of very short newspaper reviews, which almost have a language of their own. Clearly, you'll want students to develop their own style, but they may like to adopt one or two of the techniques.

LEARNING SUPPORT

You may wish to reduce the amount of reading for students who require extra **support** by asking them to focus on reviews C, D, F and G (and answers 1, 3, 4 and 7). To **challenge** students, provide a more focused way of analysing the critics' techniques by asking them to find examples in each review of: genre information (thriller, documentary, comedy); dramatic, emotional language; how the writer makes you want to watch the film. Students could compare their answers in pairs.

Answers

A 6 B – C 4 D 3 E 2 F 1 G 7 H 5

6 Choosing the right word

This exercise shows the care that is taken by the critic in selecting words which are just right to describe a particular film. Students are given practice in identifying key words.

Answers

1 remote, innocent, dark secret, forced
2 a From the snow-capped mountains … to a shark-infested water park …
   b dishonest
   c is attacked, assaulted, framed, forced to defend himself (string of passive verbs)

7 Presenting a film or play to the class

This exercise consolidates the unit so far by asking students to present a talk on a film or play to their group. If possible, they should choose a work which they found memorable.

Before students present their talks, it's a good idea to discuss the approach with them and to clear up any uncertainties.

Active listening

Emphasise to students that the IGCSE Speaking Test will be a positive interactive process. After the student has presented his/her initial ideas, the assessor will ask further questions on that topic and on related topics.

Encourage the student presenting the talk and those listening to take part in a lively follow-up discussion. Each student should contribute one positive response expressing praise or encouragement. You could practise the following beforehand:

Well done! That was a fascinating talk.

I thought that was very well thought out. I can see how much preparation you've put in.

Brilliant! I really hope I have the chance to see this film.

Students should also try to ask a question based on the talk or a related topic, e.g. *Do you think there will be a sequel? Do modern films contain too much violence and brutality? Do you think people are influenced by what they see in films?*

Recording your talks

If students record their talks, encourage them to analyse the results in their groups. You may wish to select a strong example as a model for positive criticism from the whole class.

C Working in the film industry or theatre

1 Pre-reading discussion

A The initial discussion gets students thinking about the film industry in general as an area of employment.

B The reading comprehension which follows is based on an interview with a very successful animator. He has created a set of quirky characters and built interesting stories around them. They particularly appeal to young people.

Make sure students understand the concept. The photographs in this section will be useful. Elicit examples of animated films students have enjoyed. Ask them whether they found the ideas original and inventive or childish and silly.

C Ask students *'What do you think would be difficult about producing an animated film using Plasticine models?'* Any of the following would be good answers:

- making characters seem appealing
- devising background sets
- inventing plots

D All the personal attributes on the list would be useful for an animator.

2 Vocabulary check

Answers

1 F   **2** E   **3** B   **4** A   **5** C   **6** D

3 Reading for gist

TEACHING SUPPORT

See the Introduction for a general approach to helping students with Reading tasks.

LEARNING SUPPORT

For students who will find the second question challenging, give them a copy of the text in which the parts of the text that refer to the personal attributes are underlined or highlighted.

Answers

Nick studied animation.

All the listed attributes are mentioned or suggested.

4 True/false comprehension

Answers

1 true   **2** false   **3** true   **4** false   **5** false   **6** false

7 false   **8** false   **9** false

5 Vocabulary

Answers

1   **d** individual picture which is part of a film

2   **e** people who gave him ideas or encouraged him

3   **c** basic structure made of wire

4   **a** in a real place

5   **b** names of the people who were involved with a film

Guessing meaning from context

6   ability to notice and remember details

7   a job with regular hours, e.g. from 9 a.m. to 5 p.m.

8   extremely busy

6 Spelling and pronunciation: The letter *c*

The aim of this exercise is to raise students' awareness of how the letter *c* affects pronunciation. Wherever possible, vocabulary from the reading comprehension has been recycled.

Remind students that the rules for pronunciation help with spelling, e.g. words like *notice, peace, replace* keep the final -*e* when the suffix 'able' is added, in order to keep the *c* soft.

You may wish to discuss the role of character marks and accents in some languages to denote how letter should be pronounced (e.g. *c* with cedilla in the French word *façade*). Ask students if their language(s) use accents and how much they help with pronunciation.

As always, encourage students to see that spelling rules are part of a larger language framework. As students become more proficient at analysing patterns, their skills as linguists increase.

Practice: answers 🔊 CD 1, Track 14

/k/	/s/
Oscar	Wallace
career	scene
action	centimetre
comedy	Plasticine
discovered	advice
communication	certainly
accurately	influence
particular	recipe
credits	face
	cine

/ks/	/ʃ/
eccentric	efficient
accident	delicious
	sufficient

AUDIOSCRIPT

As in the Student's Book.

As always, make sure students understand the meanings of the words, hear an accurate model, and practise saying them aloud.

Other words illustrating these sounds are: *identical, café, pronunciation, incident, spacious, gracious.*

7 Using words in context

This exercise provides an opportunity to practise contextualising the sounds. Swapping sentences and reading them aloud provides further practice. Encourage students to monitor each other's pronunciation.

8 Spelling and pronunciation: The letters *ch*

Students will certainly be aware of the commonest contrast of *ch* sounds: /k/ and /tʃ/. They are also reminded of *ch* pronounced /ʃ/.

Odd word out: answers 🔊 CD 1, Track 15

Group A: chef (belongs to **C**)

Group B: scheme (belongs to **A**)

Group C: chocolate (belongs to **B**)

AUDIOSCRIPT

As in the Student's Book.

You could follow up this exercise by getting students to write the words in context or by giving them a quiz. In the quiz, you could test their acquisition of the sounds by writing up the phonetic symbols on the board, with an example word under each symbol. Label the symbols 1, 2 and 3. Call out a word and ask students to say whether it belongs to 1, 2 or 3.

9 More practice of *c* and *ch* sounds

The discussion about a drama club production is an opportunity to practise the sounds in a reasonably natural dialogue. As always, encourage students to work in pairs and check each other's pronunciation.

10 Look, say, cover, write, check

Students continue with the visual strategy to reinforce recall of words which are difficult to spell.

D Reading for pleasure

1 Pre-listening discussion

This pre-listening task asks students to think about what reading for pleasure offers. You may like to ask a student to build up the notes on the board, e.g.

You have time to absorb the ideas and can re-read sections.

It's intellectually stimulating.

2 Listening for gist 🔊 CD 1, Track 16

TEACHING SUPPORT

See the Introduction for a general approach to helping students with Listening tasks.

Students are going to listen to a discussion in which a librarian expresses his fears that TV and films are depriving children and young people of the opportunity to form positive reading habits, thus harming their intellectual and creative development.

83

LEARNING SUPPORT

The listening script is challenging, so it may be helpful to **support** some students by giving them some key quotations from the audio before they listen. They should mark them agree/partly agree/disagree/not sure, and briefly discuss their views with a partner. This will give an opportunity to check understanding of the language. For example: *Reading for pleasure is declining in children., Video can't develop the mind in the way reading can., TV programmes rely on shock tactics to get attention., Children who watch a lot of violence in films come to accept it as just a normal fact of life., Parents should set a good example by reading themselves.*

A Jonathan's key point is that reading develops the mind, whereas TV and videos offer easy entertainment.

B The phrases the interviewer uses are: *If I could just butt in here …*, *Hang on!*, and *If I could get a word in here*. You may like to ask students how much success the interviewer has with interrupting. He doesn't succeed, even when the speaker has come to the end of a sentence, because the speaker is so determined not to be interrupted.

You could point out that *'Hang on!'* shows the interviewer's attitude – that he thinks the speaker is exaggerating. Elicit students' own personal strategies for interrupting, asking which strategies they would feel comfortable with.

AUDIOSCRIPT

You are going to listen to a radio interview. Jonathan, a librarian, is concerned that young people are giving up reading because of television and videos. Listen first for the general meaning and try to decide why Jonathan thinks videos are intellectually less stimulating than reading.

INTERVIEWER: What exactly are your concerns, Jonathan?

JONATHAN: I think it's very sad to see reading for pleasure decline in children and young people. Reading is a wonderful way to use leisure time. You can escape into an imaginary world of your own. Do you realise the average child watches 20 to 30 hours of TV a week?! Children and young people are not forming the habit of settling down quietly with a book, and getting, you know, the rewards of concentrating on a really absorbing story.

I: Well, if I could just butt in here, …

J: Children from poor homes watch most TV, maybe because their parents can't afford to pay for other diversions. However, borrowing books from the library costs nothing at all.

I: But surely a high-quality film can stimulate young people intellectually and creatively?

J: A video, however well made, can't develop the mind in the way reading can. Reading teaches you to discriminate between good and bad in subtle ways. Most videos are about quick and easy entertainment, just as quickly forgotten.

I: Oh, now, I think that's a bit unfair! Where's the evidence?

J: Most videos and TV programmes are pathetic! The characters are shallow, the plots predictable. They rely on shock tactics to get attention – violence, aggression, crime, and abuse…

I: Oh, hang on!

J: … just to keep us watching. If crime is a theme in a novel, on the other hand, a child can think it through properly and come to understand the motives behind the actions of the characters. But I think violence on the screen is different. Children aren't using their minds to discriminate about what they see – they're just soaking up violent images!

I: So you're saying violence is more harmful on screen than when it's written about in a respected novel?

J: I think children who watch a lot of violence in films and on television come to accept violence and aggression around them as just a normal fact of life.

I: So you believe films and television actually influence behaviour?

J: Why would advertisers spend millions advertising products on TV if they didn't believe it was money well spent?

I: So, how would you encourage children to switch off the TV and open a good book?

J: Parents should set a good example by reading themselves. Our library has a special young people's section with some wonderful books! Parents can encourage children to join. At the moment, they're taking the easy way out and letting their children become telly addicts! Parents …

I: If I could get a word in here …

J: … parents should talk to their kids about what they're reading. They … they ought to ask their opinions of the plot and the characters. In the end, families would be closer too.

I: I don't think you should be too hard on parents! But what you say about screen violence and so on having a more harmful effect is interesting, though I doubt whether you'll be able to prove it! I wonder what our listeners think?

3 Detailed listening 🔊 CD 1, Track 16

As the interview is quite a dense, complex passage, you may want to pause the recording in various places to check understanding.

The TV viewing figures are based on UK research. After the listening, you might like to ask students what they think the average number of viewing hours is in their own country.

Answers

1 They lose out on the habit of reading and the rewards of concentrating on an interesting story.

2 Reading uses intellectual powers which help you learn to discriminate between good and bad.

3 They come to accept violence as a normal part of life.

4 They can encourage their children to borrow suitable books from the library, and they can talk to them about what they read, asking their opinions of the books.

5 c interested and concerned

4 Post-listening discussion

Encourage students to support their arguments with reasons and examples.

5 Dialogue: Interrupting each other

Make sure students understand that the ellipsis device (…) shows one speaker in mid-flow when someone interrupts.

Obviously, students will interrupt each other more than is normal in real life, but they will get valuable practice. If they have volunteered interrupting strategies of their own, they could also use them here. The views of the two speakers are deliberately rather black and white, as this makes their frequent interruptions more natural.

The pairwork adds more useful fuel to previous discussions about the influence of TV, films and books. Some follow-up questions to ask could be:

'Can violence on TV undermine the moral values children learn in a good home?'

'Could examples of kindness and generosity on TV or in books compensate children who are being brought up in a harsh, uncaring environment?'

'If children were not watching TV, would they necessarily be doing something more challenging?'

'How useful is TV as an educational tool, teaching children to understand concepts or supporting the curriculum?'

LEARNING SUPPORT

Some students may need an opportunity to practise using some of the interruption phrases in a more basic drill before embarking on the dialogue activity. Review the phrases in Exercise 2 (or substitute alternatives), then put students in pairs. One student begins a 'conversation' with 'bla-bla-bla' and the other interrupts using one of the phrases and appropriately polite intonation, taking over the 'bla-bla' conversation themselves until their partner interrupts them in turn. Continue until they have had a chance to try out several different phrases.

85

TEACHING SUPPORT

It is important that students understand that they need to be polite when interrupting someone. Even if it is difficult for them to stop someone else from talking, they shouldn't use the phrases introduced in Exercise 2 too excitedly and certainly not aggressively. This is more important if they don't know the person in question very well. As well as encouraging students to use the phrases, you could **stretch** students' learning by introducing them to the body-language signals people use to show that they would like to say something, such as holding a hand in the air or opening their mouth to speak. As these may be culturally specific, you could ask students to say something about such body language in their country.

International overview

This can be done as a useful homework exercise using an internet search engine, if students have internet access, and the answers discussed in class.

Answers

A   Norway

B   UK

C   Iceland

D   India, Nigeria, USA

E Book and film reviews

1 Pre-reading tasks

A   To prepare students for writing reviews later in this section, they are asked here what attracts them when they choose books. It's handy to bring in a few paperbacks of different types. Ask students what they can predict about a novel from the picture on the cover, the title and, finally, the publisher's blurb.

B & C   Before students complete the notes for a review of a book they have enjoyed, you may wish to go through the points with them, reminding them of useful things they have learned from film reviewing, e.g. keeping description of the plot straightforward, concentrating mostly on setting the scene, using vivid vocabulary.

2 Reading a book review/3 Reading a film review

These exercises contrast two examples of reviews which are suitable for a school magazine.

An interesting discussion could be stimulated by asking students whether novels adapt well to the screen. You could ask them to discuss this statement:

'A film director, making a film of a novel, can show a viewer at a glance a situation which took many pages of description to build up in the book.'

You could ask if anything is lost when a book is filmed (subtlety of character development, introspective elements, comments on life and surroundings, opportunity to really absorb and think about what is happening and so on).

The first review is of *'Great Expectations'* (published in 1861), a classic English novel by Charles Dickens, one of Britain's best-known writers.

It is a thought-provoking novel in which character development is a major strength. You may like to discuss with students what they know of 19th century life.

The second review is of a modern animation, *'How to Train Your Dragon',* in which the main character Hiccup also undergoes a journey of self-awareness. Hiccup tries to go against his gentle nature by proving to his family and community that he is capable of killing the dragons that terrorise their island home.

His personal journey has some similarities to Pip's enlightenment in *'Great Expectations'*, although they appear to be very different works.

It is hoped that some of the students will have seen the film and be able to describe it before they read the article. They can then go on to explore its deeper meanings.

Comprehension check: answers

Great Expectations

1   *Great Expectations*, Charles Dickens

2   in the 19th century, in England

3   because he helps an escaped prisoner

4   He becomes more aware of his faults, and more compassionate.

5   because he is moved to tears at the end

How to Train Your Dragon

1   Dragons attack their island home.

2   because he is ridiculed by his clan/he is hopeless at fighting

3   by killing a Night Fury

4   Hiccup discovers happiness and peace of mind.

5   Younger viewers will enjoy the hilarious twists and turns; older viewers will appreciate the deeper messages.

6   Encourage any experiences students want to share about becoming more open-minded and developing empathy, eliciting, for instance, the idea of reaching out to a person who is perhaps different in some way.

4 Analysing example reviews

Students are asked to analyse why the reviews are effective, and to underline useful language for use in reviews.

5 Useful language for reviews

Students are asked to indicate which expressions would be suitable for reviewing films as well as books, and then to tick those they would like to use in their own reviews.

6 Criticising a film, book or live performance

Students are given a chance to consider more mixed comments on books, films and live performances which express both negative and positive views.

7 Effective openings for book reviews

Students are asked to rank the example book reviews in order of effectiveness. C and E are the most successful examples. They are concise and informative. The other reviews are vague, say too little in too many words, and do not make use of appropriate vocabulary.

You could ask students to substitute expressions from exercise 5 for those used in reviews A, B, D and F. For example, the phrase *It's hard to put down* could be used instead of *I couldn't leave any single moment in the book without reading it*, which is seen at the end of review A.

8 Writing an opening paragraph

Remind students of the ingredients of a good opening paragraph for a review: clarity, being concise and engaging interest immediately.

TEACHING SUPPORT

If students haven't read a novel recently, let them write about a film or TV show they like. Before students try to write an opening of their own, practise an example with the class as a whole. Decide together on a film, TV show or book that everyone in the class knows, then elicit different ways of beginning a review of it. A good idea would be to write three openings and then ask students to decide which is the best and why.

LEARNING SUPPORT

With students who find writing challenging, it may help them to prepare the task orally. They could work with a partner or small group, telling their partner enthusiastically what is good about their chosen novel (or film) and why their partner should read it / go to see it. Encourage them to focus on what is really good about it in as few words as possible. When moving on to the writing, some students may benefit from a choice of sentence starters to incorporate – e.g. *This book/film will make you …; This is the most … book/film I have ever …; Set in …, this novel tells the … story of …*; etc.

9 Writing a review of a thriller from prompts

'The Kidnapping of Suzy Q' is a novel aimed at the teenage market.

Example answer

The Kidnapping of Suzy Q by Catherine Sefton is the most thought-provoking and atmospheric novel I have read. It is set in modern urban Britain and it tells the story through the eyes of the courageous heroine Suzy. One day she is making an ordinary trip to the supermarket to buy groceries when the supermarket is raided. In the confusion, the criminals kidnap Suzy as she is standing in the checkout queue.

The criminals keep Suzy in captivity. Suzy recounts her ordeal in painful detail. I was impressed by Suzy's courage, determination and refusal to panic or give up. Several incidents in the novel reveal Suzy's ability to cope when she is threatened by them.

The story made me think how ordinary life is changed by one incident. It is also inspiring because it made me realise the inner strength ordinary people can have to cope with disaster.

The novel is skilfully written. Catherine Sefton's style is witty, and the characters are strong and convincing. The plot is intriguing and never predictable. If you like tense novels, you'll find this hard to put down.

10 Writing a review of a play based on a dialogue

Encourage students to read the dialogue aloud, as it is useful for pronunciation practice. Writing the review could be done by two students working together, checking and comparing each other's drafts. Alternatively, it would also make a good homework exercise.

Example answer

A student's answer could be similar to the following:

The gripping new thriller, *Every Move You Make* is on at the Red House Theatre for the next three weeks. It's a must for anyone who loves suspense and a fast-paced story. Based on true events, it focuses on a quiet boy called Matt who has a secret power.

Matt can break any security code, however difficult. He would never do anything wrong himself, but he is kidnapped by a gang who want to use his powers to rob an international bank.

Martin Inez gives a very powerful performance as Matt, a person who wants to be popular with his classmates. From the very first scene the film is full of suspense, as we see the gang secretly monitor Matt on electronic devices. Like me, I think you'll be on the edge of your seat as the drama unfolds.

During the play, we watch as Matt becomes a changed character. After the kidnap, he shows the strength to stand up to the gang. Even though his life is at risk, he outwits the gangsters and saves the bank. I was delighted when, in the end, Matt gets offered a top job with the police to stop internet crime.

I would definitely recommend *Every Move You Make*. It was a fantastic and thought-provoking evening's entertainment. I also realised how much I rely on my passwords being secure but in fact, they might not be. The film would also be great for the Theatre Club's regular outings.

Grammar spotlight

TEACHING SUPPORT

See the Introduction for a general approach to helping students with Grammar exercises.

Students clarify the use of *will* for prediction, and the use of the superlative + present perfect for recommendations and reviews.

You may like to elicit some more examples of the superlative structure, perhaps by writing key adjectives on the board (e.g. *funny, strange, frightening*) to prompt sentences, e.g.

It's the funniest film I have ever seen.

It was the strangest story we had ever heard.

It's the most frightening book I have ever read.

LEARNING SUPPORT

To **support** some students with this activity, elicit the rules for formation of superlative adjectives as necessary. It is useful to check that the students can explain to you when we use the + -*est* (for one-syllable adjectives and two-syllable adjectives ending in –*y*) and when we use *the* + *most* + adjective (adjectives with two or more syllables). Check their understanding of the spelling rules, and of irregular forms. Finally, a practice drill of example sentences would consolidate the work well, if time allows.

Answers

Students of English language and literature will find it particularly fascinating.

I think you'll be moved to tears at the end.

It's one of the funniest films I've ever seen.

Exam-style questions

See the Overview of *Cambridge IGCSE English as a Second Language* section at the beginning of the Student's Book for the mark scheme and criteria for marking the writing questions.

Writing

4 Concert or live performance – review

A model answer could be similar to the following, but students are free to choose any live performance they want to review. As always for Question 5, the answer should cover the bullet points given.

Example answer

If you want to be feel excited, scared and sad all at once, I suggest you go and see 'The Silver Song' at the Moonlight Theatre. Although one of us said that the musical was a little slow at times, most of us thought it was magnificent.

The heroine is played by Inara Asar, who gave a sparkling performance in the role of Lily, a likeable teenager with musical talent. Her family are too poor to pay for singing lessons, but, one day, when she is working for a rich family, a visitor to the house offers her a job in his theatre. It is a dream come true, but sadly, Lily is soon drawn into a criminal underworld.

I won't spoil the ending for you, but my whole family were on the edge of their seats. The singing is also memorable, especially in the scene where Lily has to leave her parents to start her new life. The costumes were really impressive too.

The Silver Song is a masterpiece. It has superb music, appealing songs, engaging humour, powerful performances and witty dialogue. So don't miss out! (200 words)

(Reading & Writing, Exercise 6: 16 marks (Extended).)

Reading

The reading text explores reading in the digital age. As usual, students need to:

- read the rubric carefully for context

- scan the questions to get a general idea of what the texts are likely to be about
- read for general meaning
- match speaker to statement through a process of careful checking, and elimination.

Encourage students to be patient when they match the statements to the texts. If they approach the task in a rush, and try to spot answers too quickly, they are likely to get confused by ideas which sound very similar, so being methodical is essential. It is always worth drawing attention to the way the statements use paraphrasing for the words and expressions given in the text. It may be helpful to set a time limit of about 20–25 minutes.

Answers

a	B
b	D
c	C
d	A
e	D
f	C
g	B
h	A
i	D
j	C

(Reading & Writing, Exercise 2: 10 marks (Extended).)

Listening 🔊 CD 2, Track 1

This multiple matching exercise is challenging, but worthwhile, as it should more than prepare students for what they might face in a listening exam. It is pitched at Extended level. Core-level students, in particular, may try to match words they hear on the recording with the same or similar words or phrases in the statements. Explain that this approach is insufficient. They need to listen for genuine understanding and then focus on the specific details which enable them to identify the correct answer. They should read the statements carefully first, and then scan the options for the correct answer as they listen.

Encourage students to check their answers after the first listening, and to use the second listening to double check. As this is a challenging exercise, you may choose to let them listen more than twice.

Answers

1 C **2** G **3** F **4** A **5** D **6** E

(Statement B is not needed.)

(Listening, Exercise 3: 6 marks (Core); 6 marks (Extended).)

AUDIOSCRIPT

You will hear six people talking about film making. For each of Speakers 1–6, choose from the list A–G which idea each speaker expresses. Write the letter in the box. Use each letter only once. There is one extra letter which you do not need to use. You will hear the full recording twice.

SPEAKER 1

In my job, I'm responsible for making the film set look as convincing as possible so the audience aren't distracted by items that would be out of place. That's fine if we're using specially made film sets, but if we use real locations we have to make sure any changes we make can be removed at the end of filming and there's no damage. In one film, which was set in a castle in the 19th century, there were modern light switches which needed disguising. It was difficult, but in the end I used white boxes to cover them up. When filming ended, the owners of the castle allowed us to have a wonderful party at the castle, which they also came to.

SPEAKER 2

I always feel the audience must accept the character and find him or her realistic and true to life. In one film, I had to play the part of a man who disguises himself as a woman in order to get a job. My make-up alone took over four hours, but the make-up artist did a fantastic job, and I looked exactly like a real woman. It gave me confidence that I could be convincing in my role. When my wife saw the film, she was really impressed!

SPEAKER 3

I work in make-up and I recently had to make someone up to look much older than their real age, as, over the course of the film, the character changes from being a teenager to a middle-aged adult. The film schedule had completely underestimated the amount of time this would take. On some days it was a real rush to get the make-up finished on time for the scene, which was very stressful for both me and the actor. This happens more often than I would like and can make my job very difficult.

SPEAKER 4

As the director, I usually have a clear idea in my mind of what I want to get from each actor, but I need to listen to their opinions as well. Recently, I was working with an actor who had to play the part of someone who can't be trusted. The actor and I had some disagreements, but in the end she persuaded me that her approach was the right one, and I was happy to change what I thought and go along with that. People think actors are very moody and difficult to work with, but in my experience most of them try hard to please.

SPEAKER 5

As an assistant director, I have to give the actors their instructions regarding the film schedule and the timings to be on set. It's essential the actors arrive at the correct time, as the entire schedule is delayed if someone is late. One actor at the moment gets a bit annoyed with me as he doesn't always like being told where to be and at what time. He has to be on the set very early in the morning, which he really dislikes. I've learned to keep calm under this kind of pressure, and I work at appearing self-assured even if I don't always feel it.

SPEAKER 6

Working with a good director can be a great experience, and I've learned so much from the directors I've worked with. I usually also have a lot of input into how to portray the character. As I'm already well known as an actor, I have to think about my audience and the ideas they've developed about me over many years. I wouldn't do anything that would damage their view of me, and if there's a difference of opinion with the director, we work to reach an agreement. I've developed good friendships with some of the directors I've worked with, and see them outside work.

Wider Practice

1   Why not study a short story extract in class and analyse it in terms of plot, theme, characters, language effects and the ideas it conveys?

2   You could watch a popular film in class and analyse it afterwards. Ask students to write reviews and compare them.

3   You could try to arrange a talk to the class by someone involved in TV, radio, the music business,

film or creative writing. Failing that, you could record an interview with a writer, film director, musician, etc. from English-speaking TV or radio (if possible), or show a video clip from the internet, and discuss the ideas it raises.

4   The class could make a visit to a cinema, theatre, museum and so on, and upload a review of their impressions onto a reviewing website, or design an advertising poster for it.

5   Some museums and art galleries will arrange guided talks and tours for school groups. This could also provide a basis for writing a formal report for the headteacher or school management committee about the pros and cons of the trip.

6   You could read a short play in class and perhaps even act it out. Students may enjoy discussing all aspects of theatre: the casting, costumes, scenery, stage direction, lighting and so on.

    If many students watch the same TV programmes, you could ask them to be 'casting directors' and choose actors and actresses from favourite soap operas and so on to take the parts in the play. This could lead to a discussion about the suitability of actors (age, appearance, voice, acting skills, etc.) for different parts.

7   Students could discuss how to turn a short story or novel into a film. They could discuss what they would include and what they would leave out, as well as the setting/background, special effects, the costumes they would choose and who they would cast in the various roles. They could discuss what kind of films could be adapted for the stage.

8   You could set up a debate about illegal downloading or pirating films and music.

9   The ideas below could be adapted for paired conversations, individual talks and class debates. They make excellent practice for a broad range of oral skills and build confidence for the Speaking Test. Students can record themselves using their phones, if appropriate, and analyse the recordings, or share the recording for the whole group to discuss.

- Reasons for starting a drama club / music group / theatre group at our school
- A review of an enjoyable evening spent at the theatre / a music concert / a festival of dance
- How is technology shaping our leisure time?
- Are we influenced by what we see on TV?
- Life is better with a smartphone.
- Which apps have changed our entertainment the most?
- 'Classical music is better than pop music in every way.'
- 'Drama, art and music are the most important subjects on the school timetable.'
- 'Nothing can match the excitement of a live performance.'
- Are creative artists exploited if their work is accessed on the internet without their permission?
- Is it better for our school to spend money on theatre visits or a new recreation area/common room?

91

Travel and the outdoor life

Overview

One of the main aims of this unit is to develop students' ability to produce a memorable description. Although IGCSE students possess basic descriptive skills, they often need help with making their descriptions more vivid, and with explaining why what they are describing is enjoyable and of interest to others.

Theme

Constructive use of leisure time is the main theme of the unit. Leisure is a popular topic, and the emphasis is often on the educational aspects of leisure, e.g. what do you learn from this activity? In the unit, 'active leisure time' is considered in a broad context and stresses the value of new experiences. These include: activity holidays, leisure activities, camping, foreign travel and tourism.

IGCSE students sometimes tend to treat ideas superficially. The course aims to help them develop and demonstrate more intellectual depth. The unit tackles this need by posing questions which help students to think of all aspects of a topic. For example, if students are presented with an attractive idea, such as going on a foreign holiday, they commonly have difficulty in thinking of its less obvious, perhaps less pleasing, points.

Areas for discussion in the unit are:

- How does a brochure advertising an activity holiday achieve its effects?

- What are the possible drawbacks of holidays?

- How can you be a responsible tourist?

- Can students hoping for new experiences by doing 'voluntary work overseas' make an important contribution to developing countries?

- What are the pros and cons of working for the leisure industry as a resort rep?

Language work

Students extend their range of stylistic techniques by learning more about using comparisons, relative clauses, -ing forms and the role of imagery in descriptions. Vocabulary is developed in a variety of ways, with work on adjective suffixes, intensifiers, colloquial expressions and precision in the use of adjectives. It is assumed students will already have some familiarity with the language forms. The exercises reinforce and expand their knowledge.

Punctuation of direct speech is studied. Pronunciation focuses on words with shifting stress.

The *Grammar spotlight* focuses on the position of adverbs of frequency.

A Holiday time

1 Holiday quiz

The lead-in exercise focuses students' thoughts on what they want from a holiday. To consolidate this exercise, it would be interesting to create a class survey chart of the most popular and least popular holiday activities.

2 Pre-reading discussion

The holiday brochure students are going to read is aimed specifically at young people learning English. The summer camp concept is a repackaging of the traditional language study holiday. Students at the camp do a few classroom-based lessons a day. They then continue practising their English as they try out a variety of fun-orientated outdoor activities with native speakers of English.

Before students read the brochure, encourage them to focus on describing the pictures.

Brainstorming

Students may find thinking of *bad* points about the holiday challenging. You may wish to use prompts, e.g.

'Do you think you would see enough of ordinary British life if you stayed at a summer camp?'

'Could young students perhaps feel homesick and unsure?'

Some additional good points to elicit:

- learning practical everyday English
- caring staff
- safe environment to learn new skills
- making new friends

- wide choice of activities
- discovering more about yourself
- becoming more responsible

Additional bad points:

- homesickness/feelings of insecurity
- possibly not enough emphasis on formal English
- probably very expensive
- may not like the choice of sports and activities on offer
- little opportunity to experience everyday life and customs in Britain

3 Reading for gist

TEACHING SUPPORT

See the Introduction for a general approach to helping students with Reading tasks.

Before students read, write up an example sentence containing both facts and opinions, e.g.

The sensitive, energetic instructors are aged between 18 and 25 and are qualified in first aid.

Ask students to identify the factual and the opinion phrases in the example. You could also ask *'How do you know this phrase is a fact?'*, eliciting the possible response:

Age or qualifications can be proved to be true, but personal qualities are a matter of perception.

LEARNING SUPPORT

Before readers who may require extra support tackle the reading task, check understanding of the following language: *integrated, build (confidence), upgrade, like-minded, excursion, residential centre.*

4 Comprehension: Scanning the text

The questions test scanning skills. Remind students that, although the questions might look straightforward, mistakes can be made. They need to look carefully at the detail, such as the information in the small print which is necessary to answer some questions.

LEARNING SUPPORT

Remind students that the wording used in the text will not necessarily be the same as that used in the question (e.g. in question 1, they will be looking for a different way of saying 'well known for'). Also remind them to use clues to help them find where the information is likely to be – e.g. pictures, and their knowledge of other similar texts. Ask them where you would typically find contact details (at the end) and the most important facts about a company (at the beginning).

Answers

1 leading the way in integrated language and activity camps
2 every day
3 do Stable Club/upgrade to Stable Club
4 excursions/day trips
5 special transfer service/ met on arrival and transported to the camp.
6 download it from the website
7 send in a completed form/the Pre-visit Pack

5 An eye-catching advert?

Introduce the meaning of *eye-catching,* which is used to refer to something that is immediately attractive or interesting. Elicit the ways in which adverts try to attract our attention, e.g. by use of memorable slogans (a short phrase such as Apple's 'This changes everything'), logos (a symbol such as Nike's tick) and photographs chosen to appeal to particular people. Once students have analysed the brochure in Section A2, you could ask them to design a short advert for a language school to go on a website or in a newspaper. They can use computers to do this, if you have access to them. At the end, the class can decide which of the adverts are the most eye-catching and why.

Answers

The target groups for the advert are children and their parents who will be paying for the trip. The advert aims to attract these groups by the 'identification technique': potential customers will identify with the pictures of teenagers doing fun things, and parents are reassured that the fun is balanced by learning.

There is a variety of opinion language, e.g. *Every minute of the day is filled with fun, excitement and activities; All our residential centres offer excellent accommodation and good food ...*

The language, photographs and layout suggest fun, interest, stimulation, supervision and good organisation.

6 The best way to learn?

It should be interesting to explore with students what learning English through another medium, such as water skiing or horse riding, can offer. It will raise their awareness of how and why learning takes place.

Ask *'What kinds of language would be most likely to be learned?'* Possible responses are: listening to and following instructions/explanations, language to communicate to your instructor or partner that you understand / need help / need clarification, etc., specialised vocabulary (e.g. *trot, gallop*) and words for equipment, conversational English to discuss things with your partner.

7 Quite

The meaning of *quite* as a modifier depends on the context, and, if spoken, on the intonation pattern. In the brochure, *'quite fluent'* means *'moderately fluent'* to provide a contrast with *'absolute beginner'*.

> **TEACHING SUPPORT**
>
> It is important to point out that *quite* with the meaning of *completely* is reasonably formal. In informal written and spoken English, people are just as likely to say *The film was really brilliant* as they are *The film was **quite** brilliant*. You may want to draw students' attention to phrases such as *I quite agree*, *It is/was quite extraordinary* and *quite honestly*, which, though formal in tone, are commonly used, and which students could make good use of in the Speaking and Writing parts of an exam.

8 Shifting stress

You may wish to give further examples, e.g.

*There will be an **in**crease in prices.*

*Try to in**crease** the amount of time you spend on your homework.*

(Similarly, **sub**ject/sub**ject**, **re**ject/re**ject**, **con**vict/con**vict**.)

> **LEARNING SUPPORT**
>
> As shifting stress can be a challenging area for some students, focus on a much shorter list of examples when getting the students to work out the stress rule. Once they have understood the rule, offer them plenty of practice – for example, get students to make up sentences for their partner using one or more of the stress-shifting words. They should read aloud their partner's sentences with the correct stress, while their partner checks and corrects them. If necessary, demonstrate how stress is marked in dictionary entries (usually with a stress mark immediately before the stressed syllable). Give the students a few further stress-shifting words to look up.

Marking the stress: answers 🔊 CD 2, Track 2

1   **pro**duce
2   pro**duce**
3   re**cord**
4   **re**cord
5   ob**ject**
6   **ob**ject
7   **con**trast
8   con**trast**
9   **per**mit
10 per**mit**
11 **pre**sent
12 pre**sent**

Elicit the fact that, in the examples, the stress falls on the first syllable of the nouns and on the second syllable of the verbs.

AUDIOSCRIPT

As in the Student's Book.

Monitor students' pronunciation of the example sentences, as it's important that they can show the difference.

Many two-syllabled words change their function from noun to verb, of course, without a shift in stress. You may wish to end by eliciting some examples of these, e.g. *mistake, promise, display*.

B Outdoor activities

The following sequence of exercises aims to help students describe leisure activities by highlighting useful language structures and vocabulary. IGCSE students are often asked to analyse *why* an activity they like would interest other people too. Here they are offered ideas of things to say and ways of phrasing them.

1 Pairwork

If you have a class in which students know each other very well, they could be more motivated to do an exercise like this if one of them goes to the front of the class and answers questions.

2 Reading: Identifying leisure activities

Exercise A offers practice in identifying key vocabulary. First, ask students to identify the main people, places and objects seen in the photographs. In the first photograph these are: bike, mountain, track, cyclists, clouds, sky. Once students have done this, ask them to scan the six descriptions to see if they contain any of the key words. Do this with all the photos, pointing out the skill that needs to be developed: the ability to scan images and text to pick out important details.

> **LEARNING SUPPORT**
>
> It may be helpful to ask some students to first study the photos and identify a few key vocabulary items which may not be familiar to them. Then students could read the descriptions in pairs so that they can discuss with each other what they think each activity is. Encourage them to find as many key words as possible.

Answers

A

1 mountain biking Key phrases: *hard to keep the frame straight, muddy holes, pedal my way out of, foot of the mountain* (Photograph A)

2 jogging/running Key phrases: *without stopping once, good pair of trainers, slow down gradually* (Photograph C)

3 archery Key phrases: *fit an arrow to the crossbow, pull the bowstring back, quiver, target (Photograph D)*

4 tennis Key phrases: *large outdoor court, hire a racket, friendly games with a partner, concentrating on the*

ball, I usually get to most of the shots, perform the basic strokes (Photograph E)

5 horse riding Key phrases: *the saddle and bridle, mount by putting my left foot in the stirrup, trot, rise up and down* (Photograph B)

6 swimming Key phrases: *submerging my face, artificial buoyancy aids, floating on my back, I feel as though I'm weightless (Photograph F)*

B

This approach to reading develops comprehension skills in the style of a multiple matching type of exam question.

> **TEACHING SUPPORT**
>
> Exercise B offers practice in making connections. It is worth taking your time over this and giving students as much help as possible. First, elicit information about questions A–F. With regard to question A, for example, ask: *'What does 'sociable' mean?' 'What does it mean to say that an activity is 'sociable'?'* Aim to elicit related vocabulary: *other people, friendly, outgoing.* Then ask students to find links between what you have discussed and relevant information in one of the texts. Students may even find that one of the related vocabulary words you have come up with is actually in the text.

> **LEARNING SUPPORT**
>
> Before beginning the scanning, encourage students who may need **support** to narrow down the number of texts to scan for each question by making predictions. They should note down next to each the sports that they think this might apply to: they could compare ideas with a partner (e.g. 'develops strength in the hands' – most likely to be archery?). Tell them to start with the ones they are most sure about.

Answers

a 4 Tennis

b 2 Running

c 5 Horseriding

d 3 Archery

e 6 Swimming

f 1 Mountain biking

3 Developing your writing style

This exercise will make students more aware of the variety of ways they can describe an activity they enjoy. The contextualised examples (some of them taken from the texts in Exercise 2) remind them of grammatical structures they have met before, and show them how they can be used for particular purposes.

If students have difficulty with structures such as the -ing form, it would be a good idea for them to work on some specific grammar exercises. (Suitable grammar practice books are *Recycling Your English* by Clare West or *English Grammar in Use* by Raymond Murphy.)

If they have a reasonable grasp of the structures, a discussion of the examples in the exercise should be sufficient to refresh their memories. Go into as much detail as you feel is appropriate. You could, for example, contrast the use of the infinitive with the -ing form:

We're allowed to use the school facilities.

We enjoy using the school facilities.

You could elicit further examples with *like, love, begin/start, intend, continue.*

Students can use 'since' clauses to make a comparison with their state of health, mood, etc. before they began playing a sport or game and their state of health now, e.g.

I'm fitter/have stronger arms since I started swimming regularly.

I'm calmer / happier / more flexible since I've been doing yoga.

Remind students of the way comparative structures are formed (adjective + -er or *more* + adjective).

Students can also study the use of similes, e.g.

If I can't go rock climbing I feel like a caged bird.

4 Analysing language structures

Check with students that they have underlined the correct parts of the extracts. Actually going through the exercise might uncover gaps in their knowledge which you need to follow up with some formal grammar exercises – possibly for homework.

5 Describing a favourite activity

The consolidation exercise could be set for homework, or as a classroom exercise if you have time.

If your students don't do much sport and prefer other outdoor activities such as gardening, walking or photography, encourage them to write about these. The main aim is to achieve a clear, interesting description with enough detail.

6 Reading aloud

Students may well enjoy the chance to read aloud their description, without saying the actual name of the activity and letting others guess what it is.

7 Pre-listening discussion

Ask students to study the camping picture and explore their responses to a camping trip, building on actual experiences some of them might have had.

You could ask:

'What challenges would living in a tent present?'

'What kind of clothes/equipment would you bring?'

'What might a typical day's camping be like?'

Stressful aspects of camping could include: coping with living in a small space cooking outdoors, coping with storms or cold weather.

8 Listening for gist 🔊 CD 2, Track 3

> **TEACHING SUPPORT**
>
> See the Introduction for a general approach to helping students with Listening tasks.

The listening exercise is based on a colloquial conversation between two boys relating their feelings about a camping trip. Asking students to listen for gist, will, as always, help them focus on the overall meaning of the extract.

Answers

There are several things they didn't enjoy: the girls laughing at their attempt to put up the tent, the long walk in the rain, boots which leaked, missing the chance to see the museum, no food for breakfast, cold showers.

Their intonation indicates that they enjoyed the trip overall.

AUDIOSCRIPT

Paul and Marcus have just come back from their first camping holiday with the youth club. What did they

find difficult about the holiday? Note three things.
Overall, do you think they enjoyed the trip, despite the
difficulties?

PAUL: Do you remember that first night? I mean,
           we'd just arrived, couldn't wait to get
           unpacked and go for a swim.

MARCUS: And we couldn't get the tent up.

P: Well, that was my fault. I could have sworn
           I put the instruction leaflet in. I couldn't
           believe it when it wasn't in with the rest of
           my stuff!

M: Well, don't blame yourself. We managed it
           in the end.

P: I felt bad about it, though. That gang of
           girls didn't help. Remember how they were
           all giggling, watching us struggling with
           the tent half up?

M: Well, they got their tent up straightaway,
           didn't they?

P: Getting the tent up wasn't half as bad as
           that fifteen-mile walk in pouring rain.

M: And discovering that your brand new
           waterproof boots you'd spent thirty quid
           on weren't waterproof at all!

P: I blame the girls for that walk. We wanted
           to see the aircraft museum.

M: Yeah. It was their fault we got soaked and
           we never did get to the museum.

P: All because they were 'desperate to see
           a picturesque historic village with such a
           quaint-sounding name'.

M: Yeah, which turned out to be just like all
           the other villages around there.

P: Mr Barker always let them do what they
           wanted to do.

M: He didn't listen to what we wanted. Funny,
           wasn't he? With that woolly hat and specs.
           How old do you think he was? Fortyish?

P: More like fifty!

M: Remember when we had no food for
           breakfast?

P: Because the girls had forgotten to pack
           the food into airtight containers and
           everything was full of bugs.

M: Yeah, they tried to deny it, but it was
           definitely down to them. They were
           responsible for putting stuff away.

P: We had a good time, though, didn't we,
           despite the stone-cold showers …

M: Rock-hard bread at breakfast …

P: Trying to find the toilet in the pitch dark …

M: Not being able to get any sleep …

P: Because of Mr Barker's snoring …

M: Getting up at the crack of dawn …

P: Want to go again?

M: You bet!

9 Listening for detail
Answers
1 c   **2** a   **3** b   **4** b   **5** c

10 Post-listening discussion
The sort of things the boys might have enjoyed are:
independence, exploring a new area, making new
friends, the challenges of camping, the countryside,
physical exercise.

11 Blame
Students will probably need to listen again to the recording
so they can really focus in on the expressions used.

Answers

Students should tick all the 'blaming' expressions, plus *It's
my fault*, *I feel bad about it* and *Don't blame yourself*. (Note
that in some cases the speaker used a different tense and/
or pronoun.)

Blame and guilt are sensitive areas. British people
tend to be indirect, so they are unlikely to say to
someone's face 'It's your fault' unless they are angry.
They do, however, use such language quite freely in
talking about someone who is not there (as the boys
do on the recording). Make sure that students understand
the distinction.

Suitable expressions for blaming someone to their
face are:

'I'm not really very happy about …' (formal)

*'I really don't know why you insisted on driving/bringing us
here. Now look what's happened!'* (informal)

97

Admitting guilt and telling someone they are not to blame are not sensitive areas, so the expressions listed can be used freely.

12 Comparing cultures

It will be informative to hear the language used in other cultures, and could lead to some interesting stories.

13 Functional language: Writing a dialogue

Remind students to think quite carefully about the blame language they want to use. You may want to suggest that it's unlikely in the picnic situation that anyone would say 'It's your fault'. Perhaps suggest that students disagree over whose fault it is, each one being willing to take the blame, e.g. *'It's my fault', 'No, it was mine'*.

> ### TEACHING SUPPORT
>
> Before students write their own dialogues, write one with a class as a whole and put it up on the board. This can then be used as a model for students to follow. Encourage students to focus on how we actually speak. For example, were someone to write the following sentence in a dialogue *I am afraid to say that it has come to my attention, Burak, that you have forgotten to pack the cold drinks*, most would agree that this is not how people speak. Better would be *Burak! Where are the drinks? You haven't forgotten to pack them? Ohhh, I don't believe it!*

> ### LEARNING SUPPORT
>
> Students who require an extra **challenge** can be encouraged to expand the dialogue, perhaps explaining why the drinks were forgotten, apologising, and going on to discuss what they are going to do to remedy the situation. Students who need **support** with the activity could be given a more basic structure: Speaker A: Say what has happened; Speaker B: Apologise and admit responsibility; Speaker A: Tell B they are not to blame. Speaker B: Offer to get some more drinks.

14 Colloquial expressions: Adjective collocations

In informal English, these noun + adjective and adjective + adjective expressions are common.

You may like to ask students if they know any other of the numerous meanings of *pitch*. For example, it can be

used as a verb in *to pitch a tent*, and to mean 'a field' as in *cricket/football pitch*. This could be a good opportunity for some dictionary work.

As this is a challenging exercise, you could narrow the vocabulary options and give students who find it difficult a pair of words to choose the correct collocation from, e.g.

Wasn't Jeremy's talk fascinating?

I'm afraid I don't agree. In fact, I was bored fast/stiff.

Answers
1   bored stiff (also *bored silly/bored to death*)
2   crystal clear (also used metaphorically, e.g. *His explanation was crystal clear.*)
3   scared stiff (also *scared to death*)
4   freezing cold, wide open
5   sky-blue (also *navy blue* – very common)
6   fast asleep
7   dirt cheap

Other examples you could elicit are: *wide awake, boiling hot, razor sharp.*

15 More colloquial expressions

English is very rich in all kinds of colloquial expressions. Understanding their use and being able to use them will make a huge difference to students' fluency.

Answers
1   a bite to eat
2   a drop of rain
3   hear a pin drop
4   a hair out of place
5   at the last minute

Before students try to create their own sentences, remind them that they need to use the whole phrase. You could round off the exercise by asking them to share any similar colloquial expressions from their own language(s).

16 Word building: Adjective suffixes

Remind students that *e* and *y* are dropped from the end of words when adding a suffix beginning with a vowel.

You may like to discuss the answers to the first few questions with the whole group together and then let students answer the remaining questions in pairs or small groups. Encourage students to use a good dictionary to help them with this exercise.

Answers

1   bulletproof

2   twentyish

3   ironic

4   odd-sounding, odd-looking

5   childish, childlike, childproof, childless

6   Arabic

7   boyish

8   panoramic

9   soundproof

10   Islamic

11   pleasant-sounding, pleasant-looking

12   scenic

13   pinkish

You could also ask students what other adjective suffixes they are aware of, e.g.

-ical:	grammatical, theatrical, alphabetical
-ous:	poisonous, dangerous, courageous
-ious:	ambitious, suspicious, infectious
-ful:	helpful, delightful, meaningful, peaceful
-y, -ly:	windy, spicy, friendly
-able:	memorable, fashionable, advisable
-ible:	edible, legible

17 Punctuating direct speech

Many IGCSE students can use inverted commas around the actual words used by a speaker, but they don't use other elements needed for direct speech, such as commas or capital letters. This exercise aims to encourage students to work logically, so allow them sufficient time to analyse the examples, prompting where necessary.

Remind students that if you start a new paragraph when the speaker is in the middle of a speech, you don't need to close inverted commas at the end of the paragraph. They do need to be opened, however, at the beginning of the next paragraph.

Practice: answer

'What was the best part of your holiday in America?' Naomi asked when she saw Kevin again.

'Going along Highway One from Los Angeles to San Francisco,' said Kevin, without hesitation. 'I wouldn't have missed it for the world.'

'What's so special about Highway One?' Naomi asked, 'Isn't it just another dead straight American highway?'

'Well,' replied Kevin. 'The road runs between […] full of redwood trees'. Yes,' he paused for a moment, 'it's truly magnificent.'

'What was the weather like?' Naomi asked. 'Every time I checked the international weather forecast there was one word: hot.'

'In fact,' Kevin laughed, 'we had stormy weather, but when the sun broke through it created fantastic rainbows. We visited a cove where you can hunt for jade. Anything you find is yours and I'd almost given up looking when I found this.' He reached into his pocket and pulled out a tiny green fragment. 'Here,' he said, 'it's for you.'

C Tourism: The pros and cons

1 Brainstorming

The IGCSE course is about developing and displaying depth of thought. Awareness of topical issues and an ability to discuss them thoughtfully are good skills to acquire. This exercise is very challenging, and it's a good idea for students to do it in small groups before coming into a larger group to pool their ideas.

Example answers

The following may give you some ideas of what students could produce.

Pleasures of being a tourist

*   Having new experiences – observe customs, sample local cuisine, visit local places of interest perhaps very different from home country.

*   Having more time to explore things / learn a skill / meet people.

*   You can practise the local language.

*   You go home with more understanding of a different part of the world.

Drawbacks of being a tourist

- You may be adversely affected by strange food, a different climate, different culture.
- Lack of knowledge of the area/language may cause frustrations/misunderstandings and you may even be exploited by unscrupulous people.
- You may be homesick.
- You may find the country you are visiting disappointing and very different from your expectations.
- You may get sunburnt / bitten by insects / lost in a strange place or lose your valuables.

Advantages to the host country

- Tourism creates employment of various kinds – service industries, construction, manufacturing.
- Tourism earns foreign currency.
- Tourism can create more international harmony.
- The wealth generated by tourism can be invested in the economy to improve the infrastructure – roads, hospitals, schools, etc.
- Some facilities built with tourists in mind may benefit the local population, e.g. wildlife parks, swimming pools.

Disadvantages to the host country

- The natural beauty of a locality may be destroyed by insensitive development.
- People may be displaced to make way for tourist facilities, e.g. indigenous people moved off land to create safari parks.
- The local economy may become distorted as plantations, rice paddies and pasture land used by farmers are destroyed to build golf courses, hotels, safari parks, etc.
- Local fishermen may be denied access to beaches to work.
- Wildlife may be negatively affected.

How can tourists behave responsibly when they go abroad?

- Save precious natural resources and energy, e.g. they shouldn't waste water and should switch off lights.
- Avoid buying items made from endangered species, e.g. ivory.

- Ask (using gestures if necessary) before taking photos/videos of people.
- Respect the local etiquette – dress modestly and avoid behaviour in public which may offend.
- Learn about their host country's history and current affairs.

You may like to ask a student to write up the ideas from the whole class on a board or flip chart, if there is time.

(The photograph shows the Acropolis of Athens, Greece.)

2 Tourism with a difference

Ask students what they think of 'sustainable tourism', and elicit examples of ways it could be implemented in students' own countries.

> **TEACHING SUPPORT**
>
> See the Introduction for a general approach to helping students with Reading tasks.

3 Pre-reading discussion

The reading comprehension exercise which follows is based on a magazine article encouraging British holidaymakers to visit two lovely Italian islands, Sicily and Sardinia.

Before they begin reading, it's interesting to hear students' perceptions of these islands, and also to find out how they think foreigners view their own country(ies). You could link their answers to the results of the earlier discussion about tourism as a worldwide issue.

If students have travelled abroad, you could ask what their expectations of the country were before they went, and how the visit changed what they thought.

4 Vocabulary check

Answers

1 H 2 E 3 A 4 F 5 J 6 D 7 K 8 B 9 I 10 C 11 G

Incandescently is an unusually long word. You could ask students to work out how many different words they can make from it by rearranging the letters.

5 Reading and underlining

Underlining the descriptive passages will reinforce awareness of description, one of the unit's main aims.

TEACHING SUPPORT

To help **support** your students, it would be a good idea do the underlining exercise with the class as a whole. First, elicit the fact that that descriptive language describes people or places in such a way as to help the reader visualise them. For example, *He was tall and thin* doesn't offer us much. By contrast, *Tall and sickly-thin, with bald head hidden under an old fedora, and eyes like the lifeless black holes of forgotten space* creates a mood and helps us picture the character. Once students are clear as to the purpose of descriptive language, read out the text about the Italian islands, pausing as necessary, and guiding students towards its use of description. The purpose in Exercise 5 is simply to identify imagery (another way of saying descriptive language). Students look at the effects it produces in Exercise 9.

6 Comprehension check

The comprehension questions require both short answers and the selection of the correct option about each island from either/or questions. Students also have to decide on the author's attitude to the islands by selecting the correct option from the choices given.

LEARNING SUPPORT

Tell students who may need **support** to read only about Sicily (i.e. to line 53). They can answer questions 1–3 and, for question 5, change the wording to 'Which of the following are true of Sicily?' Alternatively, the reading task could be done as a jigsaw reading with one of each pair reading about Sicily and the other about Sardinia.

Answers

1   their physical separation from the mainland

2   Markets like souks and couscous cafés in the capital remind the writer of North Africa.

3   There are some of the most beautifully decorated buildings in that part of the world.

4   any two of: fishing, cycling, walking, riding

5   **a**   Sardinia (eagles, black vultures and flamingos.)

    b   Sardinia (mountain wildness, eagles and black vultures soar over mountains)

    c   Sicily (agriturismo)

    d   Sicily (amphitheatre, temples)

    e   Sicily (Mount Etna)

    f   Sardinia (prehistoric buildings)

    g   Sardinia (childminding services available at Forte Village)

6   **c**   (The author gives a balanced view – there is no evidence that she recommends one island more than another.)

7 Post-reading discussion

It's fascinating to explore the contradictory needs of tourists and the difficult position it places tour operators in, e.g. the wish to be immersed in an exotic culture but find familiar foods from home.

You could ask *'How far should tour operators meet the needs of holidaymakers, e.g. wanting hotel comfort when staying with local families on remote farms?'*

8 Adverbs as intensifiers

Intensifying adverbs are common in English. It's difficult to give rules about their use, but you could tell students that adverbs like *appallingly, horrifyingly*, etc. collocate with negative words.

Adverbs like *staggeringly, amazingly, incredibly* are used when there is a suggestion of surprise, e.g. *The balcony had a staggeringly beautiful view of the bay.*

Before students do the exercise, check their understanding of the following vocabulary:

Blizzard:	A severe snowstorm.
Dew:	Very small drops of water that form on the ground overnight.
Dusk:	The time between day and night.
Drizzle:	Very light rain that falls in small drops.
Gale:	A very strong wind.
Thaw:	A period of warm weather that causes ice and snow to melt.
Drought:	A long period without rain which causes a shortage of water.

Answers

1   surprisingly
2   fully
3   strikingly / strangely / surprisingly
4   badly
5   seriously
6   utterly
7   dazzlingly/surprisingly
8   surprisingly
9   painstakingly/badly
10 faintly
11 alarmingly
12 strangely/surprisingly

9 Imagery in descriptions

The following sequence of exercises focuses on bringing together what students have learned so far about describing, building on the earlier work on describing a leisure activity.

Encourage students to draw on all their language resources in responding to the question on imagery. For example, a good response to '*a lovely, broad landscape with rolling plains and corn-coloured hills*' would be: 'When I hear this, I think of an open, peaceful landscape, with an unhurried way of life.'

By contrast, the description of the starker landscape of Sardinia in '*Eagles and black vultures soar over the mountains, pink flamingos flash their wings by the coast*' might elicit the response: 'It suggests a wild atmosphere, lots of contrasts, very colourful, lots of fascinating things to see.'

10 Adjectives: Quality not quantity

Students continue to investigate the power of language by observing how many descriptive adjectives are used before a noun. It's usually only one or two, and the students can reflect on the effect that well-chosen adjectives have on creating atmosphere.

Encourage students to choose an example of descriptive language and explore it.

11 Comparing two styles

Comparing and contrasting the two styles will bring descriptive techniques into sharper focus for students. Style 1 reflects the way many IGCSE students write – in simple, short sentences, with a limited vocabulary, resulting in a repetitive style. Students need to move on from this. Style 2 integrates the techniques students have been learning so far: intensifiers, a broad vocabulary and more complex sentences.

12 Developing your writing style
Practice

Students could work in pairs to draft and redraft the description. Encourage them to make use of the ideas introduced in this exercise.

Example answer
Students could produce something like this:

> The town developed around an ancient rectangular marketplace. It has many medieval buildings and a wide diversity of restaurants offering delicious food from several different cultures. The local people have a traditional way of life and dress, and are very hospitable, honest and welcoming.

13 Writing your own description

This would be a good homework exercise. Encourage students to make as many drafts as they feel are necessary.

International overview

According to the United Nations World Tourism Organisation, the top four international tourist destinations in 2014 were France, the USA, Spain and China, in that order. It should be interesting to hear students' reactions to this fact, and their opinions about the reasons.

Questions 2–4 should also produce some interesting ideas and discussion.

14 Giving a short talk

You may like to record a few of the best talks for analysis later.

15 Words from names

Some verbs such as *pasteurise* (milk) or nouns such as *sandwich* are, of course, named after the individuals who invented them. In this exercise, students match the invention to the name of the person.

Answers

1   Sandwich
2   Cardigan
3   Pasteur
4   Fahrenheit
5   Morse
6   Volta
7   Marx
8   Diesel

Encourage students to think of the alterations which are made to some of the names to turn them into verbs or adjectives: *Pasteur + -ise, Marx + -ist.*

Names, their meanings, origins and associations, are a source of great interest. Sometimes students have an adopted English name, or are aware that the name of

their country or city has a different name in English; some people moving to settle in an English-speaking country anglicise their family names.

The discussion could also stimulate exploration of how family and place names originated. Many English family names were derived from place names (*Worthington, York*), nicknames (*Armstrong*), family relationships (*Johnson*) and trade names (*Carpenter, Baker, Fletcher, Smith, Miller*).

Ask students to contribute what they know about the origins of names in their culture(s).

The impact of modern life on names could also be investigated, with students asked to reflect on trademark names such as *biro, hoover* and *iPad*, which have become a part of everyday language.

16 More homophones

This exercise gives further practice with homophones taken from the reading texts. Some are less obvious than others, e.g. *boar/bore*. This will give students more insight into the range of homophones in English.

Answers

real/reel

scene/seen

boar/bore

flower/flour

sea/see

right / write / rite

soar / sore / saw

blue/blew

two / to / too

sail/sale

herd/heard

deer/dear

D Personal challenges

1 Reading an example email

As always, the email provides a reliable example of the sort of writing students should be aiming for.

2 Comprehension
Answers

1   Tasmania

2   She was nervous. Her feelings weren't justified – she didn't feel lonely because the group leaders were so thoughtful.

3   Canoeing – the instructor made her laugh and forget her fears, she made quick progress and was happy with what she learned in a week.

4   She thinks Lucia would like the place, the people, and all the different things that can be done on an activity holiday.

5   She loved it and wants to do it again.

3 Analysing the email
Answers

1   Paragraph 1: reason for writing

   Paragraph 2: description of place and weather

   Paragraph 3: description of canoeing lessons

   Paragraph 4: why Lucia would enjoy it too

2   They should try to comment on the use of adjectives and intensifiers such as *so* and *really*.

3   Students sometimes find it difficult to say why something they like would also interest others. This paragraph gives another example of how to do this, with useful expressions for closing an email.

4 Vocabulary: The weather
Before students do the exercise, check their understanding of the following vocabulary:

Blizzard: A severe snowstorm.
Dew: Very small drops of water that form on the ground overnight.
Dusk: The time between day and night.
Drizzle: Very light rain that falls in small drops.
Gale: A very strong wind.
Thaw: A period of warm weather that causes ice and snow to melt.
Drought: A long period without rain which causes a shortage of water.

Answers

1   false

2   false

3   true

4   true

5   false

6   true

7   true

8   true

9   true

10   false

5 Spelling revision
This exercise gives students the chance to revise some of the spelling rules they learned in earlier units (see Student's Book Unit 2 Section D, Exercise 8 and Unit 3, Section D, Exercise 8).

6 Writing about the weather
Answer

We're having a good time here but the weather isn't great. Every day starts *misty* or even *foggy*. This clears up by midday and we get a little *hazy* sunshine. We had a *rainy* day yesterday and the ground was too *muddy* for walking. It's generally *chilly* and I'm glad we brought warm clothes. Our boat trip was cancelled because it was *stormy*. We're hoping for calmer weather tomorrow.

7 Discussion: Voluntary work abroad
You could begin by reading out the information about voluntary work abroad. Students then work in pairs to discuss the questions. If students struggle to think of how volunteers abroad can overcome the problems they face, suggest the following ideas: volunteers can take part in an induction scheme in which they learn about the host country; volunteers can do some training in a particular area before they go aboard; volunteers can talk to other people who have had experience of living and working abroad.

8 Building a blog from notes
Elicit the fact that a *blog* is a website which takes the form of a diary or commentary on particular subjects or events. You may like to tell students that the word blog is a combination of *web* and *log*, with web being an abbreviation of *world wide web*, and log being a kind of record of events which occur during the voyage of a ship or plane. Point out or elicit that people who write blogs are called *bloggers*, and that bloggers write *posts*. The blog could be checked by getting students to complete it on the board.

Answer

> At first I was very busy but now I have time to update my blog. I'm enjoying myself here. The weather is warm and sunny, except for last night when there was a big storm which turned (the) paths into rivers.
>
> The family I'm staying with are very kind. The house is three-bedroomed and is quite comfortable. I am very close to my 'sisters', who tell me off if I do anything wrong! Each morning I wake up to / am woken by the sound of exotic birds darting among the trees.
>
> Yesterday, I took a bus through breathtaking countryside to the local city. I went to a bustling market. Everywhere people were selling things but I am/was not sure who was buying!
>
> I'm helping to look after young children in a nursery school. The children are delightful and are very polite. The work is demanding but rewarding.
>
> I miss everyone at home but I feel I am growing up / have grown up quickly and I'm more confident now. I will upload photos tomorrow and would love to read your comments.

9 Look, say, cover, write, check

Regular short tests give students a sense of progress. As usual, in this exercise they learn problematic spellings.

10 Discussion: Working as a tour guide

You may like to check that students understand what a tour guide actually does before going into the activity in the Student's Book. They need to understand that tour guides are normally employed by a travel company to look after tourists who have booked holidays with the company. Their duties may include interpreting and explaining to tourists things they need to know about the places they are staying in, e.g. the opening times of banks and shops, how to get a doctor, etc. They will help sort out problems tourists encounter, such as getting ill, losing valuables, problems with accommodation. The job sometimes includes taking the group to places of interest and places of entertainment in the evening.

Depending on the type of trip, a guide may accompany the group to other cities or destinations on the itinerary, or even across continents. Tour guides usually wear some sort of uniform so they are easily recognisable.

Point out that, unlike a tour guide, a resort rep (= representative) is usually based in one specific holiday resort.

11 Reordering a magazine article

Answer

The correct order is: l, j, e, m, c, d, n, f, a, h, k, b, g, i.

You may like to circulate a copy of the completed magazine article.

> **LEARNING SUPPORT**
>
> For students who need **support**, give them the topic of the three paragraphs and tell them to begin by dividing the sentences by paragraph: 1 Describing Rhodes, 2 Describing her job, 3 Final conclusions and recommendations.

Grammar spotlight

Students will be familiar with adverbs of frequency, but they often misplace them in sentences, so they will appreciate some clarification about where the adverb should be put.

> **TEACHING SUPPORT**
>
> See the Introduction for a general approach to helping students with Grammar tasks.

> **LEARNING SUPPORT**
>
> Provide further controlled practice for students who need it. For example based on their daily routine (i.e. eat breakfast – *I always eat breakfast*; get the bus to school – *I usually get the bus to school*, etc.).

Answers

1 always, often, usually, seldom, sometimes, hardly, rarely, never

2 **a** I always ride my bike to school.

b Angela often goes swimming with her friends. *(already correct)*

c He usually prefers the buffet-style breakfast.

d Visitors to the Taj Mahal are seldom disappointed.

e We sometimes play tennis after college.

f Lewis is hardly ever on time – it's so annoying!

g The children rarely go to the cinema.

h She has never been on holiday abroad.

Exam-style questions

See the Overview of *Cambridge IGCSE English as a Second Language* section at the beginning of the Student's Book for the mark scheme and criteria for marking the writing questions.

Writing

2 Activity holiday – account

Students should use a friendly tone and register, use some imaginative vocabulary and details, and as always, cover the bullet points given.

Example answer

> Hi Chess,
>
> It seems a long time since we met. School is not the same without you.
>
> Remember I told you I entered that photography competition? Well, to my astonishment, I won first prize for my 'Sunset' photo! There were some amazing holidays I could choose from for the prize. I decided on bushwalking with guides in Kenya, as I have always longed to visit Africa and now was my chance!
>
> We slept in tents and were woken early by the sound of birds and animals. I thought it would be quiet in the bush, but nothing is further from the truth! After a wash in icy cold water and bread and eggs for breakfast, we set off with our local guide, Luke, who knew all the names of the trees, birds and flowers we saw. We were staying in a very wild, mountainous area and had beautiful views.
>
> One day, we were walking through the bush when suddenly, elephants appeared. We wanted to run away because we were frightened, but Luke explained they are peaceful animals. So we stayed and took photos!
>
> For tourists, Kenya's magnificent wildlife and distinctive landscapes are magical. You would love it!
>
> Love
>
> Fatma (196 words)

(Reading & Writing, Exercise 5: 16 marks).

Listening 🔊 CD 2, Tracks 4 and 5

This exam-style note-taking exercise is in two parts: A and B. It is based on similar exercises in Extended listening components so it is quite challenging. The topic is Viking culture and customs. In Part A students listen to a talk about Viking warriors given by a museum guide and take notes. In Part B they hear a conversation between two students about Viking settlements in Iceland and take notes. There are five gaps in each exercise and each gap is worth one mark, making a total of ten marks for the whole exercise.

Students should listen twice to each part. They should use the second listening to check their answers. In a class situation, naturally, they can listen as often as you think is necessary. Only one or two words are required to fill each gap in the notes.

It is helpful to check the answers by pausing the recording in the right places.

When completed, the notes should make complete sense to someone who has not heard the original recording. The correct part of speech is required.

Answers

Part A

Vikings: Longships

Between the 8th and 11th centuries, the Vikings travelled to many regions of the world in wooden longships. Some longships have been dug up from rivers in one piece, as the *clay* at the bottom of the river bed preserved the wood in good condition.

What a longship looked like

The longships were light and narrow. The red sail of a warrior longship scared away enemies. The rack along the length of the ship held *wooden shields*.

Viking weapons

Viking warriors used iron axes, spears, swords, arrows and crossbows. Children were taught *archery*, as these skills were needed for both hunting and fighting.

Before going into battle, warriors put on cloaks and helmets made from bearskins and worked themselves into a (*fierce / mad / frightening*) *rage / fury / temper*. The word 'berserk' is from an early Norse word meaning bearskin.

The swords were decorated with delicate silver patterns. The warrior valued his sword highly and it had a special *name* written on it. The weapons were buried with warriors when they died.

(Listening, Exercise 5: 10 marks (Extended).)

Part B

Iceland in the Viking Age.

Between 870 and 930, 1000 Vikings left Norway because they needed *more space.*

The first settler built a farm in an area which became the site of Iceland's *capital/capital city.*

The settlers used iron and *soapstone* to make weapons and cooking pots.

Exports: natural resources, linen and *wool.*

In 930, the settlers set up a yearly *assembly/government* called the Althing, which discussed the best ways to rule the island.

(Listening, Exercise 5: 10 marks (Extended only).)

AUDIOSCRIPT

PART A 🔊 **CD 2, Track 4**

You are going to listen to a museum tour guide talking about Viking history and culture. Listen to the talk and complete the notes in Part A. Write one or two words in each gap. You will hear the talk twice.

I am delighted to show you our museum's marvellous collection of Viking artefacts. The Vikings were fierce warriors but also clever traders and adventurous travellers.

The Vikings were superb sailors and left Norway, Sweden and Denmark and went to areas now called Western Europe, the Middle East, Canada, Greenland and Russia. They used the sun, stars and winds to navigate across stormy, dangerous seas. Their wooden longships were narrow and light, which made them versatile. They could be landed on beaches and rowed upriver when they were inland. In modern times, some of the actual boats the Vikings sailed in have been excavated intact from the bottom of river beds. It seems the thick, mud-like clay acted as a preservative, which stopped the wood of their boats from rotting away.

On our left, we can see a magnificent reconstruction of a Viking longship. The intricately carved longship you see here is a warrior ship and has 40 oars for rowing when required. The sail is painted red because the Vikings thought that would frighten the enemy. The rack that runs alongside the side of the ship was made for holding wooden shields.

Vikings were skilled craftsmen and on the wall here behind the longship you can see examples of their weapons: iron spears, swords, battle axes, crossbows and arrows.

Archery was learned at an early age, as archery skills were essential for hunting as well as for fighting. The wooden shields and crossbows you see are replicas, as unfortunately wood rots quickly and very few of the real shields and crossbows have been found.

On my tablet, I can show you a famous engraving of a Viking. You'll see he is wearing a heavy bearskin cloak and a helmet made from a bear's head. If you look closely, you can see the frightening expression on his face and his threatening body language. To develop the correct mental state for warfare, warriors dressed in helmets and cloaks made from bearskins and then worked themselves into a fierce rage. In English, we get the word 'berserk', which means being so angry that we are out of control, from an old Norse word for bearskin.

Making weapons look beautiful was also very important. Notice how the hilt of the sword is beautifully decorated with a pattern of inlaid silver. A warrior's most treasured possession was his sword and he gave the sword a particular name and had it engraved on the hilt. When the warrior died, his axe and sword were buried with him.

PART B 🔊 **CD 2, Track 5**

Now listen to a conversation between two students about Viking settlers in Iceland and complete the sentences in Part B. Write one or two words only in each gap. You will hear the conversation twice.

STUDENT 1: I'm so glad we came to the museum. It's really going to help us with our history project.

STUDENT 2: You bet. You've chosen Viking settlements in Iceland for your special topic haven't you, Jenny?

STUDENT 1: Yes, I've already learned a lot about them from the Iceland website. From 870 to 930, 1000 Vikings left Norway and settled in Iceland because the coast was so fertile and the sea was full of fish. Norway's valleys had become crowded and they needed more space.

STUDENT 2: But I thought Iceland was mountainous, with lots of glaciers and volcanoes?

STUDENT 1: That's only in the interior. The coast has always been good for farming. There's an interactive map of Iceland in the Viking Age over there. Let's take a look, shall we?

STUDENT 2: Oh yes. You can see on the map that there also used to be a lot of forests between the mountains and the sea.

STUDENT 1: Yes, it seems as if the interior is like it still is today – not really inhabited. It says here that the first settler was called Ingolf. He came from Norway and he built a large farm on the bay overlooking the sea.

STUDENT 2: And that place is now Reykjavik, Iceland's capital city?

STUDENT 1: Yes, and what a stunning location it is. The settlers must have been very resourceful. They raised sheep on their farms, fished and used local iron and soapstone to make their own utensils and weapons.

STUDENT 2: And it says they eventually exported these natural resources along with wool and linen.

STUDENT 1: Let's look at this bit here on the map in the south-west of Iceland. It is a high plain called Thing...Thingvellir, I am not sure how to say it.

STUDENT 2: Which bit?

STUDENT 1: This bit here. Thingvellir. It's surrounded by cliffs of lava. It says it's the place where the settlers held an annual assembly, making decisions about how to govern Iceland.

STUDENT 2: And the assembly was called, what's that word here - the Althing? The settlers were very advanced weren't they? They wanted to do more than survive. They thought about the future and wanted it to be safe and peaceful.

STUDENT 1: Yes, it says the first meeting of the Althing was in 930. Experts think the discussions were held outside, as no evidence of a building has ever been found.

STUDENT 2: It must have been exhilarating to meet right out in the open like that surrounded by such majestic cliffs and natural beauty.

STUDENT 1: I'd love to visit Iceland one day.

STUDENT 2: Me too. Books and museums are interesting but nothing is as good as actually being there!

Wider practice

1 If tourism is a big issue in the area in which you are teaching, you could ask local tourist officials to talk to students about employment prospects, ways of managing tourism which respect the environment and heritage, and future tourism projects.

2 The travel theme lends itself well to the study of maps. Map reading is a very useful life skill, and understanding the points of the compass is also relevant for exam topics, so it is well worth practising.

3 If you have access to the internet, you may be able to find interesting websites and download video clips which reflect the unit's themes. Consumer holiday programmes are popular and there is a growing emphasis on activity / adventure / special interest holidays. Students could watch these and do the following: listen for factual detail; compare places to stay; decide which of the places presented they'd like to visit and why; review the programmes, offering suggestions for ways in which they could be improved.

4 Students might like to do a cross-curricular project in which they investigate a topic which draws on geography, history, literature or technology, etc. and present it to the class. The following topics might give you some ideas:

- An investigation into popular pastimes – their origins and reasons for their popularity
- Any topic around the seven natural wonders of the world
- An investigation into the history, design and decoration of buildings the students are curious about
- An investigation into an ancient civilisation, describing its impact on the world.

As well as doing internet research, students could write to the embassy or tourist office of a country they are interested in, asking for information. Many organisations are very generous and will send all kinds of information about their country free of charge. Students could use this for writing a profile on the country.

5   If you know of someone who has an unusual or exciting hobby, he/she could either come into the class to describe it and answer questions, or you could record him or her talking about it and replay the talk for discussion. Sometimes a parent or relative of a student is delighted to be invited to share their experiences with the class.

6   As a change from brainstorming ideas for a topic, why not try brainwriting? Each student writes an idea about the topic on a slip of paper. No names are used. The slips of paper are collected and each anonymous idea is discussed in turn in the group.

Student life

Overview

The main aim of this unit is to develop the skills students need for writing an email of advice. Giving advice, particularly in written English, presents difficulties even for native speakers. This is partly because the tone and register are tricky to get right – subtle variations of tone can have a powerful impact on the effect of what is said, and there are important cultural differences between languages in terms of what is socially acceptable.

This unit also focuses on the techniques which help sustain an idea and develop it into a complete paragraph. This is one of the key areas where students need support if their hard work is going to translate into success.

The unit includes an analysis of tone and register in spoken English as part of a broader analysis of interactive techniques in conversation. This will help students become more familiar with the discourse strategies needed in the Speaking Test and improve classroom talk in general. In addition, there are opportunities for students to learn more about listening (there is an interview with a college counsellor) and understanding what they read (a magazine article on exam tension).

Theme

The unit is thematically linked through a number of topics of particular interest to young students. These include:

- leaving home to study – independence versus security

- coping with exam tensions and developing study skills

- making friends in a new environment

- responses to bullying.

The language study and themes have been selected to combine popular IGCSE topics with skills that are frequently tested.

There are many exercises in the unit. Why not use your insight into your particular class to really focus on those areas where development is needed, even if it means cutting other exercises short?

Language work

The language work includes detailed work on useful phrases for asking for and giving advice, modals, and idiomatic expressions. Idioms are natural in informal contexts, students enjoy learning them, and they can greatly enhance the effectiveness of tone and register. Spelling and pronunciation focus on silent letters. Vocabulary is developed with more work on word building, and punctuation is revised.

The *Grammar spotlight* looks at text messages and how 'text speak' differs from more formal, grammatical written English.

A Challenges of student life

1 Completing a checklist

The topic opens with a discussion about looking after yourself at university. If you feel this is culturally or socially outside students' likely experience, you may prefer to start off by getting them to think about transitional times in their life. You may like to ask them to think about what has been good or difficult about a particular situation, and what they feel they have learned from it. Elicit concepts relating to self-sufficiency, developing a larger range of social and practical skills, making new friends, relating to different kinds of people, understanding new rules, finding one's way around a strange area, and so on.

If you have students who have already experienced being away from home to study, then it would be ideal to capitalise on their experience and let their views be your starting point.

Let students complete the checklist by themselves.

2 Before you listen: Interactive skills

Once students have given their answers to the questions at the beginning of Exercise 2, it would be a good idea to demonstrate how to interact with someone badly and how to do it well. You can do this by choosing a student to play the role of someone about to go to university. You are their friend and want to know how they feel about leaving home. Do two role plays. In the first one, look bored, do not make eye contact, do not smile, and do not use any of the communication strategies listed in Exercise 2. In the second, do the reverse: look and sound interested, ask open questions, offer encouragement, paraphrase, ask for more information, and offer advice. Then ask the class to describe the differences in your attitude in the two roleplays and to say why your interactive skills were better in the second.

TEACHING SUPPORT

The aim of this sequence of exercises is to increase students' understanding of a lively conversation. The dialogue is a bit contrived, of course, but it will help them cope better with the Speaking Test and improve their classroom talk. Peter and Dora take an equal part in the conversation, whereas the teacher/interlocutor's role in the Test is to give students the best possible opportunity to demonstrate their oral skills. In oral pairwork in class, students sometimes tend to take turns giving their opinion, listening to each other but not really interacting. The work on interactive skills will help them move on from this to greater fluency.

---

3 Reading and listening at the same time 🔊 CD 2, Track 6

AUDIOSCRIPT

As in the Student's Book.

Once students have listened to and read the dialogue, check that they have underlined the phrases in it which show that the speakers have good interactive skills (the answers below highlight some but not all of the examples.) Ask students why it is important to show enthusiasm, kindness and affection while listening to a friend who is talking about a problem. Elicit the idea that when we give advice to someone, it should not sound as if we are giving them a command. We should try to put ourselves into the position of our friend, and imagine what it would be like to be experiencing their difficulties.

Answers
Asking open questions: Why do you feel like that?

Giving encouragement: You always seem so confident.

Paraphrasing: So, what you're really saying is that's it's the chores that are bothering you.

Asking for more information/clarification: I'm not sure I follow you. What do you mean?

Reflecting the speaker's feelings/state of mind: I can see you'll be glad to get some privacy.

Making suggestions/offering advice: Why not do it while you've still got some around to show you?

If you share a common language with your students, it's a good idea to compare and contrast ways of offering advice in the two languages. It may well be worth comparing the similarities and differences of tone and register between the two languages.

Giving advice orally

Elicit from students the unique elements of face-to-face contact: body language, the opportunity to smile / to look sorry / to tailor what we say to the person's reactions, the scope for the listener to ask questions.

You can set up the following mini role plays as extension activities if you think it's appropriate:

* Your friend is keen to leave school and take a job but you feel he/she would be wiser to stay on and get some qualifications. What do you say?

* A young man hoping to be promoted at his firm is rejected after an interview because he lacked knowledge about how the company wanted to develop in the future. He asks his manager for advice about how to do better next time. You are the manager. What do you say?

* Your sister wants to marry her boyfriend. You feel she is too young and the boy is unsuitable for her. What do you say?

4 Conversation study

This exercise encourages students to notice how we use specific phrases to make a conversation sound friendly. Put students into pairs or small groups to highlight the parts of the conversation which illustrate each of the points.

Answers
a Dora's use of paraphrase (*So, what you're really saying is ...*) shows that she is trying to understand what Peter is saying to her.

b Dora's suggestion that Peter try ironing a shirt is friendly. She doesn't tell him to do it, but simply suggests that now might be a good time for him to learn how to do it.

c Dora says, 'That surprises me. You always seem so confident.' This suggests that Dora knows Peter very well and that she has warm and positive feelings about him.

d Peter's use of the phrases 'to be honest' and 'a bit nervous' reveal that the conversation is a reasonably informal one. However, there is not much colloquial or slang language in it, which means that it is not as informal as it might have been.

5 Developing your own conversation

Tell students they are going to practise having a conversation about doing something challenging such as going away to college. Read out the five bullet points, and make sure that students understand them. You can do this by asking students to give an example of how to explain an idea clearly, be a good listener, offer appropriate advice and so on.

Give students a couple of minutes to look back at their answers to Exercise 1. Once you have put students in pairs, give them time to decide what they are going to talk about. If students respond well to this task, you could ask them to roleplay further conversations on similar topics.

> **LEARNING SUPPORT**
>
> Students who are less confident with speaking activities may find this task challenging. To **support** these students, tell them to focus on just two or three of the points from Exercise 1, and the first time they do the roleplay they should simply focus on keeping the conversation going rather than trying to correctly use phrases from Exercise 2 – they can look back at these afterwards and have a second go. Some students may prefer to write their dialogue before they record it.

6 Recording your conversation

Students can make recordings using their phones. Alternatively, if your school has recording equipment you can use that. Put students into small groups to listen back to the recordings they make. Encourage students to give one another constructive feedback: What did students do well? What could they improve?

7 Comparing languages

This exercise would best be set for homework. Encourage students to make a short recording of two conversations, one in English and one in their own language. The conversations should be on exactly the same theme. Students can then analyse the recordings, looking at the differences and similarities between their language and English. Point out that students need to consider tone as well as the interactive techniques used.

8 Reading and discussing a problem email

Before they begin reading, ask students to find out if the writer of the email has difficulties at university that they anticipate for themselves. This will help them focus on the email and provides continuity with the earlier work in the unit. The pairwork after the email provides more opportunities to exploit and reinforce advice language.

9 Reading an example reply email

The reply serves as a good example of how a friendly tone can be achieved in an email or letter of advice. Remind them that they can look back at this as an example of how an advice email could be written.

It's important after the pairwork to get feedback on the example email, to make sure that there have been no misunderstandings.

Answers

Students should underline these phrases:

One thing you might find helpful is …

Try to …

all you really have to do is …

why not …?

don't forget to …

It's not a good idea to …

You won't forget to …, will you?

10 Analysing the example email

As this is a key exercise, you may prefer to monitor the discussion through a whole-class approach. Use this opportunity to ask students why the tone of the reply is particularly tactful. Encourage them to think about how the writer, who has to express advice in writing, uses tactful phrases to compensate for the fact that she is not able to give this advice face-to-face.

IGCSE students are not expected to take the role of anyone but themselves, or to write letters/emails of advice that would be outside their experience. Emphasis is on an exchange of views between peers, and students should aim for a relaxed tone and register.

11 Advice phrases

Many IGCSE students can make basic use of modals such as *should* and *must*. Students should, however, be aiming for more sophisticated advice language. This exercise provides further practice in discriminating between registers and shades of tone and meaning.

Elicit from students the fact that intensifiers such as *absolutely* in *'You absolutely must'* make the advice much stronger. You could ask them to suggest alternatives to *absolutely*, such as *certainly, definitely, really.*

> **LEARNING SUPPORT**
>
> Check that all students can use the correct verb form after the different phrases. Go through the list with them, eliciting examples of advice you might give to someone about to go off to university and allowing other students to comment on and correct the grammatical forms as necessary – e.g. *Why not join a sports club …* (not ~~to~~ join), *You may like to try working in the college bar …* (not ~~to work~~).

12 Expressing problems

The way we express our problems is linked to who we are and the culture we come from.

You may like to highlight the indirectness of the informal statement *I'm not sure what to do.* This invites the listener to advise/suggest without asking directly for help. Advice/suggestions would then be offered in a seemingly casual way e.g. *I suppose you could always …*

If students are having difficulty thinking of problems, possible prompts are:

- A mother is waiting for her young child to return from school. He/she is three hours late.

- An expensive pair of shoes you bought ten days ago have completely fallen to pieces. On the receipt it says that faulty goods have to be returned within seven days.

- You're talking to your friend about redecorating your bedroom. You're undecided between redoing the room in white or another colour.

- You're on holiday in a foreign country. You know no one and do not speak the language. You find that your bag with your passport and money has been stolen. What do you say when you telephone home?

13 Tone and register in students' emails

In this exercise, students study extracts from emails giving advice. The extracts reveal typical weaknesses at IGCSE level: students struggle to convey ideas and attitudes with limited language resources.

> **LEARNING SUPPORT**
>
> The exercise is ideal for mixed-ability work in small groups. More able students, who have a quicker 'feel' for tone and register, may enjoy supporting classmates who may be more caught up with the basic meaning of the language. Why not let the more able students lead the groups?
>
> Extract 5 is the most suitably written paragraph.

14 Rewriting a paragraph

Encourage students to rewrite one of the paragraphs they didn't like, with help if necessary.

> **TEACHING SUPPORT**
>
> See the Introduction for a general approach to helping students with Writing tasks.

B The pressure of exams

1 Pre-reading task

Before students do the activity, it would be useful to focus the whole class on the pressures exams cause by asking them how they feel about preparing for and taking exams. You could elicit their comments and write them on the board. It will be interesting to see how your students' views compare with the opinions given in the Student's Book.

You could end this activity on a positive note by asking students whether it is possible to learn to enjoy taking exams. Some people say they enjoy exams because it gives them a chance to show what they can do and they are stimulated by the challenge.

2 Reading for gist

The magazine article comprises some interesting interviews with three students who are taking GCSE exams. By presenting not only the students' viewpoints, but also the parents' and an expert's, we are able to consider a variety of aspects of the pressure exams place, not just on the student, but on the whole family.

The role of the 'expert' can be introduced here. The concept is developed further in the later listening exercise on the college counsellor (Section D, Exercise 2). You could ask *'What kind of background/ experience do you think the expert has?'*

3 Comprehension check

The comprehension questions are a combination of tick box and multiple matching. For multiple matching, encourage students to find key words and phrases as evidence for their choices.

Answers

1 The statements which are true for Clare are: **b** and **c**.
2 The statements which are true for Khalid are:
    b, **c** and **d**.
3 The statements which are true for Felix are: **a**, **c** and **d**.
4 **a** Felix (doesn't do it unless he is interested in the subject)
    b Felix (compared to his brother)
    c Khalid (said getting home late the night before his geography exam was a mistake)
    d Clare (cut back on newsagent job)
    e Khalid (grateful for maths support from his mother)
    f Felix (exams are 'aren't so bad')

4 Post-reading discussion

It will be most intriguing to hear students' thoughts on Clare, Felix and Khalid. The discussion is a valuable opportunity to draw out some cultural comparisons about styles of exams, approaches to study, part-time work, sports clubs and family attitudes.

Particular issues to explore could be:

- Exams are undoubtedly stressful, but does stress have any positive effects? (You could elicit: it can make you work harder / some students thrive in a competitive atmosphere / you appreciate more fully times which are relaxing.)

- Is coursework a good idea, or can you end up overloaded?

- How can you build confidence for exams?

- How can the family help the student who is in the middle of exams?

- What do you think is the best time of day for revision? (Experts suggest our brains are at their peak at around 10 a.m.)

Chart: answers

a bedroom
b other room in house
c library and café

Students will enjoy comparing places where they themselves feel most comfortable doing homework, and perhaps saying why.

5 Vocabulary: Colloquial words and phrases

Making suitable use of colloquialisms helps students achieve a good, informal tone. This exercise recycles words and phrases they met in the text.

Answers

A 1 moan, put your foot down
    2 exam nerves
    3 stick to
    4 working out
    5 loads
B Other meanings:

moan: sound one makes when in pain

loads: large weights of something carried/transported

working out: calculating, being successful

stick to: adhere to (i.e. something sticky)

6 Word building

Students could use dictionaries for this word-building exercise. Encourage them to create sentences to show meanings, as this will test their understanding of how to use the words in context.

Building nouns from verbs: answers

appointment

astonishment

arrangement

entertainment

advertisement

improvement

management

disagreement

Other examples to elicit: *disappointment, postponement, enlargement, enjoyment, enhancement, encouragement.*

Building adjectives from nouns: answers

magical

musical

classical

personal

cultural

functional

mathematical

natural

Other examples to elicit: *national, political, logical, emotional, recreational.*

You could extend this exercise by considering the suffix *-ful*. The examples *stressful* and *helpful* are found in the text. Other examples to elicit are: *colourful, useful, harmful, thoughtful, beautiful.* You could also ask students which of these words have an opposite with the suffix *-less* (all the above except *stressful* and *beautiful*).

7 Language study: Giving advice

Students have come across the sort of language the expert uses earlier in the unit. The aim of this exercise is to help them use their existing knowledge to further explore contrasts and similarities between advice expressions. It also encourages them to look for meaningful patterns in the grammar and helps them work out guidelines for using modals correctly.

The questions draw attention to the special features of modal auxiliaries. The main ideas to elicit are as follows.

Answers

1 *Need(s) to* and *should* sound more indirect than *must.* Students might add that the expert uses a passive construction in **a** and **c**, which sounds less prescriptive than an active one. This would be a good comment.

2 *Need* is followed by the infinitive with *to. Must* and *should* are never followed by *to.*

3 *Should Khalid be encouraged …?*

   Does Khalid's mother need to …?

   Do his parents need to …?

4 *Khalid's mother doesn't need to …*

   Felix's parents offer … doesn't need to be linked / needn't be linked …

   His parents don't need to / needn't sit down …

5 *Ought to* can replace *should* and *need(s) to. Has to* can replace *must.*

8 Should/shouldn't have

Should/shouldn't have + past participle express blame and criticism of your own or another's actions. They are very direct, so students need to be careful of the way they use the structures when addressing people.

Practice: answers

1 Joseph shouldn't have taken a part-time job when he had exams coming up.

2 Indira shouldn't have gone to the concert when she had an exam the next day.

3 He should have checked his bank balance before he spent a lot of money.

4 I shouldn't have shouted at my brother when he was trying to be helpful.

5 I shouldn't have borrowed my sister's jacket without asking her first.

6 You should have bought some extra bread when you knew we needed to make sandwiches.

9 Using a more informal tone

Answers

1 I don't need to cook as Bruno is taking us out for a meal.

2 You should do / ought to do / need to do your homework at a regular time each evening.

3 You shouldn't have made/oughtn't to have made a promise you can't keep.

4 I shouldn't have left/oughtn't to have left all my revision to the last minute.

5 Abdul must get/had better get some rest or he will fail his exams.

6 I should have listened/ought to have listened to her advice.

7 He shouldn't have played/oughtn't to have played computer games instead of revising for the exam.

You could finish this exercise on register by asking students to consider the underlying strength of emotion in this kind of statement:

I'm a bit annoyed, I must say.

This is a typical English understatement and native speakers hearing it would guess that the speaker was angry about something. This is shown particularly by the phrase *I must say*. Contexts in which you might make this comment could be:

- Your friend returns a book he/she borrowed from you and you find that several pages are torn.

- You pay quite a lot of money for a second-hand bicycle which the previous owner assures you is in very good condition. After a few days you detect a lot of faults.

> **LEARNING SUPPORT**
>
> Some students may find this exercise challenging. **Support** them by providing the word which begins each answer: 1 I; 2 You; 3 You; 4 You; 5 Abdul; 6 I; 7 He (or elicit this from the students if going through the exercise orally). You can also simplify the instruction by telling them to use *should, should have, must or need* (i.e. removing the extra complication of *ought* and *had better*). Check also understanding of *vital*, which will influence students' choice of modal. Some students tend to overuse *must* – recap by asking them the difference between when we use *must* and when we use *should* (*must* is stronger and can sound too direct).

10 Spelling and pronunciation: Silent letters

Silent letters are often the cause of spelling errors – students can't hear them so they don't include them in words they write.

Before beginning the exercise, you could write a word, e.g. *castle*, on the board and ask if all the letters in it are pronounced. When you have established that the *t* is

silent, you could ask for other examples. These could be categorised according to particular letters.

Some possibilities are:

silent *l*   *chalk, palm, would*

silent *c*   *muscles, scene*

silent *p*   *pneumonia, psychology*

silent *w*   *sword, wreath, who*

silent *k*   *knot, kneel, knight*

silent *g*   *design, reign, gnat*

silent *gh*   *straight, bought, caught*

silent *t*   *thistle, fasten, soften*

silent *h*   *exhaustion, vehicle, heir*

Monitor students' pronunciation as they practise saying the words aloud.

11 Crossing out silent letters

Answers

1 g   **2** w   **3** h   **4** w   **5** gh   **6** c   **7** l   **8** l   **9** u
10 g   **11** gh   **12** h

Elicit other examples of words with these silent letters.

12 Adding silent letters

Answers

1 brightest, knows, talk
2 wouldn't, listen
3 circuit
4 Whereabouts
5 half, whole
6 write, answers
7 lights
8 wrist, knee
9 white
10 Honesty
11 scent
12 whistle, wrong
13 wrote, pseudonym
14 reigned
15 psychic

13 Detecting patterns

The aim of this exercise is to help students use what they already know about silent letters to come to conclusions about meaningful patterns. This will help them with pronunciation when they come across unfamiliar words, and with spelling.

They might need some help to detect the patterns, so you could start with an example. You could write *psychic* on the board and ask them to think of other words which start with *ps* (e.g. *psychiatrist, psychology, psalm*). Make sure students are clear that when the letters *ps* come at the beginning of a word, the *p* is silent.

Other patterns students might notice and which help towards rule formation are:

pn at the beginning of words has a silent *p*: *pneumonia, pneumatic.*

gn usually has a silent *g*: *design, assign, gnaw*

wh has an almost completely silent *h* in the question words: *what, which, why, when, where* and in the numerous other words beginning with *wh*: *white, wheel, whisper*, etc.

st usually has a silent *t* when followed by *l* or *e*: *whistle, fasten.*

As always, it is helpful for students to compare and contrast patterns in their own language(s) with English patterns. You could encourage them to reflect on anything unusual they have noticed and to share this with others.

14 Idiomatic expressions

hustle and bustle: noise and activity

light as a feather: very light

risk life and limb: to take dangerous chances

15 Look, say, cover, write, check

Using a visual strategy will help students recall the actual 'look' of words which use silent letters.

C Studying effectively

1 Punctuation reminders

These punctuation reminders will help students who are struggling and provide revision for more proficient ones.

The topic is homework, which ties in with the study skills theme in general. Homework is not universal, so it's a good idea to make sure students understand what it actually is, if necessary. Elicit their approach to tackling homework – you could make a list of tips on the board. Questions to raise can include:

- Should the TV be on and social network sites be on screens during homework time?
- How long should you spend on homework?
- What should you do if you can't understand your homework?
- Should you work at a desk or table?
- What time should you start your homework?
- Is it right to get help from parents or friends to complete homework?

Answer

I need a few quiet moments to myself when I get in from school. I have a drink and relax for a while. Then I get out my homework. I work at a desk in the corner of the living room. It's peaceful but not silent. I like French and maths homework the best.

I've got a few reference books which I keep on a shelf above my desk. I borrow my brother's paints for artwork, and I use my sister's laptop for IGCSE essays. I've used my dad's tools for some technology projects too. They don't mind me borrowing their things as long as I look after them.

Our school has a homework link on the school website. This means that you can use the homework page to check the homework you've been set. It also prevents students getting too many subjects for homework at once. About two years ago, I had English, history, German, physics, biology, maths and technology homework on the same night. It was a nightmare. The homework page prevents these problems. However, it also means teachers refuse to accept silly excuses for not handing in homework.

2 Rewriting an email

TEACHING SUPPORT

See the Introduction for a general approach to helping students with Writing tasks.

In this exercise, as well as deciding on paragraphing, students are asked to analyse the tone and register. First they need to disentangle the actual sense of the email. Then they should work out the writer's intention (to console and advise), and discuss why he does not succeed in achieving a suitable tone.

To help focus on improving the tone, ask students to picture the situation and to imagine how Harry, who has failed an exam most of his friends have passed, is feeling. Ask them questions along the lines of: *'Will he want to be criticised? To be given lots of advice? To be reminded he has failed? Have you ever been in a similar position? Can you remember what it felt like?'* Aim to elicit the need for a sympathetic but controlled response which focuses on what Harry can do, rather than his failings. This involves leaving out anything that could be interpreted as disapproval or criticism.

Encourage students to decide what's worth saving and what they should discard, and let them discuss suitable alternative phrases, e.g. *I'm keeping my fingers crossed for you.*

Example answer

This is just one possible answer, which students may like to compare with their own.

Dear Harry,

I was really sorry to hear that you're unable to join us on the trip because you have to resit your exam. You must be feeling really fed up and I do sympathise with you.

It might be a good idea to contact Oscar, as I know he's resitting too. How about revising together? I'm sure he'd be glad of your support and companionship.

An approach I found helpful which you may like to try is to get hold of the syllabus and underline the relevant sections. I know you've probably done this (if so ignore me), but I found checking past papers to identify typical questions helped a lot. There's a lot of time pressure in the exam, so it's definitely worth practising the answers in the specified time.

Let me know as soon as you get your results. I'll be keeping my fingers crossed for you. We'll miss you a lot on holiday and it won't be the same without you.

Lots of love,

Ruben

After setting the context and discussing how Harry must be feeling (see suggestions above for whole class discussion of this), pair students and ask one student to scan the letter and underline two criticisms Ruben makes of Harry, and the other to underline three good pieces of advice that Ruben gives Harry. They should then compare notes before moving on to drafting their own version. Tell students to write their email in three paragraphs – elicit what should go in paragraph 1 (sorry to hear Harry can't come), paragraph 2 (advice to Harry – use the ideas from Ruben's email) and paragraph 3 (say something encouraging).

3 Reading aloud

Students can try out on a small audience the effect of the tone and register they have achieved.

4 More idiomatic expressions

Before students start the exercise, it's worth making sure they understand the literal meaning of the component words of the idioms.

It's interesting to encourage students to relate the idioms to similar ones in their own language(s).

Answers

1 a   **2** b   **3** d   **4** b   **5** b   **6** a

5 Increasing your stock of idioms

Using idioms effectively is obviously more difficult than just understanding them. You'll need to emphasise that idioms have a precise meaning and are only applicable in specific situations. You might like to ask students to keep records of those idioms they like and to use them as much as possible until they are really sure they know the appropriate contexts for them.

6 Sentence correction

These sentences, which are taken from students' actual writing, are quite challenging to rewrite. Students may like to treat them as problem-solving exercises, working on them together to identify the intended meaning and then rephrasing them.

To **support** your students, do this exercise as a whole-class activity. Read out the sentences in turn, encouraging students to identify the errors and suggest replacement words or phrases. In item 1, for instance, *be wisdom* is incorrect – you can *be wise* but you can't *be wisdom*. Elicit ways of rewriting the phrase, e.g. *If you were wise/It would be wise/If I were you*. After this we see the verb *follow* in the middle of the sentence, which links to *advice* at the end. *Follow someone's advice* is a correct phrase. Students should then identify that *professor advice* is incorrect – it is missing a possessive apostrophe. In addition, *teacher* should be used instead of *professor* – anyone who teaches can be called a 'teacher', but 'professor' is normally reserved for an academic in a university. This means that the last part of the sentence should read *your teacher's advice*. Finally, encourage students to try different ways of rewriting the whole sentence, e.g. *If you were wise you would follow your teacher's advice./It would be wise to follow your teacher's advice./If I were you, I would follow your teacher's advice.*

This activity may be too challenging for some students. Replace with alternative sentences, each containing one or more grammar/vocabulary mistakes based on language that these students have been studying recently.

Possible answers

1   You would be wise to follow/If I were you I'd follow your teacher's advice.
2   Try to develop a positive attitude to/frame of mind for your work.
3   Remember that a good friend can be a tremendous help.
4   You should never smoke cigarettes/you should avoid cigarettes – they bring a lot more pain than pleasure.
5   Many people would agree with the points in your letter.

International overview

As always, it is worth checking basic understanding of what the table shows just to make sure that your class has assimilated the facts. For example, you could ask students how many students chose Germany for their studies.

It is also useful practice for saying large numbers, which students often struggle with.

Styles of teaching and learning vary a lot across the world. Find out how students like to learn things and ask whether going abroad to study, where there might be a different teaching style, would be difficult. Ask if they would prefer to study at a university where there is a lot of freedom and emphasis on group work and problem solving, or in more structured classes or lectures where everyone is taught in the same way at the same pace.

Answers

1   10
2   France
3   Canada

D A range of advice

1 Pre-listening tasks

Elicit or teach the meaning of *counselling* (the professional help given to people with personal or psychological problems) and that someone who does this is called a *counsellor*. Ask why people turn to counsellors for help. Elicit ideas such as: greater family mobility means separation from older relatives who people used to turn to with problems; competitive societies put more strain on individuals making them feel stressed and in need of support; there is a high rate of family breakdown in some countries.

Students can then do A and B in groups or pairs and give feedback to the whole class. Possible disadvantages of counsellors include the difficulty of checking their credentials, the difficulty of knowing whether any advice is indeed sound, the risk of becoming dependent on counselling, the expense if you have to pay.

See the Introduction for a general approach to helping students with Listening tasks.

2 Listening for gist: A college counsellor ◀) CD 2, Track 7

After you have played the recording once for gist listening, ask students if any of the questions they wrote have been answered.

119

LEARNING SUPPORT

For less confident students, provide a list of possible student problems that the counsellor may mention (the suggested list includes lexical items students will need to know later in order to answer certain questions in Exercise 3). On first listen, students tick off those that they hear: *Financial hardship – getting into debt* (yes); *Exam stress* (yes); *Parents not listening to them* (yes); *Having to share a bedroom* (yes). Stop the audio after 'more space and privacy at home' and check answers. Before listening to the second part of the audio for the first time, provide students with the script of the interviewer's questions (only) to support them as they listen, asking them to listen for the gist of the counsellor's answers.

AUDIOSCRIPT

Listen to the interview. Which of the questions that you wrote are answered?

INTERVIEWER: What are some typical problems students bring to you?

COUNSELLOR: A very common one is, um, not having enough finance to get through college, um, getting into debt. And they come needing advice.

I: How can you help?

C: We break down their spending and see if there are any economies – moving to a cheaper flat near the college saves rent, and travel costs, um, for instance. We also talk about funds they can tap into like, for instance, outside agencies that can give small grants … and I help them write letters. The college itself has a hardship fund they can apply to.

I: Is that reasonably successful?

C: Yes, it helps, but as a counsellor I'm also concerned that financial problems bring about other problems. So I look at whether needing financial assistance is putting an extra strain on their personal relationships.

I: Are there other times when problems seem to peak?

C: Before exams. Er, maybe they're finding exams stressful, they're worried they can't retain information … it … it just goes, and they get mental blocks leading to being stressed in the exam period.

I: What do you offer?

C: I do things like study techniques, summarising their notes very briefly into key words. I emphasise that, you know, quality is better than quantity: do a bit at a time, but really try to take it in. Relaxation and exercise are important, too, in helping them to cope. I try and see if there are underlying problems. I mean, why should exams be a problem now if they've done all right before? Is something in their personal lives worrying them and, you know, we get them to talk about those things as well.

I: I see you normally are prepared to go quite deeply into things?

C: It depends. For example, if young people are still living with their parents and, um, they don't feel they're listened to, that their needs are not catered for, then we need to tackle that. I get the … the rest of the family to come and see me, too. And I help students to say how they feel to their parents. One problem, for instance, might be overcrowding, having to share a bedroom, that sort of thing, and I suggest ways that a student can get more space and privacy at home.

I: So you look at each case in an individual light?

C: As a counsellor I think it's very important to make them feel comfortable, not be judgemental. Everything is confidential – I don't discuss a student's problems with anyone else without their permission. Unless … well, there is one main exception … something illegal is involved. Good quality counselling can't happen without trust.

I: So you would never openly criticise what a student is doing?

C: I try to get away from being critical. Often students have suffered too much from that. The most straightforward cases are where people want clear advice, for example, on choosing the best course for them, but counselling is not quite like that. In my view, it's primarily about supporting people who are confused or unhappy to explore their own issues. What they're going through now may be linked back to bad childhood experiences, for instance. It's … it's no good me just telling them what to do – it's essential they see things for themselves.

I: In general, how do you cope with what must be a fairly draining kind of job?

C: We see so many people! We always have appointments unless it's an emergency. This allocates a set amount of time to each student. And, um, it helps if you remember you're not responsible for their problems. Only they can, ultimately, make changes in their lives. I couldn't afford to be any other way. I'd be swamped!

3 Detailed listening 🔊 CD 2, Track 7

Let students listen again to complete the notes. Only **one** or **two** words are required to fill each gap. Check the answers by pausing the recording in the right places.

The occasional spelling or grammar mistake will not matter as long as the answers are clear.

Answers

a into debt
b hardship
c key words
d relaxation
e exercise
f parents
g illegal
h trust
i unhappy
j childhood
k changes

4 Rewriting an email giving advice

Before students begin to rewrite the email with a more tactful tone and register, encourage them to consider Roberto's problem and what could be done about it.

Example answer
This is a possible version of the email, for students to compare with their own attempts.

Dear Roberto,

I was sorry to hear that you are having a tough time getting on with your little brother. I know small children can be very annoying and it's not an easy problem to resolve.

My younger brother Tom used to drive me up the wall. Like your brother, he was always interfering with my things and even damaging them. I used to get bad-tempered and impatient with him, and we often had a strained atmosphere at home. Eventually, I decided to discuss the problem with my parents and, to my surprise, they saw my point of view. Thomas now agrees not to touch my things, and anything really precious I put somewhere he can't reach it.

Nowadays we get on quite well. I play football with him and give him a hand with his homework. He has become more of a friend than an enemy. Do you think this approach could work for you? You could always give it a try.

Looking forward to hearing from you.

All the best,

Daniel

5 Building a letter from a list of points

The main challenge in this exercise is for students to select some relevant points from the list given. They need to work on expanding a few points with more detail.

Discuss some of the dangers of using the internet for homework, such as the temptation to get distracted and sidetracked by irrelevant websites, or the problem of filtering internet material effectively. After students have brainstormed some ideas of their own about how to resolve the problem, you could take one point from the

121

list and show how it could be expanded with interesting details or examples.

For example:

> It's a good idea not to leave it too late in the evening to start your homework. For example, I usually prefer to have a short rest and a snack when I get in from school, and then get down to it. I concentrate better earlier on, and I have the rest of the evening free to relax or see friends. If you start your homework late, you may find you have to stay up late to finish it, which makes you feel tired the next day.

6 Pre-writing discussion

You could ask students whether bullying is a problem only for younger children, or whether it can happen in other contexts, e.g. between workmates or among teenagers. You can also discuss what causes it.

It will be interesting to hear students' ideas on what could be done to resolve the problem. There are no simple formulas to prevent or cure bullying. Some ideas to elicit, which could be adapted for the email of advice in the next exercise, are:

- Bullying is wrong and must be stopped.
- The victim must report the bullying to someone in authority.
- The victim is not to blame and shouldn't feel guilty.
- Adults must take responsibility to resolve the problem.
- They should make sure the bully understands that his/her behaviour is at fault and must be changed.
- Bullies are often inadequate people and bully others to cover up their sense of inferiority.
- A meeting between bully and victim, when each listens to the other's point of view, can be productive.
- Some schools set bully and victim to work on a joint project so they can get to know each other as individuals – this has been shown to have positive results.

7 Email completion

This exercise offers more much-needed practice in developing ideas into interesting paragraphs. You may

wish to suggest students turn back to the example email in exercise 9 for guidance.

Grammar spotlight

With students' books closed, you may like to open the discussion on 'text speak' by asking which features of their mobile phones they use most frequently. They could discuss the advantages of texting – it's convenient, usually cheap, etc.; also its disadvantages, such as whether people feel disappointed to receive a text on a special occasion instead of getting a greetings card in the post.

Before asking students to answer the questions in the Student's Book, it would be helpful to elicit a text message or use one of those from the exercise and write it on the board. Students can then identify how it is different from a proper sentence: missing pronouns, articles, prepositions, special abbreviations, etc.

Answers
1 Hi Libby! I hope your weekend in Dublin went well.
2 I'm sorry, but I can't come tonight. I'll phone you when I get home.
3 I'm on my way but I'm going to be 20 minutes as there is a lot of traffic. Please wait for me.
4 Dear Mr Poulos, I would like to accept the position you have offered me. Many thanks.
5 I'll text you before I come round to make sure you are in.

Exam-style questions

See the Overview of *Cambridge IGCSE English as a Second Language* section at the beginning of the Student's Book for the mark scheme and criteria for marking the writing questions.

Reading

The text is taken from the University of Sydney website. It recycles the themes and language of the unit and is very useful practice for the similar reading exercises in Reading and Writing papers, which can often be an advertising text in some shape or form. The first 8 questions require short answers, mostly testing understanding of factual detail. The final question (9) for the Extended students only, requires them to identify four points from the text.

Remind students to take care with their answers, and not rush their work, as this is where many marks can be gained through patience and attention to detail. Students can usually copy the required words and key phrases from the text, but, as always, they need to take care with spelling. The number of questions in the Student's Book is 13, which reflects the number set for Extended candidates. If you have Core students who might struggle to answer 13 questions, you can, of course, reduce the exercise. For example, you could cut down the number of questions to nine, which is the number on the Core paper. Alternatively, you could set four of the questions for the whole class to tackle as a group and check those answers together, and when confidence has been built up, ask students to do the remaining nine questions without help.

Answers

1 1856

2 heart surgery / ear implants / Ebola virus (Any one 1 mark)

3 Eastern Suburbs (1 mark)

4 leadership skills (1 mark)

5 Any two from:

   manage stress levels / regulate sleeping patterns / boost your mood (1 mark)

6 Any two from:

   three catered meals a day / laundry service / support network (2 marks)

7 Any time (in the year) (1 mark)

8 Tap your student card on the reader by the door (1 mark)

9 (On Extended papers only) grants / scholarships / counselling (service) / mentors (4 marks)

(Reading & Writing, Exercise 1: 9 marks (Core), 13 marks (Extended).)

Writing

2 Exam Advice – email

Students should use a friendly tone and register for giving advice and as always cover the bullet points given.

Example answer

Hi Eleni,

I was sorry to hear you are feeling nervous about your exams. That's a shame because I used to get nervous too and it's a horrible feeling.

Here are a few tips. A revision plan is always a great idea, if you haven't already got one I know you would stick to it, and it helps you feel confident, because you can see your progress. You will soon have loads done! If you haven't already got some, why not make playlists for your work? You can choose the best music for getting into just the right mood to concentrate and it can help you remember things too.

Relaxing, eating well and early bedtimes are vital when we have the pressure of exams, so remember to take care of yourself. You used to love running, which is great exercise for stress. Do you still do that? If you take enjoyable breaks from learning, you will go back to studying feeling refreshed.

In the exam, don't forget to read the questions carefully and underline the key words. Even if a question doesn't make sense at first, ideas will start to come, and you will get great results.

Loads of luck,

Adriana

(198 words)

(Reading & Writing, Exercise 5: 16 marks (Extended).)

Wider Practice

1 You could set up role plays and ask students to imagine they are addressing very different groups of people. Encourage them to adjust their tone and register to their audience.

   Topics could include:

   • encouraging an elderly person to use a mobile phone or tablet

- comforting a parent whose son/daughter is about to leave home to study overseas
- explaining to a small child what to expect on the first day at school.

Students who are less confident at speaking could be given prompt cards with key phrases on them to help remind them what to say. Also they could focus on simpler situations, such as learning to apologise correctly for accidently breaking a cup or vase when visiting the house of someone they do not know well.

2   Students could further explore the pros and cons of the internet as a tool for study. They could discuss how they evaluate the usefulness of a website, share website addresses they have found helpful, and say how they resist being distracted by links to irrelevant sites, etc.

3   If students are interested enough in the theme, you may like to invite an ex-pupil who speaks English well, and now attends a university, to visit the class and give them his/her opinions of university life.

Similarly, university officials (student union officers, careers advisors, lecturers, welfare officers) could be invited to answer students' queries.

4   You may like to collect further examples of letters/ emails which contrast tone and register. A formal register, using longer words of Latin origin, passive forms and no contractions, could be contrasted with the style of informal registers.

You could present students with a situation, perhaps a dispute between neighbours about noise levels. Ask one group to imagine that they have no wish to fall out with their neighbours. They should write an email to the neighbours explaining the problem and asking politely for more peace and quiet. The other group should read the email and take offence. They seek legal advice and send a reply, cold in its tone and register, to their neighbours.

The search for adventure

Overview

This unit focuses on narrative technique. When writing a story students are expected to use their imagination to build a story around something that could conceivably happen in their real lives. They can expect a wide variety of stimuli, e.g. recounting an incident on a journey, losing something, a burglary, a storm, an accident, a fire. They are usually given a scenario to work from which gives them a brief outline of what happened.

Theme

The theme of exploration has been chosen for this unit. Many of the exercises are sea-related because dramas at sea provide key ingredients for a good story: heroism, adventure, rescue missions, etc. The thrill of adventure appeals to students and is a popular exam topic.

Areas for discussion, which are relevant to other aspects of the course, including the Speaking Test, are:

- Why are people so fascinated by the sea?

- What do we mean when we talk about 'heroism'?

- How can negative experiences that cause hardship and struggle be turned into something positive so that we ultimately come to benefit from them?

- Is the desire for adventure also a wish for greater self-knowledge and personal development?

- What lessons can be learned from dangerous, frightening or disappointing events?

Language work

Structuring a narrative means ordering the events coherently and making the links between events clear. Whilst most IGCSE students will have met the narrative tenses they need to use before, 'putting them all together' still presents a challenge. The unit deals with this through exercises analysing how and why narratives work, and through follow-up activities.

Students who show they have a wide vocabulary and can manipulate structures to dramatic effect are likely to be more successful. The unit helps students build up these skills by vocabulary expansion exercises, using emotional and dramatic language, and writing more complex sentences. Reported speech, which students will probably already have met, is revised.

The *Grammar spotlight* focuses on the interrupted past continuous.

A The call of the sea

1 Visualisation

Let students have as much time as they need for the visualisation so that they can freely associate with any aspect of the sea which comes into their mind. Writing down what they visualised might best be done in their own language.

2 Discussion

Students compare statements encompassing the romantic and adventurous aspects of the sea with their own views. Many of the ideas are followed up in greater detail later in the unit, so it's useful to hear students' views and encourage them to be as speculative as possible.

3 Sea vocabulary

> **TEACHING SUPPORT**
>
> See the Introduction for a general approach to helping students with new vocabulary.

The vocabulary work prepares for many of the lexical items later in the unit. It's a good idea to remind students to make a note in their vocabulary records of unfamiliar words.

> **LEARNING SUPPORT**
>
> Pair students for this activity and give them three categories each to deal with. When they have had time to check the meaning of all the items in their list, students should look at their partner's categories and ask their partner to explain the meaning of any words they don't know. Follow this up with a quick quiz – give definitions for some of the words, and ask pairs to come up with the words.

Answers

sea associations: hive

on the beach: spanner

sea creatures: squirrel

words for boats: tram

occupations: solicitor

watersports: abseiling

Photograph left A: jetty

Photograph B: driftwood

Photograph C: seal

Photograph D: trawler

4 Writing a descriptive paragraph /
5 Reading aloud

In the next two exercises, students consolidate this stage of learning by writing a descriptive paragraph and reading it aloud to their groups for comments. As always, encourage positive feedback and constructive criticism.

LEARNING SUPPORT

Provide students who require extra **support** with the following structures as models to incorporate: I could see + noun + verb with -ing ...; I could feel + noun + verb with -ing ...; I could feel + noun + verb with -ing .... (e.g. I could hear waves lapping on the beach, I could feel the sand squelching under my feet).

6 Pre-reading discussion

It's interesting to learn from students what part the sea has played in the history of their country. For example, the imperial power of Britain was built on the country's naval strength. The sea is a potent symbol of independence and plays a large part in British cultural traditions.

Tell students about *Robinson Crusoe*, written by Daniel Defoe and published in 1719. Based on the true story of Alexander Selkirk, a Scottish sailor, it has been called the first English novel. The condensed version of the story in Exercise 8 on page 171 uses some of the formal style of Defoe's novel, a style of narration we would now find old-fashioned.

The idea of a castaway on a desert island captured the public imagination and the book was an immediate success. Many subsequent stories, films and radio programmes have been based on this concept.

7 Reading and sequencing

TEACHING SUPPORT

See the Introduction for a general approach to helping students with Reading tasks.

Check students' understanding of the following vocabulary, which appears in the events listed in a–k:

Shipwrecked (adjective): to be left somewhere after your ship has either sunk in a storm or been broken up by hitting rocks, e.g. *We were shipwrecked on a desert island for weeks.*

Salvage (verb): to rescue important objects from a wrecked ship, e.g. *Before the boat sunk, we were able to salvage some of its cargo.* Note that *cargo* refers to the goods transported by a ship.

Before they begin reading, you could ask students to predict the content. They could discuss what makes a good story, e.g. strong characterisation, powerful scenes, dramatic incidents, an intriguing or fast-moving plot. If appropriate, encourage them to use insights they have gained in other parts of the curriculum, e.g. from the study of literature.

It may be interesting to discuss how Crusoe might have made a calendar. Ideas such as using sticks or stones or shells/scratching numbers on wood etc. would all be plausible.

LEARNING SUPPORT

Some students may benefit from a glossary or from pre-teaching of further lexical items in addition to those listed above – *slave, plantation, trading ship, survivor,* etc. Consider splitting the text into three as a jigsaw reading for these students: Crusoe's early life (to line 21), life on the tropical island (to line 43) and how he escaped (to the end). In threes, each should feed back to the other two on their own section of the story, before they carry out the sequencing activity together.

Answers
The order of events in the story is:

1 i   **2** c   **3** e   **4** a   **5** k   **6** h   **7** j   **8** b   **9** f   **10** g   **11** d

8 Comprehension check

Before students do the exercise, check their understanding of the adjective *self-pitying*, which describes a person who feels sorry for themselves because of a misfortune or difficulty they are experiencing.

Answers

1   Crusoe's father wanted him to be a lawyer.
2   He survived storms, was taken as a slave, had a plantation in Brazil.
3   Crusoe's cry 'Am I all alone?' emphasises his sense of isolation.
4   to salvage everything of value
5   Because he made useful things (with his hands) (baskets, pots, a boat and other necessities).
6   a footprint
7   A ship arrived which had been taken over by mutineers. They landed on the island. Crusoe trapped them and freed the captain, who took him to England.
8   A *mutineer* is a person, especially a soldier or sailor, who refuses to obey orders and attempts to take control from people in authority.
9   c

9 Language study: Narrative tenses

The idea of this exercise is to help students use the grammatical knowledge they already have and apply it to the study of tenses in the *Robinson Crusoe* text.

The difficulty for many students at this level is not in understanding the theory of tenses or the underlying rules, but in applying their knowledge in different situations. Seeing how tenses are used in authentic texts is a dependable way to reinforce and extend understanding, which students can then build on in their own writing.

You could pair a student who struggles with grammar with someone who is more able if you think the pairing is appropriate and will be of benefit to both of them.

After students have worked out their own ideas for formation and usage, you could open up the discussion to the whole class. Why not ask an able student to record notes on the board?

The past simple

The past simple of regular verbs is formed by adding *-ed* or *-d*, e.g. *I joined a big trading ship*. Exceptions include: *was, knew, ran, found*.

The past simple is common in storytelling as it shows one completed action or event following another and it moves the story forward. Paragraphs 6 and 7 of the story contain good examples.

The past continuous

The past continuous is formed with *was/were* and the *-ing* form of the verb, e.g. *I was breaking my father's heart*.

It is used for actions in progress in the past, often interrupted by another action, e.g. *He was escaping the anger of his countrymen and I gave him refuge*.

In storytelling it is often used for background information and descriptions setting the scene. You could extend the discussion by eliciting a further example such as:

It seemed like any other ordinary day at the market. Stallholders were selling fruit and vegetables, shoppers were buying food for the weekend, dogs were barking and children were playing near the fountain. I was walking towards the café to meet a friend when I noticed a strange object lying on the ground……

The past perfect

The past perfect is formed with *had* + the past participle, e.g. *I had always wanted to go to sea*.

It is used to show that something had already happened at the point in time we are talking about, before another action, e.g. *I sowed barley I had taken from the ship*.

Once the earlier point in time is established, we don't need to keep using the past perfect – it's more natural to use the past simple.

You may wish to draw a timeline on the board to help students understand this tense.

10 Beginnings and endings

The beginning of the Robinson Crusoe text gives us a lot of information in two short paragraphs, which get us quickly into the action of the story. The last paragraph brings his stay on the island to a definite end.

In the opening two paragraphs, the tenses are present perfect, present simple, past simple passive, past perfect, past continuous and past simple. The verbs in the last paragraph are in the past simple.

11 Discussion: Heroism

A Possible answers in relation to Crusoe could be:

He makes the best of his situation – he has no self-pity or bitterness.

He lives with dignity, courage and self-reliance.

He treats Friday with respect and never tries to exploit him.

He's brave when he rescues the captain.

B For this part of the discussion you could ask *'Is it only people faced with extraordinary problems who can be called heroic? Can ordinary people who show exceptional qualities be called heroic too, e.g. people with disabilities who manage to succeed against the odds, or elderly people who lose a partner and face old age alone?'*

C Encourage students to give examples of their own heroes and heroines. Ask them to identify the qualities/ attributes which make them heroic. You could say something like *'In what way would you like to be like your hero or heroine? How could you achieve that ideal?'*

D The discussion could then be extended along these lines: *'How can we benefit from 'ordinary' struggles in our everyday life? For example, you may have something in your life which seems negative, perhaps not getting on with a brother or sister, or finding a compulsory school subject very difficult. How can a negative experience be of value so that in the end it becomes positive?'*

Students may come up with ideas like:

We can learn more about ourselves and so understand other people better.

We can learn to empathise with people who have problems.

We can learn persistence – the importance of not giving up.

E Examples of things he might have learned from Friday are: a knowledge of herbs for treating illnesses, human values – no knowledge of money so no greed for material things.

12 Continuing a story creatively

Let students identify with Crusoe and think through the possibilities. After such a long time away, will anyone remember him? What is likely to have changed? How will Crusoe's experiences have changed him? Is he now better prepared for the real world, or has he been disadvantaged by his unique experience?

Before students begin writing, ask them what form their continuation of the story will take. Elicit that it should be written in the first person and that it could be written as a diary entry. Then consider its tone. Robinson Crusoe is on his way back home and will have much to think about: what life on the island was like, what life at home will be like. The writing should therefore have a reflective tone.

> **LEARNING SUPPORT**
>
> To help **support** students who find this challenging, you could put some ways of beginning this piece of writing on the board, e.g. *It is hard to believe that I am on my way home: there were times I thought I would never see England again. / Can it be true? Have I really left the island? / We are nearing England, and I should be pleased, but all that is in my mind is the island I have left behind.* Additionally, you could provide some sentence starters, e.g. *I keep thinking about … / I wonder if … / I am really worried that … .*

13 Writing from notes

Answer

We were standing on the deck of the ship when the captain shouted that the English coast was in sight. I felt very strange. After so many years of solitude, the noise, bustle and crowds (or: the noise and bustle of the crowds) at/on the dock almost overwhelmed me. I was walking towards (the) town when I heard a voice call my name. I turned and saw my sister. She embraced me warmly. I knew from the tears in her eyes (that) she had forgiven me for hurting our parents. She told me she had almost given up hope when she got the message (that) I was alive.

14 Comparing cultures

You may prefer to ask students to research a favourite story, perhaps one from their childhood, for homework and then present it to the group.

15 Showing surprise: Stress and intonation

🔊 CD 2, Track 8

In *wh-* questions the sentence normally has a falling intonation, with the main stress towards the end:

*When did you arr**ive**?*

However, when we want to show surprise, the voice rises and the question word is stressed instead:

***When** did you arrive?*

Let students listen carefully to the examples and have a chance to hear the contrasts.

When the question is first asked, the stress and intonation are normal. When the second question is asked the speaker shows surprise and wants clarification.

Pause the recording after each question and let students practise the intonation patterns. Finally, they can make up questions and answers of their own.

AUDIOSCRIPT

As in the Student's Book.

B Adrift on the Pacific

1 Pre-listening tasks

TEACHING SUPPORT

See the Introduction for a general approach to helping students with Listening tasks.

Students are going to listen to an interview about a couple, Maurice and Vita, who attempted to sail in their own boat from England to New Zealand. Unfortunately, the boat was hit by a sperm whale and it sank. They survived for several months on a life raft before they were rescued. The couple's courage and dignity come across on the recording, and it is a powerful tale of endurance.

Narrative questions

Remind students that a complete narrative should answer the questions *Who, What, Where, Why, How* and *When*. To help them focus on the content of the story, students make up interview questions beginning with the above words before they listen, e.g.

What happened?

Why did you want to sail to New Zealand?

Where did the boat sink?

How did you survive?

Who rescued you?

When did you return to England?

LEARNING SUPPORT

Revise the basic formation of past simple questions with students, eliciting the rules from them and giving them some examples to practice (e.g. They bought a boat – *Why did they buy a boat?* / She saw something in the water – *What did she see in the water?*). Ensure they are clear how to deal with questions where the question pronoun is the <u>subject</u> rather than the object – ask them to discuss and explain the difference between *Who rescued you?* And *Who did you rescue?* (i.e. there is no *did* when the question pronoun is the subject).

Vocabulary check: answers

1 F   2 B   3 E   4 C   5 A   6 G   7 D

2 Detailed listening 🔊 CD 2, Track 9

Let students listen to the recording once and find answers to their own questions.

3 Checking your answers

Students can discuss the answers to their own questions. Elicit some examples from students of questions which were answered/not answered in the interview.

AUDIOSCRIPT

Listen to the interview with the couple who survived. Try to note down answers to the questions you wrote.

INTERVIEWER: Why were you making the trip?

MAURICE: Well, Vita and I had decided to emigrate from England to New Zealand in our 32-foot boat, the *Sandpiper*.

I: When did disaster strike?

VITA: We left Southampton in June and we were near Panama in the Pacific Ocean when what we had often dreaded actually happened. Our boat was hit by a 40-foot sperm whale. A small hole appeared in the hull and she began to fill with water.

I: How long did the boat take to sink?

129

M: It took an hour to go down.

I: How did you react? I'm sure I'd have been petrified!

M: Well, er, actually there was no panic. We sort of went onto automatic and um, did all the right things. As experienced sailors, I suppose we were prepared for this sort of emergency. We had just enough time to get out onto a life raft and we found ourselves adrift in an ocean covering a third of the earth's surface.

I: What did you do first?

M: Oh, for the first three days we rowed towards the Galapagos Islands. With hindsight this was not such a great idea because it was exhausting work and we used up most of our energy and water supplies.

I: So what happened then?

V: We felt increasingly desperate. We headed for the equatorial counter-current that we hoped would take us to the Central American coast. We continued towards that coast for three weeks. Then, to our horror, a hostile current dragged us back out to the middle of the ocean.

I: How did you actually manage to cope with being stuck on a life raft?

M: The raft was 4 foot 6 inches – just small enough for us to sit on! We lived and slept where we sat. We were completely confined. It was like being in a tiny prison cell.

I: What did you eat?

M: We fished over the side, grabbing turtles, birds and sharks with our bare hands or improvising fishing lines. We became emaciated and malnourished. At times it seemed death was not far away.

V: There was absolute silence on the ocean – apart from the lap of the waves or the screeching of the gulls. It was eerie. Sometimes the sea was very rough. The waves crashed around us and the dinghy which we were towing kept flipping over.

I: Did you see any ships?

M: Only eight ships passed us all the time we were adrift. The first seven sailed by oblivious to us. We fired flares, waved and set fire to our clothes in turtle shells. Nothing attracted them.

I: So when did you actually see the boat that rescued you?

V: After 119 days adrift. We'd spent about 45 days without seeing a ship. Then I heard something. I told Maurice I thought I'd heard the engine of a boat and he thought I was going mad. But I shouted and the boat turned towards us.

M: The relief was overwhelming! We knew for the first time since the disaster the joy of being alive.

I: Who actually picked you up?

V: We were rescued by South Korean fishermen and returned to Britain a month later. We were so weak and ill it took five more months before we could walk properly.

M: And it took another nine months before we felt really well.

I: What actually kept you going when there was little hope of rescue?

M: We took it one day at a time. If we'd really thought about what might happen, we might have been overwhelmed. We just concentrated on staying alive. Hour by hour. Day by day.

I: Do you have any plans to get to New Zealand?

M: No. But we still love the sea so we've settled on the Isle of Wight.

4 Listening and note-making 🔊 CD 2, Track 9

Students should now listen again and complete the notes.

Possible answers

a They were emigrating to New Zealand

b Near Panama in Pacific Ocean/hit by sperm whale

c Didn't panic/got onto life raft

d It was exhausting/used up energy and water

e very small and cramped

f turtles, birds, sharks, fish

g 119 days

h Vita shouted

i 5 months to walk properly, 9 more months to feel well

j took one day at a time

5 Discussion: Motivation and adventure

A Each year many people take part in risky expeditions to climb mountains, cross seas, etc. You could discuss the extreme mental resolution required, and hardships undertaken out of choice rather than necessity.

Possible questions could be:

Are they in search of a dream?

Do they want fame and success?

Are they encouraged by their group to do more and more risky things?

Are they afraid of failure and letting people down?

Are spiritual goals important – do they want to discover their own inner potential and limitations when put to extreme tests?

Are they bored and dissatisfied with ordinary life?

You could ask which of these ideas, if any, students would apply to Maurice and Vita.

B The discussion is now extended to consider the wider implications of adventurous projects.

You could finish the discussion by asking whether it's possible to develop as a person and build inner strength in ordinary circumstances, or whether it's necessary to go to extremes to do it.

6 Ordering events

It's a good idea to revise the use of time expressions by putting a few examples on the board and checking that students understand their function:

I'll ring you as soon as the email arrives.

Is he going to ring a long time after, or just after the email arrives?

He waited until the rain stopped before going out.

Did he go out when it was raining?

Answers

The statements should be numbered as follows:

2, 5, 6, 4, 7, 8, 9, 11, 10, 3, 1

They could be linked as follows:

First they left England for New Zealand. When the *Sandpiper* was damaged by a sperm whale, they escaped onto a life raft before the boat sank. First they rowed towards the Galapagos Islands. Next / After that / Then they attempted to get to the Central American coast but a hostile current dragged them back out to sea. They tried to attract the attention of passing ships but they sailed by, unaware of the couple's situation. Eventually they returned to Britain.

You could suggest students check the order of events by listening to the recording again and using their notes for reference.

7 Expressing emotions

Remind students that emotional expressions such as *to our horror, to my dismay*, etc. make a narrative more dramatic and personal.

You could extend this exercise to discuss modifiers, e.g. *great, intense, serious, enormous*, and the ways these collocate. For example, we say *to our great relief/ astonishment* and *to our intense relief*, but not *to our intense astonishment*. Unfortunately, there are no rules. Familiarity can be improved by wider reading and practice.

Possible answers

1   … when, to my alarm/horror,

2   … yesterday, to our great relief/joy,

3   … when, to his alarm/concern,

4   … and, to my delight / amazement / astonishment,

5   … saw, to his alarm / concern / horror / excitement,

6   … when, to my amazement/astonishment

Tenses: answers

1   past continuous, past simple

2   all past simple

3   past continuous, past simple, past continuous

4   past continuous, past simple, past perfect

5   past continuous, past simple

6   past continuous, past simple

131

Students need to understand that the phrases introduced in exercise 7 are used to describe emotional reactions to dramatic situations, e.g. *My friends and I were sitting on a bench outside the zoo when, to our great astonishment, we saw a Sumatran tiger walking towards us.* Another thing to remember is that these phrases are quite formal. In informal language, when describing more ordinary surprises than tigers appearing in front of us, we don't usually say things such as *To my horror, the supermarket had run out of chocolate biscuits.*

8 Dictionary work: Prefixes

This exercise is quite high level, so you could treat it as a good opportunity for dictionary practice.

The prefix *mal-:* answers

1   malnutrition
2   malignant
3   malfunctioning
4   malpractice
5   malevolent
6   malicious

The prefix *counter-*: answers

1   counterbalance
2   counterproductive
3   counterattack
4   counteract
5   counterpart
6   counterarguments

You could round off the exercise on prefixes by discussing some other examples and their meanings, e.g. *miscalculate, outgrow, overcompensate, intercity, derail, reconsider.*

9 Revision of reported speech

Incorporating some reported speech adds variety and immediacy to a story. Many students will already be familiar with the rules. You could revise them by discussing the example from the dialogue and encouraging students to formulate the rules, e.g. tenses shift one tense back, many modals do not change, pronouns change to reflect who is being spoken about, infinitives do not change.

Remind students that *that* is often omitted in reported speech, especially after *say* and *tell*, e.g. *She said (that) she wanted to be alone.*

The rules governing reported speech are often broken in informal spoken or written English. A way of avoiding reported speech is to simply quote someone. In modern informal English, *be like* is often used to do this instead of *said. Be like* can be used in either its present or past form, e.g. *And I'm like, 'why did you do that?' and he was like 'I've no idea!'* However, students do need to master the rules with regard to reported speech so that they can become competent users of more formal styles of written and spoken English.

Some students may need further practice with basic tense shifting in reported speech ahead of the harder examples in Exercise 10. If so, practise a simple drill in pairs – one student makes brief statements about themselves for the other to 'report back' to them, e.g. *"I came to class by bus" – Laura told me she had come to class by bus.* Provide practice the other way round too: *Malik's brother said he would meet him at 7 – "I'll meet you at 7."*

10 Reporting verbs

You could elicit other examples of reporting verbs such as *accuse, deny, apologise, think, offer, advise, reply, encourage, agree, recommend, complain.*

Possible answers

1   She declared/explained she was attempting to break the world record for sailing non-stop around the world.
2   She revealed that she was being sponsored by several businesses.
3   She admitted/confessed her worst fear was personal failure.
4   She acknowledged she was doing it because she was hoping to beat the present world record of 161 days.
5   She said she was taking food and drink to last her up to 200 days.
6   She revealed that the food included 500 dried meals, 150 apples, …

7   She confessed that when she was thousands of miles from shore, and if she was injured, then she would be scared.

8   She mentioned that she had been taught to stitch her own flesh in an emergency.

9   She said that if there was a crisis, she thought the answer was not instant action but to think about it.

10 She declared/revealed that she knew she could handle the boat and she would find out whether she had the strength to beat the world record.

You could elicit other examples of direct speech changing into reported speech and introduced by different reporting verbs, e.g.

'This hotel is badly heated.'

He complained that the hotel was badly heated.

11 Writing a report of an interview

TEACHING SUPPORT

See the Introduction for a general approach to helping students with Writing tasks.

LEARNING SUPPORT

Provide a basic writing frame for any students who need more **support**. For example: Silvia Camilletti is a … yachtswoman, who … This morning I spoke to her at/on … where …

I began by asking her about …

I was particularly interested to know … She told me …

Example answer

Silvia Camilletti, 24, is planning to sail around the world single-handedly. She is hoping to beat the present world record of 161 days.

I interviewed Silvia on her yacht, as she made last-minute preparations for her adventure. As we spoke, Silvia was organising boxes of food supplies in her kitchen. 'I am taking food to last me 200 days,' declared Silvia. The food includes 500 dried meals, 150 apples and 144 bars of chocolate.

I was intrigued to know why Silvia wanted to undertake such a dangerous voyage by herself. She assured me that she was not doing the trip to prove herself. 'I have always been involved in challenging projects,' she insisted. Undoubtedly, however, she may face serious problems. Silvia confessed, 'When I'm thousands of miles from shore, and if I'm injured, then I'll be scared.' Silvia also revealed she has been 'taught to stitch her own flesh in an emergency'.

Whatever the risks she faces, Silvia is a brave young woman who is determined to test herself to the limits.

'I know I can handle the boat and I'll find out whether I have the strength to beat the world record,' she said.

International overview

The quiz highlights many interesting facts about the world's oceans. An interesting aspect of the topic for students to look up on the internet or in printed material could be how we use the oceans as a resource. Possibilities include investigation into the mineral wealth of the ocean, the food it provides or wave power. Alternatively, students could explore the world of fishing, either by researching a traditional fishing community or finding out more about a commercial fishing company. Other aspects of the oceans to focus on include the development and use of coral reefs, or pollution of the oceans from sewage, dumping of chemicals and pesticides, oil spillages, etc. Students could present their information to the class, or they could interview each other, taking the part of journalist and representative.

The use or abuse of the world's resources are popular reading comprehension, note-making, summary and listening topics in the IGCSE syllabus, so any additional preparation will continue to build confidence.

Answers

1   **b** the Pacific Ocean

2   true

3   **c** the Caspian Sea

4   **c** Russia

5 **a** Indonesia

6 **b** gold

C A remarkable rescue

See the Introduction for a general approach to helping students with Reading tasks.

The text comes from a popular newspaper. It's aimed at a general audience and is a typical example of a human interest story.

The questions on the reading text finish with a guided summary which gives extra practice in a difficult skill area, whilst reinforcing tense usage.

1 Pre-reading tasks

The first pre-reading exercise gives students practice in structuring a narrative. Losing something is a common, annoying experience and most students should be able to relate to it.

2 Reading for gist

LEARNING SUPPORT

Some students may meet plenty of unfamiliar vocabulary in this text, but most of the meanings can be deduced from the context, so discourage them from using dictionaries here. If they find this difficult, demonstrate how to use context clues to guess meaning; for example, *in pursuit* - we are told that the sheepdog is a 'trainee', which suggests it is not experienced. It has just seen a sheep, so what is it likely to do? (follow it – *so set off in pursuit means set off following the sheep*).

Answers
Some examples of the tenses include:

Past simple
spotted, rounded, plummeted, called, abseiled, rang, asked, ran, etc.

Past continuous
was running

Past perfect
had been watching, had survived, had been knocked unconscious, I'd been giving him

3 Vocabulary check
Answers
1 stranded
2 plunge
3 spotted
4 plummeted
5 resigned
6 forlornly
7 collie
8 distraught
9 jagged
10 sheer

4 True/false comprehension
Answers
1 true 2 false 3 true 4 false 5 true 6 false
7 false 8 true 9 false 10 true

5 Narrative structure
Although IGCSE students are not expected to display great sophistication in shaping a narrative, this exercise will increase students' awareness of possible starting points in a story. It will also help them become more aware of the shifts in viewpoint and time which are typical of longer and more detailed newspaper reports.

All the points given in the Student's Book are possible reasons for telling the story in that particular style.

6 Writing a summary from notes
Answer
Farmer Aidan McCarry was walking with his sheepdog Shadow near Ballybunion when Shadow started chasing sheep. Unfortunately, he fell over a cliff towards the sea. His owner contacted the coastguard and a rescue team abseiled down the cliff. However, Shadow could not be found and the owner returned home feeling distressed. Two weeks later a man rang. He said a birdwatcher had noticed Shadow on a rock. A student rescued him. The dog was thin but well. The vet said Shadow probably survived by drinking fresh water.

7 Vocabulary: Adjectives

Answers

ecstatic, happy, pleased, satisfied, indifferent, irritated, miserable, distraught, heartbroken

obese, fat, overweight, plump, slim, thin, skinny, scrawny, emaciated

You could ask students to use these items in sentences of their own – as a homework exercise, for example.

8 Homonyms

Homonyms are, of course, very common in English. *Train*, for example has different meanings depending on whether it is a noun or a verb. This is an area of language learning which often puzzles students, so it can be worth making comparisons with other languages the students share.

Answers

1 *Spotted* is an adjective meaning 'with a pattern of spots'.
2 *Sheer* in *sheer madness* is an intensifier meaning 'absolute'.

Practice: answers

1 *mine*: noun, verb, or pronoun
2 *sound*: noun, verb, or adjective
3 *stamp*: noun or verb
4 *dash*: noun or verb
5 *file*: noun or verb
6 *book*: noun or verb
7 *light*: noun, verb or adjective
8 *match*: noun or verb

9 Revision of defining relative clauses

The aim of this and the following exercise is to revise the difference between defining and non-defining clauses and to help those students who, even at IGCSE level, are still writing mainly in simple sentences to vary their style of writing. Sentences that demonstrate variety in length and complexity as well as accuracy show greater skill. Using defining and non-defining clauses accurately is one way to achieve this.

Practice: possible answers

1 They prefer stories which have happy endings.
2 The man who won the lottery has donated a lot of money to charity.

3 The student who survived the plane crash received an award for bravery.
4 The shoes that I bought last month have already fallen apart.
5 The factory where my grandfather worked is now a tourist hotel.
6 The doctor who helped us comes from Guatemala.

10 Revision of non-defining relative clauses

Practice: possible answers

Students could treat this exercise as a problem-solving one and work together to come up with the extra information for each sentence.

1 Rahmia Altat, who gave up her job last year, now does voluntary work.
2 We heard about the heroic acts of the rescue workers, which impressed us all.
3 Nurse Mara, who attended the meeting specially, demonstrated the lifesaving techniques.
4 Drowning, which is a common cause of death in children, can usually be prevented.
5 Smoke alarms, which are quite cheap, should be fitted in every home.
6 My cousin Gina, whose parents died when she was a baby, is being brought up by her grandparents.
7 Mrs Nazir, who had never entered a competition before, won a trip to the Caribbean.
8 The new hospital, which opened last month, is the biggest in the country.
9 Our sailing teacher took us to an island, where we had a picnic lunch.

11 Functions quiz: Consoling and sympathising

The quiz provides more practice in choosing appropriate responses to sensitive situations. IGCSE students can find it hard to get the balance of sympathy right.

Possible answers

1 a or e
2 a or c
3 a
4 a, b or c

135

5 I'm sorry, you must be really disappointed.

6 Are you? Why? It looks all right to me.

7 Oh no! How terrible!

The expression 'Oh dear!' is a useful sympathetic response in many situations and is heavily used by British people.

12 Spelling and pronunciation: The suffix -tion or -ion 🔊 CD 2, Track 10

This exercise will boost students' awareness of the sound and spelling pattern of this suffix, pronounced /ʃn/ or /ʒn/.

After practising the pronunciation, students should mark the main stress in each word. Marking the stress, as always, helps develop listening and pronunciation skills.

Answers

1 exhi**bi**tion

2 **fa**shion

3 occu**pa**tion

4 demon**stra**tion

5 **pa**ssion

6 in**ven**tion

7 qualifi**ca**tion

8 defi**ni**tion

9 recog**ni**tion

10 ig**ni**tion

11 pro**mo**tion

AUDIOSCRIPT

As in the Student's Book.

The matching exercise will ensure that the meaning of each word has been understood properly.

Answers

A qualification

B occupation

C invention

D passion

E exhibition

F definition

G promotion

H ignition

I recognition

J fashion

To round off the exercise, you could elicit more examples of words ending in *-ion*, e.g. *inspiration, comprehension, expression, attention.*

13 Language study: Adverbs

Students often make spelling mistakes when forming adverbs. They tend to overgeneralise about the *-ly* ending and don't make the adjustments that are necessary to take account of the spelling of the adjective. The rules aren't complex, however, and mastering them needn't take long.

After the brief 'refresher' course in the functions of adverbs, students can go straight into the basic spelling rules for adding suffixes. Or you could adopt a problem-solving approach by giving them some examples and asking them to look for meaningful regularities in the spelling changes.

Examples

comfortable	*We sat comfortably.*
incredible	*We were incredibly lucky.*
guilty	*'I haven't taken anything,' said the thief guiltily.*
merry	*She laughed merrily.*
rhythmic	*They danced rhythmically.*
terrific	*It was terrifically expensive.*

Practice

Your students may like pondering over the career possibilities offered at sea. An interesting discussion could explore the pros and cons of living on a ship for long periods, raising issues of: family separation, being on call at all hours for emergencies, little privacy, cramped living conditions, coping with the discomfort of living on a ship in storms and gales, etc. On the other hand, the basic needs of everyday life are provided for you (food, accommodation, leisure facilities, uniform, etc.), there's friendship, opportunity to travel, and opportunities to develop your potential within a wide range of interesting occupations on offer. You could also explore the distinction between civilian and military vessels, and discuss which sort of ship would be preferable to work on, and why. You could finish the discussion with a focus on the rapidly growing cruise ship trade (there are more than 400 cruise ships currently operating worldwide) and ask students if work on cruise liners appeals to them.

Answers

surprisingly	normally
definitely	electronically
necessarily	daily
directly	immediately
quickly	ably
hygienically	heavily
healthily	temporarily
economically	technically
usually	suitably
fully	capably
properly	efficiently
totally	happily
appropriately	responsibly
dramatically	frantically
accordingly	

14 Look, say, cover, write, check

The spelling list will, as always, help students recognise spelling sounds and patterns by developing visual awareness.

D Reacting to the unexpected

1 Pre-reading task: Making notes

This next phase of exercises pulls together the skills students have been building up and gets them actually producing narratives. They start by making notes on something which happened to them. Encourage them to keep their notes and ask them to write up the ideas for homework.

2 Reading an example narrative

The example narrative shows the style and format students should aim for.

Comprehension check: answers

1   She was watching the children on the beach paddling and throwing pebbles.

2   no

3   mouth-to-mouth resuscitation

4   She is only **dimly** aware of the crowd gathering around her.

5   They are going to arrange for him to have swimming lessons.

3 Analysing the narrative

Remind students that their narratives need to be properly paragraphed. Many students produce blocks of text when they are writing narratives.

4 Dramatic expressions

Dramatic expressions can increase the pace and excitement of a narrative. Encourage students to use them. Other dramatic expressions to elicit include *was thunderstruck, quick as a flash, in the nick of time,* and show how they could be used.

Answers

1   E

2   A, B, C or D

3   B, C or D

4   A, B, C or D

5   F

6   A

Students could read their own sentences out loud.

5 Pre-writing discussion

Make sure students understand what a windsurfer does and what the sport is all about, especially if they have little experience of watersports.

6 Ways of developing an outline

The outline of a story about a windsurfer who is carried out to sea when strong winds blow up is provided. This gives students a basic plot to work from so they can concentrate on structuring the story well and providing interesting background details.

Put students into small groups to develop the story from the outline. Make sure that there is a mix of abilities in each group. Encourage students to discuss the best way of opening the story, how to make it more interesting by adding details, and what dramatic expressions might bring it alive for the reader.

137

TEACHING SUPPORT

This exercise does not involve the search for a correct answer, which means that students could be **stretched** and encouraged to give their opinions and to supply reasons for those opinions, e.g. *I think we should open the story with 'I had no idea what was going to happen' – this makes the reader really wonder what took place! What do you think?*

LEARNING SUPPORT

The task may be more manageable for students who need extra **support** if you break the story into two halves. When they have finished, you could have two groups read their versions consecutively so that they hear the complete story read aloud. You could also provide students with a short tick list of features you want them to include, e.g. two time expressions, one non-defining relative clause, one dramatic expression, etc.

7 Building a story from a dialogue

Students write a narrative based on a conversation about an incident on a school trip to the seaside. The teacher lost her purse and one of the children helped her look for it. Students may not immediately see how they can produce a composition from a conversation, so it's useful to clarify how they can transfer the information revealed in the dialogue into a story told from Ethan's point of view.

Discuss with them how to shape the narrative and how to change the pronouns, etc. before they start. Using some direct and reported speech would add interest and variety to their stories.

8 Post-discussion task: Correcting and writing a report

Before they get started on proofreading the report, elicit from students the pros and cons of the idea of giving funds for the explorer's expedition. You could elicit suggestions before the class read the report, having made sure first they understand the rubric, or, elicit ideas after they have read the report, when it will be reading comprehension. However you approach it, the following are useful points to discuss:

Good reasons for giving funds to support the expedition:

- students interested in project/want to find out what happens

- good example to students of explorers' courage, bravery and determination

- local people involved – good to support them

- hopefully, explorers well prepared

- they may have learned survival skills/done training

- could find things out on expedition which benefits our knowledge e.g. climate change factors.

Reasons against giving funds to support the expedition:

- waste of money – giving to inexperienced teenagers who just want to have fun

- dangerous – things might go wrong and end in disaster

- lack of experience and preparation

- wouldn't be able to give money to help a different cause with a tried and tested reputation e.g. Fire Service.

Students should enjoy improving the report, as it is quite a straightforward exercise and they will produce a perfect report at the end with good audience awareness e.g. *'I have spoken to other students in my year to find out of their views'/'At school, we are all looking forward to reading the Antarctica Expedition blog'.*

You could draw attention to the formal tone and register, e.g. *'The positive points of supporting the expedition are that, firstly'/ To sum up, I believe that '.* You could ask students to comment on the fact the report sounds polite.

Finally, asking students how small extra words get into our writing unnoticed is also worthwhile. It will be interesting to hear their view on why we make mistakes when writing.

Answer

The extra words which should not be there are highlighted in bold and crossed through.

This report will consider **at** the pros and cons of supporting the young explorers going to Antarctica. I have spoken to other students in my year to find out **of** their views and these are given in the report.

The positive points of supporting **to** the expedition are that, firstly, the people taking part are from our town, so we would be helping local people. In addition, many of us admire the explorers because they are prepared to take risks and are testing **in** themselves to the limits. Their courage is a shining example and **for** encourages us to think about the importance of having challenging projects ourselves.

On the other hand, a few students have said it would be better to give the money to the Town Emergency Services rather than a group of teenagers who ~~they~~ want to have fun. Also, the trip might ~~it~~ end in disaster. While it is true that exploring the coast of Antarctica is dangerous, in my view, the people going

on ~~if~~ the expedition are taking the project seriously and are well-prepared. They have spent a long time learning ~~how~~ survival skills. They are also going to do some research ~~there~~ in Antarctica which will increase scientists' knowledge of climate change.

To sum up, I believe that we should support ~~our~~ the expedition. The explorers ~~who~~ deserve our help. The project is a worthwhile and inspiring ~~one~~ challenge. At school, we are all looking forward to reading ~~on~~ the Antarctica Expedition blog.

Grammar spotlight

TEACHING SUPPORT

See the Introduction for a general approach to helping students with Grammar tasks.

The *Grammar spotlight* gives further practice with the interrupted past continuous. Students will hopefully have developed an appreciation of the way this structure, which is not too difficult to master, can make a real difference to their writing. It should certainly help consolidate the work they have done earlier in the unit.

LEARNING SUPPORT

Some students may be puzzled by the extra words sometimes used between the auxiliary verb and the main verb (e.g. *Alan was alone on the desert island trying* …). Demonstrate that this makes no difference to the structure of the past continuous form, putting brackets around the 'extra' words (*alone on the desert island*). Also point out that there may be more than one past continuous verb before the verb that 'interrupts' (*the class were listening quietly and making notes when the teacher put* …).

Possible answers

1   Tomaz was sitting on his life raft feeling hungry and scared, when, to his relief, a rescue ship appeared on the horizon.

2   The shipwrecked couple were having a conversation about what to do next, when they saw/noticed a rowing boat coming towards them.

3   Alan was alone on the desert island trying / hoping / struggling to make a fire without matches, when, to his amazement, he saw / noticed / spotted some children walking / running / skipping along the beach.

4   Lorna was desperately searching for her mobile phone when, to her horror, she felt a large hand cover her mouth.

5   The class were listening quietly to Mr Hamsun's science lecture and making notes when the teacher suddenly put his hand in his pocket and threw a fistful of fabulous diamonds onto the desk.

6   Anton was walking with his children in the woods when, to his amazement, he spotted a mysterious, veiled woman dressed in golden robes.

Exam-style questions

See the Overview of *Cambridge IGCSE English as a Second Language* section at the beginning of the Student's Book for the mark scheme and criteria for marking the writing questions.

Reading

Students should feel confident with the multiple matching reading exercise which focuses on the views of four record-breaking young explorers. It reflects the unit's theme of adventure, heroism and risk taking and the recycled language points include narrative tenses, emotional expressions and adverbs. Remind students to use the methodical, step-by-step approach they have practised in earlier units (checking context in the rubric, scanning questions, reading for general meaning and then reading the question again carefully and skimming the texts to find the answer.) As always, if more than one person seems correct for the answer, they should check the detail in both text and question extra carefully again and apply the process of elimination they have learnt previously.

Answers

a   Person D
b   Person B
c   Person A
d   Person A
e   Person B

f   Person D

g   Person A

h   Person C

i   Person B

j   Person C

(Reading & Writing, Exercise 2: 10 marks (Extended).)

Writing

In Paper 2 (Extended), two prompts are provided for the writing in Exercise 6. If you think your students need them, you may like to elicit two additional prompts from the students themselves.

5 Visit to underground caves report

Detailed technical knowledge of underground caves is not expected; any reasonable description of the challenges of exploring caves would be sufficient. Students can draw on their earlier learning in the unit about exploration, risk and adventure. Students should aim to express their reasons clearly and back up their opinions with some examples. As always, they can use the comments given but they are free to make up their own ideas. The report should sound formal or semi-formal.

Example answer

When we arrived, the caves looked ordinary, but when we went inside, we were amazed at the strange atmosphere. It was a sunny day but inside the caves it was so dark and silent. Some of us found that scary, but I didn't mind because we had torches and the guide had a big flashlight too.

We followed the guide who led us down some very steep entrance steps, reminding us to hold on tightly to a safety rope. She explained that the caves were ancient but had only been discovered recently and they are important for our eco system. During the walk, to our surprise, occasionally there was not enough space to stand up, so we had to crawl slowly like turtles.

When we finished exploring, we got ice creams and sat outside in the sunshine. Some classmates

admitted they had felt panic at first, thinking something could go wrong and there would be a disaster underground. Gradually, however, we realised that the caves were mysterious but safe. Overall, it was wonderful exploring a place very few people had seen before. It was cold though, so I would advise next year's group to bring warm jackets for their visit. (200 words)

(Reading & Writing, Exercise 6: 16 marks (Extended).)

Wider practice

1   The sea is a fascinating topic and students may enjoy researching many of its other aspects, e.g. the creatures that live in it. If appropriate, cross-curricular links may be made with other subjects which students are studying, e.g. geography, science.

2   Students could extend the theme of adventure and exploration further by investigating space travel or life in space. They may like to research the lives of famous astronauts, look into space missions, find out about everyday life on a spacecraft or investigate space tourism. Presenting their mini-projects to the class in the form of short talks would be enjoyable for everyone.

3   Students could extend their storytelling skills by choosing a current news topic which absorbs them and tracing its development over several days. This could then be presented to the class.

4   Students could explore poetry or extracts from literature, from their own cultures or English literature, which focus on bravery, heroism, adventure and exploration.

5   Students may enjoy a competition where they have to walk a new route in their area. They could be told to look at familiar territory through the eyes of an explorer, making notes and taking photos. The class could vote for the person who finds out the most interesting or unexpected things and they could perhaps win a small prize.

Animals and our world

Overview

The main aim of the unit is to further develop students' ability to express reasoned opinions and arguments in emails/letters, articles and reports. There is also further practice in note-making and summarising. Unit 4, Our Impact on the Planet, focused on presenting 'for and against' arguments. This unit looks at a wider variety of arguments using the topic of animals. There is also a multiple matching exam-style question based on a text about birdwatching and an exam-style report writing question about whether to help fund a tiger sanctuary or a bird reserve.

Sometimes students are asked to present views and opinions explaining how or why a thing could happen. For example, in a discussion on endangered species, rather than being asked to take a stand for or against a proposal to help endangered species, students could be asked to express their opinions in a more measured way, e.g. *'Why do endangered species need our help and how can we ensure their protection?'*

Theme

Students consider a number of questions on the theme of animals, including:

- How can zoos be more animal-friendly?
- How can medical understanding and health standards be improved without resorting to experiments on animals?
- How can we ensure working animals are treated fairly?
- What can we do to help protect endangered species?

The items include a magazine article about animal experiments, a talk about a virtual-reality zoo, and a leaflet about 'adopting' zoo animals. There is also a multiple matching exam-style question based on a text about wild birds.

Language work

The language work further develops the skills needed to present a convincing argument. These include opinion language, rhetorical questions, and ways of adding emphasis. There is a range of vocabulary expansion exercises related to animals. Spelling and pronunciation work focuses on plurals, and students practise the functions of disagreeing informally and expressing disappointment.

The *Grammar spotlight* focuses on the past perfect passive.

1 A fresh look at zoos

1 Animal vocabulary

The unit starts with some key vocabulary the unit. It's a good idea for them to work in pairs for Exercises 1 and 2.

Answers

A   eagle

B   lizard

C   wolf

D   gorilla

E   rhino

F   leopard

mammals:	bear, camel, cheetah, dolphin, elephant, gorilla, kangaroo, leopard, lion, monkey, rhino, wolf
reptiles:	crocodile, lizard, snake
fish:	salmon, shark
birds:	eagle, parrot, penguin, vulture

2 Definitions

Answers

1 b   2 a   3 c   4 a   5 b

3 Pre-reading discussion

Allow the discussion about zoos to be as open as possible so that students have a real chance to think through the issues for themselves.

> **TEACHING SUPPORT**
>
> See the Introduction for a general approach to helping students with Reading tasks.

D *'I wasn't sure about the rights and wrongs of zoos'* tells us he has thought about both sides of the argument. *'On balance, I feel that'* sums up his view of zoos and pulls the contrasting ideas together.

E The final paragraph ties together the whole structure effectively. It shows audience awareness by including a reference to his classmates.

4 Reading an article for the school website

Encourage students to underline the opinion language as they read.

5 Comprehension check

Answers

1 because their teacher wanted them to see a modern zoo
2 very positive – he thought the animals seemed happy
3 the origins and habits of the animals
4 They protect animals from predators, provide a caring environment, and educate people about wildlife.
5 Bad points about zoos to elicit could be:
   - Wild animals find conditions cramped; they lack space and privacy, and they are herded together when some animals are naturally solitary.
   - Animals are frustrated because they can't get enough exercise or respond to hunting instincts.
   - Animals become lazy as they have no need to search for food.
   - Animals suffer by having to live in unnatural climatic conditions.
   - Zoos are unnecessary – we can see animals in their natural habitat by watching wildlife programmes on television.

6 Analysing the article

Answers

A The opening paragraph is effective because it explains the background to the zoo visit. It shows audience awareness because it provides typical school details.

B Paragraph 2 questions attitudes to zoos with phrases such as *'I was pleasantly surprised by what I found'*, *'people had said that zoos are full of smelly cages … Metro Park Zoo, however …'* and *'In my opinion'*.

C The phrase expressing disagreement is *'nothing could be further from the truth'*.

7 Typical opinion language

Answers

Opinion language used by Michael:

I just wasn't sure

As I see it, nothing could be further from the truth

On balance I feel that

to my mind

I think

Other possible opinion language:

In my view

Let's put it this way

I believe

If you ask me

As far as I'm concerned

As far as I can see

Disagreeing with other people's views: answers
Students should tick:

Some people accuse them of … but nothing could be further from the truth.

Many people say that … However, …

8 Making your mind up

Answer
Michael used the phrase *On balance, I feel that …*

9 Writing a paragraph

Students could either work individually on this or in a group with others who want to write about the same topic.

10 Reading aloud

Reading aloud provides a good opportunity to compare and contrast language structures and content. If you prefer, this could be done in groups rather than as a whole-class activity.

11 Expressions of contrasting meaning

Before students start the exercise, it's worth pointing out that there is more than one possible answer each time. For example, *a bare, cramped room* could be contrasted with *a well-furnished, gracefully proportioned room*. The main aim of the exercise is for students to explore different possibilities and then choose the one that seems best to convey a contrasting meaning. At the end of the exercise, they can share their answers and you can discuss different shades of meaning.

Possible answers

1   a lively / interesting / informative lesson
2   a well-polished / shiny / smart pair of shoes
3   a healthy/fit child
4   a tasty/delicious meal
5   a graceful/elegant dance
6   a tidy / neat / well-maintained garden
7   attractive, easy-to-read/clear handwriting
8   a gleaming bicycle in perfect condition
9   a peaceful/calm, friendly/tolerant person
10   a soft, comfortable bed

12 Before you listen

The electronic zoo, also known as a virtual zoo, is a zoo which is planned for the future. It uses a range of sophisticated technologies to provide the visitor with a multi-media experience. Some very small live animals will be kept, but all the larger animals will be viewed on high-quality screens. There will be sound and climatic effects. The speaker stresses the educational aspects of the zoo.

You may wish to prepare students by asking what 'electronic' means and elicit the fact that electronic technology is the basis of televisions, computers, etc.

Tell students a little about the zoo. For example, you could say *'Visitors will get the impression they are actually visiting the natural habitat of the wild animal – you will really feel as if you are in an African national park or in a tropical rainforest, seeing and listening to the birds that live there.'*

Possible questions for students to write could be:

How will the effect of actually visiting the natural habitat of an animal be created?

Why is it better than an ordinary zoo?

Are there any live animals?

What kind of information can visitors get about the origin and habits of the animals?

How will we find out the sounds animals make?

Will the zoo be very expensive to visit?

Where did the idea come from?

13 Vocabulary check

Answers

audio-visual: involving sound as well as things to look at

filmed on location: filmed in real places, not in a studio or on a film set

live exhibits: real animals on display

natural history: the study of plants and animals

14 Listening for gist 🔊 CD 2, Track 11

TEACHING SUPPORT

See the Introduction for a general approach to helping students with Listening tasks.

LEARNING SUPPORT

The speaker gives a lot of quite dense information, so you may want to let students listen more than once and pause the recording at intervals. Students need to be prepared for quite difficult talks for the listening tasks. This is an example of a more challenging monologue.

You can pause the recording to focus attention on a word or phrase and check understanding by means of a false statement, if you like. For example, you could pause it after 'The zoo is very different from conventional zoos...' and say to the class 'The zoo is *similar* to conventional zoos. Yes?' If the students are unsure whether to contradict you, and say 'No,' replay the sentence as often as necessary.

AUDIOSCRIPT

Now listen to the radio talk. Does the speaker answer your questions about electronic zoos?

PRESENTER:	I'm delighted to introduce our next guest, David Wallace from Christopher Parsons Productions, who is going to talk to you about an interesting new development in zoos.
DAVID:	Thank you, Sarah. It's a pleasure to be on the programme to discuss the spectacular new concept called the 'electronic zoo'. The zoo is very different from conventional zoos in that it aims to give a much broader impression of the life of many kinds of animals. It's going to do this by using the most advanced photographic and electronic techniques to reveal nature in a completely new way.
P:	Oh, I say! That sounds really interesting!
D:	The electronic zoo is a unique concept because, although no actual live large animals will be kept, the latest audio-visual technology will enable visitors to learn far more about the habitat and behaviour of large animals. It also overcomes the accusation people make about zoos – that it's unfair to keep large animals in captivity. The concept of 'magic windows', for example, uses three large TV screens and six soundtracks. Wildlife will be filmed on location in its natural habitat, and the most interesting and varied behaviour will be used for the zoo. Visitors using 'magic windows' will have the illusion of being in, for example, a penguin colony or an Alaskan river where the bears are fishing for salmon. People won't feel they are passively watching a film or a video show. They'll have the sense of observing behaviour in 'real time' – I mean, animal behaviour exactly as it occurred during the filming.
P:	How wonderful!
D:	There will also be behavioural film from the world's best natural history libraries. This will avoid the disappointment visitors often feel because the animals they came to see are asleep.

P: Oh yes, that's often happened to me.

D: There'll be interactive videos, too – you can slow down or replay the animals' actions on screen by pressing a button. The electronic zoo will also have a wide range of live animal exhibits, and these will be small species: small fish, reptiles, birds and insects. You could say the natural world will be represented in a more comprehensive way than conventional zoos, since ninety-five per cent of all animals in the world are smaller than the size of a hen's egg.

P: Hmm! Yes, I suppose they are, when you come to think of it.

D: One of the special characteristics of the electronic zoo will be the use of natural sounds. The most dramatic and beautiful sounds animals make in their own habitat will be reproduced using CD and computers. And there'll be artificial grass, bushes and so on, to create the atmosphere you would find in the natural world.

P: I'm sorry, David, it sounds absolutely marvellous, but I have to interrupt you there as we're running out of time. If you'd like to know more …

15 True/false comprehension

LEARNING SUPPORT

After students who may need extra **support** have attempted the exercise once (assuming they had already listened to it at least once beforehand – see the suggested preparation activity with Exercise 14), allow them to look at the audio script and find and underline the answers to the questions to see if their answers were correct. If they got any incorrect answers, help them to find the wording in the script that tells them the correct answer; for example, *This will avoid the disappointment visitors feel because the animals … are asleep*. It may then be useful to let them listen to the audio a further time.

Answers

1 true **2** false **3** false **4** false **5** false **6** false

16 Post-listening discussion

The talk may arouse a lot of interest in the impact technology will have in the world of the future. You may like to ask students what would be better and worse about a future where it will be easier and easier to simulate experience, and how far, today, 'virtual reality' has become the norm.

The target group of the electronic zoo is really anybody who is interested in finding out more about animals, particularly those who feel at ease with new technology. It might appeal more to the younger generation as they are very at ease with using new technology in their daily life and are confident using it.

17 Functions 🔊 CD 2, Track 12

Encourage students to express their views on the appropriateness of using large animals in the circus.

Silvia's voice goes down as she expresses disappointment. You could present a model of a disappointed tone, e.g. 'I was looking forward to seeing (name a person students will be familiar with from TV) at the theatre in real life, but she didn't give a very good performance.' You could ask students to relate their own experiences of disappointment arising from unfulfilled expectations, such as a boring film, meal or party.

Adjectives and comparative structures are important in this exercise so you may like to revise the *not as ... as ...* form (which can be tricky), with the relevant adjectives (*spectacular, fascinating,* etc.) for description.

You may like to ask pairs of students to take the parts of Malik and Silvia and read the dialogue aloud. Students usually like doing this, and you can ask the rest of the class to decide how disappointed 'Silvia' manages to sound.

AUDIOSCRIPT
As in the Student's Book.

Expressing disappointment, etc.

You could ask students to tick any expressions they recognise from the dialogue.

18 Practice dialogues

Students progress from the prompted dialogue to making up their own conversations.

You may like to round off the exercise by introducing the colloquial word *hype*, as in 'There was so much hype

about the electronic zoo but when I went it was rather a letdown.'

B Animal experimentation

1 Pre-reading discussion

TEACHING SUPPORT

See the Introduction for a general approach to helping students with Reading tasks.

The following sequence of exercises focuses on the rights and wrongs of animal experimentation. The magazine article puts forward a highly positive view of the issues, and students then go on to explore why this may or may not be a complete picture of all that animal experimentation involves. It's a difficult text, so students do a variety of tasks to prepare them for it, intellectually and linguistically.

After students have commented on the photograph, you could raise the question of using animals for dissection in science lessons (if their studies involve this) and ask them how they feel about it. You could ask if they have been immunised, and say that the vaccination against polio, for example, was discovered through animal experimentation.

Ethical questions

Make sure students have understood the concept of ethics before they go on to discuss the ethical questions in pairs or small groups. Ethical questions will be central to later discussions on the treatment of animals, but they are very culturally based. What is 'ethical' in one culture isn't necessarily seen as right in another. You could check this by asking about wider issues that students may have a view on. It might be most helpful to choose examples that relate directly to students' culture(s).

Other ideas are:

- Should a couple of over 60 years be allowed to adopt a baby?
- Is it right to keep people who have almost no chance of recovery alive for years on life support machines?
- Should terminally ill people be allowed to end their own lives?

Finally, students are asked what they think about animal experiments, after having had a chance to review the various ethical issues. They are offered some further useful vocabulary for giving opinions.

2 Predicting content

Answer

As the writer is a campaigner for medical experiments on animals, the arguments are likely to be rather extreme.

3 Vocabulary check

Answers

An *emotive* issue is one which arouses strong feelings.

A *controversial* issue is one about which people disagree strongly.

4 Reading for detail

Students can't make good notes from a text they haven't understood. The questions aim to check understanding before going on to the more challenging note-making exercise. You will need to allow enough time for students to read the text in detail.

Answers

1 research using animals
2 the discovery that blood circulates through our veins, knowledge of the way the lungs work, the discovery of vitamins and hormones
3 Animals are given human diseases so that researchers can study their reactions.
4 Researchers want to prevent suffering but they may have to cause animal suffering to do so.
5 They might help animals by finding a cure for animal illnesses.

5 Vocabulary

Answers

1 F   2 E   3 C   4 B   5 A   6 D

6 Post-reading discussion

In order to support students with this discussion, you could elicit some ideas for and against the idea that experiments on animals are humane and necessary. Arguments for include the following: *Scientists do not set out to hurt animals and because they do everything they can to minimise suffering, the experiments they perform can be described as humane.* Arguments against include the following: *If human beings are more intelligent than other animals, then humans ought to use that intelligence more wisely – nothing gives people the right to willingly hurt other living creatures.*

7 Note-making and summary

This exercise is useful practice for note-making and making lists of points. The follow-up exercise reinforces students' summary writing skills. It is a challenging exercise so allow students enough time.

Before students begin the bullet points, it would be useful to draw attention to three key words in the exercise: reasons, achievements and steps.

Answers

The experiments aim to find cures and treatment for human illnesses.

Reason for experiments:
- to find cures and treatment for human illnesses

Achievements:
- advances in medical understanding
- advances in the practical applications of medicine

Steps to make experiments more humane:
- reduce the number of animals in each experiment
- replace animals with alternatives where possible
- refine experiments so they cause the least possible harm to animals

Encourage students to draft a summary paragraph, using some of their own words.

Example answer

> Animal experiments aim to discover cures and treatments for human diseases. The experiments have improved advances in doctors' understanding of illness and in the applications of medicine. To improve the welfare of animals, scientists aim to cut down the number of animals required for each experiment. If it is possible, scientists avoid using animals and use other methods. They have also refined their experiments so that animals suffer less.

8 How the writer achieves his effects

A The aim of this exercise is to study devices the writer uses to achieve a dispassionate style. You could ask *'Does the writer seem aggressive and angry about medical experiments being the right thing to do?'* Questions along these lines will help students become more analytical about the artifice the writer is using.

This, and the subsequent exercises, would be challenging even for native speakers, so there are a number of prompts in the Student's Book to help students think along the right lines.

B Students should find the checklist helpful in exploring the devices the writer uses. *'He makes us laugh at people who campaign against medical experiments'* is incorrect. Being 'fair' to the views of people who are against his work is one of the ways he appears objective.

Examples in the text of these points are:

He suggests animals are well cared for by saying *'The worst these animals have to put up with is living in a cage with regular food and water …'* (lines 57–58).

Statistics are given on the numbers of people affected by polio, the numbers of animals used for experiments, and the numbers of dogs dying of distemper.

Factual information is given about advances in medical understanding, medical treatment for diseases, and advances in surgery.

A reassuring, caring image of researchers is put across by saying *'People who experiment on animals are just the same as the rest of us'* (lines 80–81) and *'because we like animals'* (line 83).

He seems to try to understand the point of view of his opponents by admitting that the animal experiments cause suffering: *'The golden rule of laboratory animal welfare is to minimise any distress involved'* (lines 60–61).

You could also ask:

'Does he use a lot of emotive, upsetting language?' (No, the opposite is true.)

'Does he quote from famous authorities?' (No, although this is a common technique used for adding weight to an argument.)

9 Finding the right angle

This is a good opportunity to contrast the notion of a 'for and against' approach to an argument with the 'how' approach, which requires reasoning and explanation from different standpoints. To give another example, you could ask *'Are you more likely to be asked for your opinions for or against reducing road accidents, or for your opinions as to how they might be reduced?'*

TEACHING SUPPORT

Exercise 9 refers to the angle of an argument, while Exercise 10 mentions *bias* in an argument. Students need to be clear as to the meaning of these related concepts:

An *angle* refers to the approach that a writer takes to a topic. For example, looking at the subject of experimenting on animals from the perspective of how those experiments have led to improvements in medicine.

Bias refers to the way that someone's viewpoint is affected by their prejudices. We can show bias for or against something. For example, we might expect a scientist who experiments on animals to show bias in favour of colleagues who do the same, but bias against animal-rights campaigners who want to put a stop to such experiments.

10 Understanding bias in an argument

A The aim of this exercise is to show how the impression of objectivity can be reduced when we consider how much the writer has left out of his argument. Students try to find points against medical experiments on animals. 'Points against' is a slight oversimplification: what students are doing, in fact, is considering a wider variety of aspects of the issue in order to establish a more complete picture.

B Each point is quite condensed, so it's worth taking each one in turn and making sure students understand what is being said.

You could finish the work on understanding bias by asking students to sum up how fair they feel the writer is to the topic, now that they have had a chance to consider more aspects of the issue.

11 Writing an article for the school blog

TEACHING SUPPORT

See the Introduction for a general approach to helping students with Writing tasks.

Students are asked to transfer their understanding of medical experiments on animals and the language used for opinion and persuasion to writing an article to post on the school blog. The question is intellectually quite challenging and has a different slant from the 'for and against' compositions they have written before.

Make sure students understand that they are writing a measured argument. They can show this by using contrast expressions such as *whilst, although, even though,* e.g. *Whilst animal experiments have led to important medical advances, there are other ways in which health care can progress.*

Key points to include could be: the limitations of medical experiments (animals react to drugs and experiments in

different ways from humans); the alternatives to research on animals (e.g. more tests on human volunteers which can be more reliable, the use of medical technology such as lasers and ultrasound techniques); preventive measures to reduce human illness (e.g. better health education, the provision of clean water supplies).

Allow students enough time to ask any questions and to write the composition, as they are likely to find it a demanding task. Remind them of the need to use a firm closing paragraph. The main idea to convey is that there are alternatives.

LEARNING SUPPORT

To **support** students, simplify the task by offering a ready-made list of three points 'for' and three points 'against' animal testing – e.g. (For) Animal testing can help make medical treatment safer for humans; it can help us find cures for diseases; laws make sure that the animals are well treated. (Against) We could test new medical treatments on humans or using technology instead; animals are not a reliable way of testing treatments designed for humans; some laboratories treat animals better than others.

12 Prepositions after verbs

It is always useful to practise prepositions with students of all levels. Total (or near total) accuracy with prepositions takes a long time to master.

Other examples to elicit are:

I can only *guess at* his whereabouts.

Animals *differ in* many ways *from* people.

I want to *complain to* the manager *about* their attitude.

Practice: answers

1   experiment on
2   bother about, dying from/of
3   surprised at
4   object to
5   contribute to
6   quarrel with
7   depend on
8   died of
9   provide him with
10 respond well to

Some other verbs that can be followed by the prepositions in the exercise are:

worry / gossip / think / speculate / argue **about**

look / wonder / hint / smile / throw **at**

hear / depart / benefit **from**

accuse / remind / dream **of**

concentrate / bet / rely / congratulate / agree **on**

listen / dedicate / appeal **to**

collaborate / sympathize / help / agree **with**

13 Spelling and pronunciation: Regular plurals 🔊 CD 2, Track 13

However familiar students are with plurals, they still present problems and are at the root of many spelling mistakes and pronunciation difficulties.

Ask students to read the list of nouns silently and to double-check the meanings of more tricky words, e.g. *wasps, spiders.*

Students now listen to the 16 words listed and identify the pronunciation of each ending. The words are spoken twice.

Answers

/s/: cats, insects, wasps, goats

/z/: hens, dogs, spiders, birds, cows, monkeys, bees

/ɪz/: faces, cages, horses, houses, roses

AUDIOSCRIPT

As in the Student's Book.

14 Spelling and pronunciation: Irregular plurals

Ask students to practise the pronunciation of the irregular plurals. Other examples to elicit could be:

-es: branches, watches, wishes

-ves: ourselves, wives, thieves, shelves, halves, lives, loaves (A common exception is *roofs.*)

Change in the vowel: foot – feet

-es: heroes

-ies: babies, families

15 Vocabulary
Answers
1   sheep, lambs
2   bears, wolves, wildcats
3   deer, geese, foxes
4   mice
5   crocodiles, rhinos, teeth
6   fish
7   caterpillars, butterflies

16 Look, say, cover, write, check
The word list recycles vocabulary students have met and helps them learn problematic words.

C Animals in sport and entertainment

1 Discussion
The following sequence of exercises explores the role of animals in sport and entertainment. You could begin by asking students if they are involved with animals in any sport they do, e.g. horse riding. Ask them to describe what they enjoy about the activity and whether the animal enjoys it too.

Horse racing is popular in Britain and many other countries. You could ask whether training animals to perform under pressure and in public is unkind in any way, or whether it depends on how the animals are treated.

Field sports or bloodsports are much more controversial, and there are many groups actively campaigning either in their defence or against them. It will be interesting to hear students' views on such sports (and also to see if they modify their opinions later, after considering the letter in Exercise 9.C.3).

2 People's opinions
Asking students to put a tick or cross will help them focus on what they are reading. The sentence structures contain examples of emphatic forms, which they will be studying in more detail in later exercises.

3 Letter completion: My views on animal charities
Students do not always realise how difficult a cloze exercise can be. You may like to complete the first

(or more) of the sentences as a group, to help students think about how to do this type of exercise.

Answers

1   **c** I think
2   **c** foolish
3   **a** argued
4   **b** but
5   **c** insist
6   **c** yet
7   **a** unfair
8   **b** As I see it
9   **b** and
10 **a** nothing could be further from the truth
11 **c** Nevertheless

To finish, you may like to discuss the angry tone of the letter, which is in contrast to the cool and more measured tone of the article on animal experiments.

4 Vocabulary: Words for feelings

TEACHING SUPPORT

See the Introduction for a general approach to helping students with new vocabulary.

LEARNING SUPPORT

You may wish to recommend that some students use dictionaries for this exercise, as the level is fairly demanding.

Answers

1   horrified
2   uneasy
3   immoral
4   apologetic
5   absurd
6   saddened

You could ask students to use some of this vocabulary in sentences of their own in order to help them remember the new words.

5 Language study: Adding emphasis

There are many different ways to express emphasis in writing. The structures in this exercise have been selected

as some of the most straightforward to learn, so hopefully students will be confident in using them later.

You may like to ask students to read the sentences aloud to show the emphasis through the intonation pattern. You could discuss the fact that in speech we are less reliant on changes in structure to show emphasis, as we have the chance to change our tone of voice.

You may like to make it clear to the students that these sentences are not questions, even though they use the word *what*.

Answers

Emphatic forms in Exercise 9.C.2 are:

What I find most awesome about bullfighting is …

What makes me cross is …

What I love about horse racing is …

6 Practice
Answers

1   What she admires is/are attempts to reduce animal suffering.
2   What we need is/are better fences to stop animals wandering onto the road.
3   What the safari park wardens worry about is animals escaping.
4   The place where you can see owls, eagles and hawks is a falconry centre.
5   What we didn't understand is/was that animals are adapted to live in certain habitats.
6   What I didn't realise is/was how animals depend on each other.
7   The people who are responsible for the reduction in rhino numbers are hunters.
8   The place where the golden eagle prefers to nest is in treeless, mountainous country.
9   What ought to concern us is/are endangered species in our own country.
10 What I want is the right to object to things I think are wrong.

7 More practice
Answers

1   Having a purpose in life has made her so happy.
2   We all shouted, 'Do tell us more about your adventures.'
3   Do take lots of photos when you visit the wildlife park.

4   I never realised that baby rhinos were so affectionate.

5   Raising funds for charity is so worthwhile.

6   Your granny does enjoy her garden, doesn't she?

7   You do look tired/You look so tired today.

8   Thirsty animals are so miserable.

9   Gordon felt so sorry/did feel sorry for the animals he saw at the circus.

10   I do worry about you, you know.

11   Do turn off the tap properly when you have finished washing.

12   Do come in, Sophie. I'm so pleased to see you.

8 Comparing languages

It will be interesting to hear students describe how they add emphasis in their own language(s).

9 Writing sentences

Possible example sentences could be:

Do help yourself to anything you would like to eat.

Helping at the animal rescue centre was *so* worthwhile.

Do speak up, I am a little deaf.

Seeing a lion in real life was *so* exciting.

D Animals at work

1 Thinking about working animals

The following sequence of exercises considers the role of working animals, including police dogs and dogs for the blind. The topic then focuses on animals which are kept by people to generate income. The discussion points centre on the responsibilities people have towards their animals, and what can be done about cruelty to working animals. Students also consider whether intensive farming is ethical.

A   Ask students to look at the pictures of animals and elicit ideas about what animals are used for in their country(ies).

B   Other responsibilities owners have towards animals could include: giving them water, sheltering them, keeping them in a reasonably clean and comfortable condition, making sure they get enough rest and exercise, getting a vet for them if they are ill.

2 Discussing ethical issues

Students may have strong opinions about whether animals are overworked or treated harshly by their owners. Encourage them to be specific about any problems they may have observed, as this helps them think through their ideas more analytically.

You could extend the discussion to consider the use of animals to help people in difficulty (rescue dogs, dogs for the blind, etc.) or to detect criminals (police dogs, guard dogs, anti-poaching dogs). Such dogs often have a high level of intelligence and training. Exploring more about how they can help humans fight crime or save lives might be a nice follow-up.

3 Building an email from prompts

Example answer

Dear Sir,

I am writing in response to recent articles saying that people who keep animals for profit are 'cruel and heartless'. My family make a living from keeping sheep. In my view, our life is harder than the animals'!

In lambing time, for example, there is no day off and no rest. My father gets up as soon as it is light and hurries out to the first task of the day without even bothering to have a drink. He works for several hours without a break. He checks the lambs that were born in the night or attends ewes that are having difficulty giving birth. He brings poorly lambs indoors to be bottle-fed.

He tries to get round the flock four or five times a day, often in snow or cruel winds. If there is a specific problem, he has to go out several times a night with a flashlight. Although expensive, the vet is always called when needed.

It is true that every ewe or lamb that dies is a financial loss to us, so it is in our own interest to care for the sheep.

The sheep are eventually sold at the market. How could/can we live any other way? But we are certainly not the 'ruthless exploiters' of your article. In fact, nothing could be further from the truth.

Yours faithfully,

Orla O'Connor

4 Assessing the argument

Encourage students to re-read the email when it is correct to get a sense of textual flow, as this is difficult to do when they are building it up from the prompts. You could ask a very able student who has a good command of intonation to read it aloud to the group, or you may prefer to do this yourself.

5 The closing paragraph

As always, ask students to pay particular attention to the end of the email, which finishes with an opinion. Explain that this is appropriate for this type of composition, and compare it with how you might end a 'for and against' essay.

6 Vocabulary: Young animals

Answers

1   cub
2   duckling
3   chick/chicken
4   calf
5   kitten
6   pup/puppy
7   kid
8   foal
9   calf
10 calf
11 cygnet
12 cub

7 Comparing languages

You could ask what animal characteristic students would like to have for themselves. They could decide whether they would like to grow a woolly coat for cold days, have the strength of an ox, swim underwater like a fish or dolphin, have the grace of a wildcat or the speed of a cheetah, and so on.

8 Vocabulary: Collective nouns

Answers

1   cows, elephants, deer
2   sheep, goats
3   fish
4   dogs, wolves
5   bees, locusts, ants

Point out that *flock* is also the collective noun for birds.

You may like to extend this exercise by considering the names of the sounds animals and birds make (e.g. *buzz, bark, moo, roar, squawk, twitter*, which are onomatopoeic in English) or by eliciting the names of animal homes (*kennel, pen, stable, cage, nest, lair*, etc.). Please note that activities on onomatopoeic words are extension material and are not required as part of the syllabus.

9 Discussion: Intensive farming

Intensive farming of animals may or may not be familiar to students, so the discussion will need to be adapted to their experience. Pesticides are used on a more global scale, although very small farms may not use them as much. Depending on their background, students may have positive views of intensive farming: because it uses more technology, the results are more dependable, it can produce greater quantities of food and it is labour-saving. They might feel it is kinder to farmers than traditional, back-breaking methods where whole crops are ruined through uncontrolled diseases, possibly leading to financial ruin.

It would be useful to check students' understanding of the 'food chain' concept. They may be familiar with this from their science lessons.

Reasons people may object to intensive farming (which is called factory farming by those who criticise it) usually centre on the conditions in which the animals are kept, e.g. hens may be kept in dark, windowless sheds, with very little space to move around, and their feeding controlled automatically. People claim that animals kept in these conditions usually produce tasteless meat, eggs and so on. There is also concern that livestock which are fed regular doses of hormones could pass these on to consumers in the food chain.

Students are asked to think of possible solutions to the objections people make to intensive farming. There are no easy answers, but solutions might include helping farmers financially to produce food on a smaller, more kindly scale, and giving subsidies to help them adopt organic methods and reduce the use of pesticides. Food companies could be obliged to give fuller information to the consumer through more comprehensive labelling of products.

10 Punctuation

It would be useful to revise students' grasp of the main points of punctuation before going into the exercise.

Example answer

Dear Sir,

Like many of your readers, I want to buy healthy food which is produced in a way which is fair to farm workers and animals. Furthermore, I don't believe food production should damage the environment.

Many farmers in our area say that it is cheaper to rear animals under intensive conditions than it is to give them a decent life. However, if farmers were given subsidies, they would be able to afford more space and comfort for animals. Farmers get subsidies for intensive methods, so why not pay them for a kinder approach?

Similarly, many of the farms around here use harmful pesticides which can get into the food chain. Farmers say it is less expensive to use pesticides than to use more natural or 'organic' methods, which require a bigger labour force and so would be more expensive. What is more expensive in the end – subsidies to the farmers for organic farming or a damaged environment?

In my view, we have a right to know what is in our food. Tins, packets and fresh food should be labelled by food companies as 'free range' or 'factory farmed', or if pesticides were used, so that we know exactly what we are eating.

I realise my ideas might lead to higher food prices, but I have no doubt at all it would be worth it.

Yours faithfully,

Shahar Rishani

11 Checking the text flow

Encourage students to read the letter again when they have corrected it, to get a sense of textual flow.

12 Further thoughts

It will be interesting to hear students' views on Shahar's arguments.

Some of the ways intensive production of food might be unfair to farm workers could include: low wages, long hours, and working in unsafe conditions (e.g. spraying pesticides, driving machinery) without adequate protection. Also, workers might feel 'dehumanised' by having to treat animals as units in a production line. You could tell students that supermarkets in some countries are now choosing to promote 'ethically produced food' to attract more customers and as a way of demonstrating support for fair treatment of workers.

13 Rhetorical questions

It can be artificial to think of rhetorical questions out of context. However, when they have assimilated the pattern, students should be able to incorporate this device into their writing styles.

TEACHING SUPPORT

Rhetoric is the art of speaking persuasively by using certain techniques to make your listeners find it hard to disagree with you. One feature of this form of communication, commonly used by public figures such as politicians, is the rhetorical question, which is not a question at all, but a statement put into the form of a question. The point of the rhetorical question is to make a statement more dramatic. *How can we ever forget our beautiful queen? said the heart-broken king on the death of his wife*, hoping that this will make more of an impact on the audience than *We can't forget our beautiful queen*. Rhetorical questions are very useful in compositions because they are such an effective way of making a point.

LEARNING SUPPORT

You may want to **support** students with analysing and forming rhetorical questions by doing Exercises 13 and 14 orally with them.

14 Turning statements into rhetorical questions

Answers

1   Is a vegetarian meal always healthy?

2   Who can say the farmers are wrong?

3   Which is more important/better: to save an animal or (to) save someone's life?

4   Who knows the extent of the problem?

5   Wouldn't we all be happier knowing that our food was free of chemicals?

6   Isn't it about time we remembered endangered species at home?

7   Shouldn't we consider farm workers before worrying about animals?

Asking students to find examples in the email and letter they have corrected will reinforce learning. They should underline the following: *How could/can we live any other way?*, *Why not pay them for a kinder approach?* and *What is more expensive in the end … environment?*

E Helping animals in danger

1 Discussion: Could you help animals?

Students may need some further clarification about how human activities have a harmful effect on animals. You may like to elicit the ways new roads and housing developments restrict wild animals' range of movement and reduce the scope they have for roaming and finding food. Rather than perceiving a need to live alongside wild animals, people who settle in these areas may see the animals as a nuisance, perhaps causing traffic accidents or foraging for food near rubbish bins. Agricultural development often leads to pesticide use, and this and the resulting run-off into streams and rivers are harmful to wildlife. The idea that we should develop ways to coexist peacefully with wild animals is explored in the report for the headteacher about a scheme to alert local people to the presence of elephants in their area (in Exercise 5) and in the exam-style listening section at the end of the unit.

International overview
Answer
Asiatic lions, tigers and snow leopards are the most endangered species on the chart.

2 Reading for gist

TEACHING SUPPORT

See the Introduction for a general approach to helping students with Reading tasks.

LEARNING SUPPORT

Encourage students who require extra **support** to try to work out the meaning of unfamiliar words from the context by looking at the words around the difficult word and eliciting or suggesting substitute words that could be used instead of the unfamiliar word. Focus on the following words in this text: *breeding ground, cost-effective, plaque, acre, orphaned, poacher.*

3 Reading comprehension
Answers
1 Most animals are available for adoption.
2 It uses the money for breeding programmes to save animals from extinction.
3 an adoption certificate, regular copies of 'Zoo Update', and four free entry tickets
4 to save a corridor of rainforest in Central America, as a sanctuary for wildlife
5 They are in Thailand, and they provide natural sanctuaries for Indo-Chinese tigers orphaned by poaching.

4 Writing a report for the headteacher from notes

TEACHING SUPPORT

See the Introduction for a general approach to helping students with Writing tasks.

The report is a substantial piece of work which involves many skills, so it is helpful to allow enough time for it, and to encourage students to write more than one draft.

You may like to allow students to discuss the example answer and compare it with their own writing. It shows how material in the Student's Book, particularly the previous few exercises, can be used as a resource and combined with original writing.

LEARNING SUPPORT

For writers who may struggle with the exercise, simplify the task: the students just have to make the case for adopting a zoo animal. Therefore delete the 'Points against' section from the notes. Revise and elicit from students the language you could use to present your first argument and then to add further points: *Firstly …, In addition, Furthermore, … Most important of all …* etc. Demonstrate how to take sections of the notes provided and expand them, eliciting ideas from the students; for example, *invitations to special events (e.g. see newborn animals)* might be expanded to: *The school would receive invitations to special events at the zoo, which could include seeing newborn animals – this would be very educational for the younger children.*

Example answer

Report to the headteacher on the adoption of a zoo animal

Our local zoo, the Queen's Zoo, has an animal adoption scheme, with many animals to choose from, and if we use the funds in this way, there are many benefits. Firstly, adopting a zoo animal means we would get plaque at the zoo with school's name on it, which would make us all very proud. We could also get discounts on entrance tickets and in the gift shop. Furthermore, we would be invited to special events such seeing newborn animals. Perhaps most important of all, however, is the fact that the funds would help support breeding programmes, which encourage animals from endangered species to breed in captivity. When they are ready, the animals are returned to the wild.

On the other hand, if we adopt a zoo animal, we cannot support other conservation projects, which are also worthwhile. Rainforests contain a wealth of wildlife but habitats are under threat. Rainforest conservation projects such as Rainforest Action Costa Rica, provide a safe haven for a vast number of wonderful birds and animals by protecting their habitat. In addition, there are some very special projects which help animals who are hunted for their body parts. Tiger numbers have fallen below 4000 due to hunting. The Tiger Trust does very valuable work rescuing endangered tigers in Thailand, for example.

I have discussed the adoption scheme with the members of the Wildlife Club, and we believe the school should use the funds to adopt a zoo animal. The club would prefer to adopt a tiger or a Tamarin Monkey, if possible. We agreed there is nothing like seeing a living, breathing rare wild animal in real life and observing its behaviour. It will be more meaningful for younger students than just listening to the reasons why animals need to be protected. It helps older students with their science projects, especially those thinking of a science career or who want to work with animals. Finally, the adoption scheme is not just about having fun at the zoo, it helps the zoo's breeding programme, which has a very important role in preventing endangered species from extinction.

5 Improving paragraphing and punctuation in a report for the headteacher

You may like to ask students to underline key phrases which show the awareness that the report has been written for the headteacher and why these phrases are important.

For example:

- …encouraged the little children to practise the right way of feeding a baby elephant who has lost its mother. As a result they understood as much as the older ones (*shows awareness that the headteacher would like evidence that the event benefited students of all ages and abilities*).
- …we felt extremely lucky that we had been given the chance to meet a true wildlife pioneer and we all learned so much (*shows appreciation of the school's efforts to arrange the meeting*).
- I would certainly recommend it for next year's group, if the opportunity is still available (*makes a polite recommendation, implying need for permission*).

The correct version should be as follows:

Mr Bavsar's talk about his work in southern India was so inspirational. Mr Bavsar explained why he started his special project, the Elephant Information Service. One night a child woke up to see a small elephant calf standing by his bed. Somehow, the elephant had got into the house and gone into the bedroom without disturbing the boy's parents. The elephant made a strange noise and then turned around and left the way he had come, without causing trouble.

As Chief Wildlife Officer, Mr Bavsar was asked to investigate the incident. When he visited the family, they said they were not distressed but they were shocked. They said that if they had known wild elephants were so near, they would have been better prepared for potentially dangerous situations. This made Mr Bavsar realise that animal and humans could co-exist peacefully, as long as they took sensible precautions to avoid conflict.

Mr Bavsar set up the Elephant Information Service and now there are early warning systems in the area. The Service alerts families when animals are nearby by sending texts, flashing warning lights and making phone calls.

The whole class loved Mr Bhavsar's talk. He was so knowledgeable and showed us his personal photograph collection of the rare and beautiful animals he has cared for, including elephants. Elephants sadly, are often orphaned when their parents are killed by hunters and have to be cared for in an elephant sanctuary before being returned to the wild. Mr Bhavsar even brought in a large toy elephant, a blanket, and feeding bottle and encouraged the little children to practise the right way of feeding a baby elephant who has lost its mother. As a result they understood as much as the older ones about the needs of infant elephants.

Overall, we felt extremely lucky that we had been given the chance to meet a true wildlife pioneer and we all learned so much. I would certainly recommend it for next year's group, if the opportunity is still available.

Grammar spotlight
The past perfect passive

TEACHING SUPPORT

See the Introduction for a general approach to helping students with Grammar tasks.

As always, if students have difficulty grasping the idea of the past perfect as a time in an earlier past, or need more practice with the passive form, it might be useful to refer them to a grammar book. The past participle of irregular verbs is often an obstacle in the correct formation of the structure, so it may be helpful to give students a few irregular verbs to learn each week. This can be more manageable for them than learning long verb lists.

LEARNING SUPPORT

Students who find the basic structure of the past perfect passive tricky may benefit from some controlled oral practice. For example, set up the following scenario. *Our local zoo raised so much money from their adoption scheme that they spent some of it on improving the zoo. When we went to visit last week ... The animal enclosures had been painted. Lots of new trees ... Some broken windows ... New play equipment for the monkeys ... The elephants' very small enclosure ... A completely new visitor centre ... etc.*

The example in paragraph 2 of the article on page 199 is: *Small ponds had been dug out ...*

Answers

a   If the Siberian tiger cub had not been found in time, it would have died in the snow outside its den.

b   The tiger cub's tail had been badly damaged by severe frost.

c   His leg had been badly bitten too.

d   The wildlife officials who found the cub said they had been shocked by the cub's condition. 'We believe the poor little thing had been attacked by a predator and the severe temperatures made everything worse.'

e   After a year, the tiger cub had made a full recovery and was returned to the wild.

Exam-style questions

See the Overview of *Cambridge IGCSE English as a Second Language* section at the beginning of the Student's Book for the mark scheme and criteria for marking the writing questions.

Reading

Four birdwatchers of very different backgrounds share their thoughts in this exam-style multiple matching text. The text introduces a fresh angle on the impact of humans on the natural world. In birdwatching, humans are involved in animal activities in a way which does not disturb them. Each person has a different reason for watching birds. It will be very interesting to hear what the students think of birdwatching as a hobby and to find out if they enjoy, or would enjoy, birdwatching themselves. As always, encourage students to be methodical and apply the techniques they have learned. They should take their time to underline the context given in the rubric, so that they can predict likely content, scan the questions, then read for general meaning and finally, match each statement to the texts by a process of logical deduction. When the statement seems to apply to more than one person, they should take extra care to read for the subtleties of detailed meaning. For example, question j asks 'Which person mentions the equipment they use for watching birds?' Some students might think this applies to both B, Ricky, and D, Pablo, since B says, 'There are several large hides – wooden shelters with benches where visitors can sit and watch birds through big windows.' If students are unsure, point out that B does not actually say he uses the equipment himself, the hides are there to be used by visitors, so B can be eliminated. The best answer is D, Pablo, as he specifically mentions equipment (binoculars) he personally uses when he does birdwatching in the woods.

(The upcoming exam-style writing exercise involves a bird reserve with birdwatching facilities.)

Answers

a	C	f	A
b	B	g	A
c	A	h	B
d	D	i	D
e	A	j	D

(Reading & Writing, Exercise 2: 10 marks (Extended).)

Writing

In Paper 2 (Extended), **two** prompts are provided for the writing in Exercise 6. If you think your students need them, you may like to elicit two additional prompts from the students themselves. Or you could provide additional prompts along the following lines.

4 *'The interactive videos were wonderful.'*

   'You can't touch or smell the animals.'

5 *'Animals do so much for us, they deserve our concern.'*

   'Animals get too much attention these days.'

6 Supporting a wildlife charity – report

As always, students can draw on the animal-related topics and language in the unit to answer this question. As always, they can use the comments given but they are free to make up their own ideas. The report should sound formal or semi-formal. Two additional prompts could be:

'The sanctuary encourages tigers to breed.'

'Birds bring so much joy into our lives.'

Example answer

To help me make up my mind about which charity we should support, I asked my friends in the wildlife club for their views and this is what they think.

Firstly, some are strongly in favour of supporting the tiger sanctuary. There are fewer than 4 000 of these magnificent creatures alive in the wild, which is very sad. Tigers are constantly hunted for their beautiful skins and body parts. Students claim they would be distressed if the species became extinct.

The sanctuary protects tigers and encourages them to breed.

On the other hand, many students like the idea of giving money to the local bird reserve. They said that birds bring joy into our lives, especially the songbirds we can see and hear every day. Volunteers at our local bird reserve work to protect natural habitats, educate visitors and keep the woodland paths clear. Furthermore, the reserve provides superb birdwatching facilities.

On balance, I would be in favour of supporting the bird reserve. Tigers get support from all over the world, but the work of small bird reserves can be forgotten. This is our chance to ensure our local reserve is remembered. (192 words)

(Reading & Writing, Exercise 6: 16 marks (Extended).)

Listening 🔊 CD 2, Track 14

This is a challenging exercise, so you may like to let students listen more than twice. Remind them that they should listen for genuine understanding, rather than simply matching words on the recording with words in the statements.

You may like to pause the recording when checking the answers in order to focus on a particular word or phrase. Encourage students to discuss why this particular word or phrase is important in making the right answer correct. You may also like to explore the fact that there is no evidence on the recording for statement C.

Answers

Speaker 1 **D**   Speaker 2 **G**   Speaker 3 **A**

Speaker 4 **E**   Speaker 5 **F**   Speaker 6 **B**

(Statement C is not needed.)

(Listening, Exercise 4: 6 marks (Core), 6 marks (Extended).)

AUDIOSCRIPT

You will hear six people talking about wildlife. For each of Speakers 1–6, choose from the list A–G which idea each speaker expresses. Write the letter in the box. Use each letter only once. There is one extra letter which you do not need to use. You will hear the full recording twice.

SPEAKER 1

We went camping in an area where grizzly bears and other dangerous wild animals live. We never actually encountered any dangerous wildlife but we still took bear spray with us when we went out, just in case we met any. We were also warned not to keep food in the tent, as this attracts animals too. We were told to put food in the campsite's storage lockers to keep it away from wildlife. I think camping in an area where wild animals live is safe as long as you follow the campsite rules and avoid taking silly risks that could endanger the lives of other campers as well as your own.

SPEAKER 2

Wildlife was here long before people settled in this region. Things we have done to the environment, including agricultural development, housing projects and road building, have destroyed much of the habitat of many wild animals. I heard recently of plans to cut down a large section of forest, in order to extend an industrial area near here, which would be terrible for the wildlife living in the forest. If we were more appreciative of our wildlife heritage, we'd all benefit. I certainly support the idea of underpasses for safer road crossings for wildlife.

SPEAKER 3

Grizzly bears and other wildlife living near us are a problem as they frequently cross the main road and come into the town. Parents get worried about their children being attacked and sometimes animals get hurt, just because people panic and don't think clearly. I'm hoping to go on a course to learn more about wildlife, so I can teach my community how to respond to the wild animals living locally without causing any harm to them.

SPEAKER 4

I think we should all do more to care for wild animals and protect them, as they are part of our heritage. However, let's not forget that wild animals can still be a real problem for the human population. My uncle is a sheep farmer and he has money worries because his sheep keep being killed by dangerous wild animals. Lambing time is when his sheep are most vulnerable, and he has to take special care as he can't afford to keep losing sheep. He once had a lucky escape from a wolf when he went out late one night to try to protect his flock.

SPEAKER 5

I attended a town council meeting last night where we discussed the idea of building underpasses so wildlife can cross roads safely. Lots of people were in favour of the idea, but, although it sounds very good in theory, in practice I doubt that animals would use the crossings. They might ignore them. I think other ideas, such as more lighting after dark and lowering the night-time speed limit, are better and would be a lot cheaper too. There's another meeting next week, and I'll definitely attend so I can put forward my views.

SPEAKER 6

We have packs of wolves and other dangerous wildlife living not far from where our sheep graze. They used to be a real danger, and our sheep were always being attacked, especially at lambing time. Then we got some financial help from the government to train guard dogs, and install spotlights and special alarm systems. These measures have really helped keep the predators away, and we hardly lose any sheep now. I would recommend these measures to any farmer who's troubled by wolves or other predators, as they've really worked well on our farm and given us so much more peace of mind.

Wider Practice

1   You may like to further discuss the concept of peaceful coexistence with wildlife, given the fact that in many parts of the world wild animals are a danger to people, cause accidents and threaten jobs. The report in Exercise 5 and the exam-style listening at the end of the unit, which give suggestions of ways to overcome problems wild animals cause, without hurting the animals, could be a useful aid for the discussion.

2   Having studied animal rights in detail, it would be interesting for students to discuss the rights of people. This could be a fascinating topic, following on well from the work they have done on ethical questions and extending their personal and social education.
Students might enjoy working out their 'rights', which you could tailor for their particular situation. With rights come responsibilities. Defending

'responsibilities' is another challenging problem-solving exercise.

Some possible rights/responsibilities for young people could be:

- to have an education/to make the most of my educational opportunities
- to have my own opinions and views/to listen to the opinions of others and to try to understand their points of view
- to meet friends of my own age and join clubs/to explain to concerned adults what they need to know about my friends and agree a time to come home
- to have access to medical care/to look after myself and to do what I can to stay in good health.

3   The topic of animals lends itself well to cross-curricular work. You could arrange for teachers of biology and geography to talk to the class about ecology, the food chain and so on.

4   There is a lot of factual information available about animals themselves: animal families, origins, habits, breeding patterns, endangered species. Students could find out about an animal they are interested in and give a talk to the group.

5   Watching or listening to a controversial discussion about farming or zoos, or animal management, could provide a basis for debate, as could inviting a speaker on the topic to class.

6   Supporting an animal or wildlife charity might be worth considering. Students would receive a lot of information, and it would give them a valuable sense of making a difference to some issues of global concern.

7   Students could be asked to research hobbies and leisure-time pursuits which involve animals, and give a short talk to the class.

8   Students could watch a film of a circus or similar event, where animals are being used for entertainment purposes, and write a review.

The world of work

Overview

This unit consolidates the skills needed if students are to show evidence of language ability in reading, listening or speaking skills and the ability to sustain quality in their writing, whether that is in writing reports, articles, emails or letters.

Theme

The theme of the unit is work. This is approached through developing more understanding of the skills and qualities needed for work, common problems faced in the workplace, and the way in which school prepares you for work. Students sometimes lack confidence because they think they will need exceptional academic qualifications to have a chance in today's competitive job market. In fact, recent research shows that employers particularly look for good communication skills. Improving communication skills has been the focus of this course and is an attainable target for them all.

The issues raised are:

- How do surveys and the portrayal of teenagers in the media influence public opinion and adversely affect their chances of training or employment?

- How does stereotyping operate at work, and why might it be harmful?

- How does school promote maturity and responsibility for work?

- How can employment levels be increased (using examples and knowledge based on students' own countries)?

The texts include factual material about the work involved in developing and producing a new chocolate item for the market, and some are used for a role play. There is also a magazine article about the employment of people with disabilities. Listening exercises are an interview with a human resources officer working for a chain of electrical stores and an exercise with short conversations based on work scenarios.

Language work

The unit consolidates the functions and skills approach of the earlier units. New language work focuses on expressing figures and approximations, and criticising statistical information. Pronunciation focuses on linking sounds.

The *Grammar spotlight* looks at superlatives of long and short adjectives, and at adverbs of degree.

A The rewards of work

1 Discussion

The introductory discussion focuses on why people work. The reasons are wide and varied. Encourage students to come up with ideas such as:

- to earn money/raise their standard of living
- to use skills and qualifications
- to have fun
- to travel
- to enjoy company benefits: car, health insurance, tax-free loans, etc.
- for security
- to get out of the house
- for standing in the community
- to give routine and structure to the day
- to make a difference to society
- to have a break from domestic chores and commitments
- to express different aspects of their personality
- to get a sense of achievement
- to enjoy using specialised equipment only available at work
- to enjoy wearing a uniform/special clothes.

You could also ask *'What is the effect on people when they lose their job?'*

This could elicit interesting ideas which can be developed later in the unit, where there is a focus on unemployment.

2 Skills and qualities for work

The matching exercise encourages students to focus on what is really essential for an occupation.

Answers

1 C   2 J   3 E   4 I   5 H   6 G   7 D   8 F   9 B   10 A

3 Pre-reading tasks

A   Students are going to read about how a new type of chocolate bar is researched, developed, tested out on consumers and launched. You could introduce this topic by telling them briefly about a new type of product you have tried yourself, what you liked about it, why you tried it and whether you are going to go on using it.

B   The text itself focuses on the challenges, in business terms, of making a new product successful. The exercise can be more fully exploited if you also highlight any business-related vocabulary students bring up while discussing the pre-reading question. Possible words might include: *consumer, market, lifestyle, competition, profits, sales.*

Challenges involved in making a new product successful which students may suggest are:

- You have to know who is likely to buy it (the target group).
- You have to understand how it will fit into the existing market for this type of product.
- You have to have the financial resources to make the project feasible.
- You have to work out a realistic figure for how much it will cost to make it.
- You need an effective marketing strategy – social media, television, the internet, newspapers, magazines, hoardings, etc., so people know about it and are tempted to try it.
- You have to be able to sustain the sales.

4 Predicting

Speculate with the students what the workers in the photo of the chocolate factory are doing and whether the work appeals to them. You could draw attention to the protective hair net and discuss hygiene issues, etc.

5 Reading for gist

TEACHING SUPPORT

See the Introduction for a general approach to helping students with Reading tasks.

This text is long and the vocabulary level is quite high, so you may want to ask students to stop reading at the end of each section to check general comprehension. For example, at the end of the introductory section you could ask '*What are the main ingredients of chocolate bars?*'

You could explain that a chocolate bar consists of chocolate plus other ingredients such as caramel, nuts, fruit, whereas a bar of chocolate is usually a larger flat piece of chocolate, divided into small squares made of just milk or plain chocolate.

If you are reading around the class, it is a good idea to allow enough time to ensure everyone is keeping up with the meaning of words which might be unfamiliar. Even for the higher attaining students, there are many insights into marketing which may be completely new. You can, as always, pause occasionally at the end of sentences, and discuss with students what an unfamiliar word might mean in context. Encourage any responses which show some understanding.

For instance, after the sentence 'One of the key criteria for producing a new chocolate bar is that it should be difficult for rival companies to reproduce' (lines 43–45), you could ask students '*What does 'rival companies' mean here?*', and elicit 'rival companies' means 'other companies that make chocolate'

You could also ask '*What does "reproduce" mean here?*' and elicit that it has a similar meaning to 'copy' You could then go on to ask '*So a new chocolate bar must be difficult for other companies to copy. Why would that be so important?*'

Understanding every word is not essential as long as the overall meaning is understood.

Provide students who may need extra **support** with a vocabulary matching task covering some of the key words. They should match words from list A with definitions from list B. *A: brand, launch, manufacturers, ingredients, packaging, consumers*; B: the people who make a product; the people who buy a product; what a food product is made of; a product made by a particular company; the paper or box that a product is inside; start advertising a new product. The students will find the text easier to follow if they have some prior knowledge of how companies develop new products, so brainstorm ideas about this from students before reading the text, using some of the words from the vocabulary matching.

6 Reading comprehension

Answers

1   to try to identify opportunities for new products

2   If not, it will quickly attract competition from competitors.

3   They want people's opinions on the taste of the chocolate, and the impact the advert had on them.

4   Poland, Russia and Australia

5   a – impressed

6   The paragraph should include the following points:

   • too easy for rivals to copy

   • price not right, too expensive for the market

   • might not come out right in the production process

   • might be difficult to make the taste consistent. The following point could also be included, as it is implied:

   • might be taking too long to get the product right.

7 Post-reading discussion

Students may express surprise at the amount of effort and money that goes into researching and developing a new product. You may also wish to discuss the idea that chocolate is not as good for us as other kinds of food. You could ask whether chocolate advertising should be on children's TV schedules. Comments from students based on the idea that chocolate manufacturers help the economy, or that banning chocolate limits freedom of choice, or the fact that chocolate eaten in moderation can be good for us (it contains essential nutrients) would be good. There is no right answer. You could also remind students that Silvia, in Unit 8 was taking 144 bars of chocolate with her on her round the world trip because chocolate is a compact, high energy food.

8 Vocabulary

Students can work in pairs to produce a lexical set for business. Monitor the exercise and encourage them to use dictionaries.

Answers

producing, companies, manufacturer, brand, competition, machinery, investment, factory, produced economically, price-sensitive market, formula, production, price, products, projects, consumers, buy, mass-production, process of development

Collocations

Suggest that students work together, using dictionaries, to come up with collocations for *stiff*, *sensitive* and *delicious*.

Point out that *stiff* in the text is used metaphorically to mean 'harsh' or 'difficult', but it can have a literal meaning, as in *stiff neck*. *Sensitive* in the text suggests something fragile or easily affected by outside pressures.

Possible answers

stiff: neck, punishment, opposition, climb, interview, exam

sensitive: skin, eyes, instrument, person, animal, plant, relationship, topic/subject

delicious: drink, food, meal, scent / smell / perfume

As always, ask students to record new items in their vocabulary books, with an example of how each word could be used.

9 A rewarding job?

The aim of this exercise is to develop students' understanding of the variety of feelings people involved in the chocolate bar project might have, and to think about the skills and qualities they would need for their work.

Possible answers

feelings: elated, happy, satisfied, enthusiastic, interested, disappointed, irritated, bored, despondent

skills and qualities: creativity, ability to work in a team, perseverance, attention to detail, ability to work on your own

10 Sharing ideas

Possible answers

The skills and qualities mentioned in Exercise 2 which are relevant are: patience, good communication skills, artistic flair, business acumen, imagination.

11 Understanding visual data

Students should now be familiar with graphs and bar charts. A basic understanding of straightforward charts is a real life skill. In an exam, students are unlikely to have a direct question on statistical data, but statistics may be referred to in listening and reading texts, so it is important that they understand how statistics are used to illustrate and reinforce opinions and facts.

Ask students to re-read the opening paragraph of 'A bar Is born'.

Possible answer

Students should come up with an answer along the lines of:

> The bar chart reflects information in the first paragraph by showing that Switzerland, Ireland and the UK consume the most chocolate. It also gives information about China and India. Extra information is given by showing how these countries compare with several other countries and exactly how much each country consumes.

12 Product development meeting and role play

Encourage students to read and understand the context for the multiple matching exercise carefully. Some questions involve inference so students should take care that they have grasped the implications of information given in the text. Remind students to: read the rubric, scan the questions, read the texts for general meaning, and finally tackle each question methodically, re-reading the text(s) to help them decide, especially where answers seem 'close.' If students feel the question applies to more than one person, they should study the evidence in the text with extra care. For example, question 3 asks, 'Which person wants to produce a chocolate bar aimed at the widest age range of customers?' Students might think this applies to both the sales executive, and the marketing executive, as both mention a wide range of customers. On closer reading

however, the marketing executive uses the key words 'older teenagers and adults' which is a more limited age range than the sale executive, who refers to 'families, to include adults and children of various ages.' In fact, the sales executive is describing every age group, so the marketing executive can be eliminated and the sales executive is the most correct choice. Students' knowledge of vocabulary and topic will be crucial in helping them make the right selections. As always, it is a good idea to ask students to provide evidence from the text to support their choices, in order to discourage the temptation to answer through guesswork.

Answers

1   Head Engineer
2   Sales Executive
3   Sales Executive
4   Designer
5   Head Engineer
6   Sales Executive
7   Designer

Role Play

The role play enables students to act out the occupational roles which were suggested by the text. This is done through role-playing a meeting to discuss the feasibility of researching and developing a new chocolate bar. The role play includes a discussion of problems with the formula, technology, price, the target group, advertising strategies, etc.

The aim is to enable students to activate as much passive knowledge as possible. However, it would be useful to revise the functions of interrupting, offering advice / suggestions / opinions and expressing disagreement, so students are well prepared. See the contents chart at the front of the Student's Book for the relevant units. Tell them that the emphasis will be on fluency, spontaneity and activating passive knowledge.

Students should do the role play in groups of four. Let them have some time to quietly read and absorb their role information individually, and check any problems with comprehension. Alternatively, you could draw together all the people with the same role. Make sure they understand what is expected of them, and clarify any misunderstandings before they begin. If appropriate, you or the students themselves could record or video the role play and play it back, pausing in key places, so that students have the chance to identify the good points of the interaction and where it could be further improved.

B Facts and figures

1 Approximations

Answers

The stress in *per cent* falls on *cent*.

1 H   **2** C   **3** B   **4** A   **5** F   **6** D   **7** E   **8** G

Elicit from students the idea that approximations are used to make bare statistics more understandable, by comparing them to amounts that the general public find easy to imagine.

The disadvantage might be that approximations can be used to slant information so that it creates a positive or negative impression. It is not, strictly speaking, a disadvantage, but simply something that students should be aware of.

2 Questioning statistics

A   The aim of this exercise is to develop students' ability to criticise authoritative-sounding statistics.

B   The answers to the questions might reveal that the survey was carried out by a market research company on behalf of a political pressure group that is opposed to working mothers and wants to influence public opinion against them. The size of the sample might reveal that it was too small to be meaningful. The questions could be too vague – 'absence' is a general term, and absences might be due not to illness but to things like dental appointments which are arranged differently by the two groups in the sample. (Working mothers might arrange appointments after school hours, whereas non-working mothers might take their children out of school for appointments.) Moreover, the two groups of children may not be similar in terms of age, social background, etc., making comparison less useful.

The reasons why the questions are important are that you need to be sure the information was gathered objectively and that the results have not been distorted in the interests of a particular pressure group.

C   The same kind of questions should be asked here. In the second survey, it would be very important to know if the intake of the schools surveyed is similar, to ensure that 'like is being compared with like' (a phrase

which means that two things which are similar in some way are being compared).

3 Criticising statistics

Before students read the reactions in the speech bubbles, you could ask *'How do you think local teenagers felt when they saw this written about them? Pleased? Angry? What do you think they said?'*

Elicit some reactions expressing indignation and a refusal to believe the results. Drill appropriate responses, including those in the student's Book. Check that students sound annoyed and disbelieving, before asking them to practise in pairs with the information in Exercise 2.

4 Young lives: Good or bad?

Students work in pairs to analyse the statements about teenagers.

Answers

Statements giving a positive impression are: 2, 3, 6, 7, 10.

Statements giving a negative impression are: 1, 4, 5, 8, 9.

You could encourage students to think about the situation in their own country by asking:

'Are teenagers in your country less materialistic than those in the survey?'

'Are they more community-minded than the teenagers in the survey?'

'Where do teenagers you know get their spending money from?'

5 Rewriting in a more formal style

TEACHING SUPPORT

See the Introduction for a general approach to helping students with Writing tasks.

The aim of this exercise is to consolidate work done in earlier units about appropriateness of style, tone and register. The letter, which is too informal for its purpose, could be analysed in small groups. It is packed with inappropriate expressions (*Hi you guys, got me mad, Talk about …, dead worried*, etc.), so all the students should be able to find some.

After they have analysed the letter in pairs, ask students *'When would you write a letter in this style?'*, eliciting something along the lines of 'When you write to a friend, or perhaps to a college newsletter if the normal tone of the newsletter is very student-centred and informal.'

You could ask a student to come to the board and write up examples of inappropriate language under the headings given.

Before students attempt to rewrite the letter, suggest some phrases they could use, e.g.

With regard to/With reference to the comment about …

I disagree with/object to the comment that …

LEARNING SUPPORT

Check understanding of the terms in the bulleted list, eliciting examples. Provide some sentence starters if they need support with the rewriting (e.g. *I feel annoyed that …, I disagree that …, I really can't agree that …, With regard to …*, etc.).

Example answer
A copy of the letter could be circulated to students for comparison with their own attempts.

Dear Editor

I am a student at a local high school. I have just read your report 'Young Lives Shock!' and I feel most annoyed about the way it describes teenagers. We are not 'unconcerned about employment'. My friends and I are very worried about the chances of getting a job in a town with high unemployment like this one.

I also disagree with your report's suggestion that 'teenagers value their spare-time jobs more than their studies'. Like the teenagers in the survey, I too have a part-time job to earn extra spending money. My parents are unable to afford to buy me the trainers or kind of phone I would like. I work in a café twice a week after school. It does make it hard to concentrate at school the next day, but I do extra homework to catch up.

With regard to the comment 'the youth of today show a strong preference for the company of their peer group over that which their parents can offer',

---

I think it is more natural to want to spend time with friends of your own age than to stay at home with your parents. However, I would like to point out that teenagers do respect their parents.

I would be most interested in hearing the responses of the other readers to this survey.

Yours faithfully,

Ollie Debeer

International overview
1   approximately 24%, 27%, 33%
2   The trend is up.

The steady increase in the global take-up of tertiary education and training is an interesting development. Students will enjoy exploring the reasons why this has occurred. Possibilities include: more opportunities for tertiary education; the need for further qualifications in order to compete in the job market; more support and encouragement from families; increasing affluence; a wish to delay finding work, perhaps because of poor employment prospects. There are no right answers.

C Job stereotypes

1 Pre-listening discussion
The pre-listening activity focuses on the topic of shopping from a consumer's point of view. To help students decide on how they would improve shops, you could explore common pet hates about shopping, e.g. queuing for service, ignorant salespeople, difficulty in getting the goods you want/refunds, etc.

2 Predicting content
Students predict the content of the talk before listening. Make sure they understand the concept of a human resources officer, as it will not be common in all cultures. (The term human resources is often abbreviated to HR.) HR staff are employed in many large organisations. They are involved in recruitment and interviewing, but often their key function is staff welfare and helping staff do their jobs more effectively. (In the past, the usual job title was Personnel Officer.)

3 Vocabulary check

Answers

personal sales targets: levels of sales which individuals are aiming to achieve

influential: able to influence or have an effect

wide spectrum: a broad range

4 Listening for gist/5 Detailed listening

🔊 **CD 2, Track 15**

TEACHING SUPPORT

See the Introduction for a general approach to helping students with Listening tasks.

As always, allow students to listen first for general meaning and then for specific information. Let them listen as often as they need, bearing in mind that they are likely to only listen twice in an exam.

LEARNING SUPPORT

To increase accessibility, encourage students as always to focus on key words in the listening exercise in order to get the gist. Remind them that they don't need to understand every word a speaker says to enjoy listening and to understand the general ideas. It may be helpful to pre-teach/elicit the meaning of some language, e.g. *to get the sack /to sack someone, to display (things in a shop), goods, to take someone on, rival store.* It would also help to have a brief pre-listening discussion about the kind of things students think a sales assistant in a shop selling electrical goods might be required to do.

Answers

1 c **2** b **3** a **4** b **5** a **6** a **7** c

AUDIOSCRIPT

Listen to the recording. Which of the points that you ticked are mentioned?

What I do is I visit electrical stores in the high streets up and down the country. I'm really trying to advise the managers on staffing so that, you know, they can get the best out of their staff.

One common problem is er … well, for example, say a sales assistant is not meeting personal sales targets. Their figures are, you know, a bit … iffy. Managers are wondering, like, are they up to the job, should they get the sack or not? I suggest, 'how about offering the assistant more training and more development?' Of course, training … it would have to be in a specific area. I mean, we get a sales assistant who knows everything about hi-fi but nothing about the white goods like fridges and dishwashers we sell. So they have a gap where product knowledge is concerned. And this can be rectified if they go on a training course. Sometimes we let them take a microwave or camera home so that they can get familiar with it in their own time. On the other hand, a few, er …, quite a few, sales assistants need training in exactly how to sell. Selling involves opening the sale and actually closing the sale to make sure the transaction is complete – clinching the deal, if you like.

Another common gap is display. In a shop, goods should be displayed so they appeal to the customer, they're easy to find, er …, well there's no point in creating confusion, is there? An assistant may be sent on a course to train them in how to set out the goods logically, taking into account the height, colour, …

It's funny, but the most frustrating aspect of my job is that managers want very quick results. Well, who wouldn't want their shop to be the best? But they want to sack people or discipline them rather than invest more in training and keep people. Managers find it hard to accept that the personnel officer is influential. When it comes to recruiting staff, it's usually the case that managers want people just like themselves – same background, all that – well, when what you actually need are the skills and attributes for the job. I get managers to see that, well, people from a wide spectrum can meet the needs of the job. Er, yeah, I'd say I … I feel most satisfied when I've persuaded managers to take on people who, er, don't fit the norm.

Sometimes, and this is in its way a much more serious thing, the store's sales are falling too. If a rival store has opened up, it'll be taking our custom or maybe the population in the area is declining – er, it's just that people are moving away. In this case, it's no good projecting sales by looking at the figures of the previous year. I'd help them project new targets, more, er, realistic targets, taking these factors into account. I try to get on well with the managers. They have to feel they've got the power. After all, you know, they do work hard and it can be a bit of a treadmill. I never make them do anything – if it went wrong, they'd blame me. I can influence but not, well … at the end of the day, they've got to feel the decisions come from them.

6 Post-listening discussion

The aim of the discussion is to explore stereotyping. The human resources officer says that sales managers want to employ people who are like themselves. It will be interesting to hear students' perceptions of the kind of person she has in mind.

You could now write the occupation *pop star* on the board and ask students *'How would you describe a typical pop star?'*, perhaps inviting one of them to draw a caricature on the board. Elicit ideas about appearance, lifestyle, clothes, spare-time interests, and so on. Students could then discuss the other occupations in pairs.

Ask for feedback on the group discussion which follows. Students will probably not have any particular difficulty in distinguishing between the popular stereotypes and reality, but you could ask *'Are all librarians serious? Do they all wear glasses? Are they all fond of reading?'*, for example.

To help students focus on whether stereotypes are a good or bad thing, you could ask *'Are school or college leavers put off some occupations by stereotyping? How far have you found stereotypes to be true to life? Who do you know who doesn't fit the stereotype for their occupation?'*

7 Common work-related expressions

Answers

1 talk about work
2 an ambitious person
3 money given when he retired
4 not working
5 person who does menial jobs at work
6 have control over how and when I work
7 a high-achieving person
8 manual workers, officer workers

8 Pronunciation: Linking sounds

Tell students that if a word ends with a consonant sound, it will link with the next word if that word begins with a vowel sound. Ask them to listen to you reading the advert, so that they can hear how some words are pronounced distinctly and others 'run into' the next word. Before they practise reading the advert aloud, remind them that, as always, pronunciation is part of meaning – for the meaning to be conveyed clearly, the pronunciation must be satisfactory too.

Seafront restaurant: answers

Brighten‿up

Get‿a job

If you need‿extra cash

Lots‿of vacancies‿in

It's fun,‿it's

Headlights Hairdressing: answers

career‿opportunities

Learn‿in‿a

got‿energy and‿enthusiasm

Contact‿Elma

9 Writing a job advert

Possible answer

GENERAL‿ASSISTANT FOR LABORATORY

Saturday help needed to wash up, sweep‿up and generally tidy the laboratory. £8.00 per‿hour plus travel‿expenses.

Contact‿Amy Jones 013452–78642 a.jones@labresearch.com

Monitor the pairs as they read to each other, and correct any faulty pronunciation.

D Recruitment with a difference

1 Pre-reading task

The reading text is about a fast-food restaurant which employs deaf staff. The text is based on an interview with the restaurant manager, who relates how his feelings of anxiety changed to enthusiasm when he realised how smoothly the system worked and all the benefits it offered to the disabled employees.

A Possible advantages of fast-food restaurants are:
  • good when you are in a hurry
  • clean, hygienic surroundings

167

- informal – you can go alone or with a group of friends
- relatively inexpensive
- consistent quality of food
- familiar menu wherever you are.

B Encourage students to write open questions, e.g.

Why did you decide to employ deaf staff?

How do the staff communicate with customers?

What roles do the staff have in the restaurant?

What training do they have?

How do hearing people communicate with them?

What difficulties have you had?

How do customers react?

How successful has it been?

2 Vocabulary check

hearing impairment: reduction in ability to hear

recruiting: finding new employees

agile: quick in movement

criteria: standards for judging/deciding something

mentor: more experienced person who inspires and advises

3 Reading for gist

Students should enjoy finding answers to the questions they wrote.

4 Comprehension check

LEARNING SUPPORT

To **support** students with this activity, tell them in which paragraph the answers can be found: 1 para 4, 2 para 5, 3 paras 8–9, 4 para 11.

Answers

1 The management were aware of the large numbers of deaf people in society and felt they had a duty to help them.

2 They used the same criteria as when they select hearing applicants.

3 In previous jobs the employees felt isolated but here they feel normal, which is very positive for them.

4 They become more energetic and better tempered.

5 any two of: learned basic sign language; changed his attitudes towards disabled people; gained a sense of personal fulfilment because he has made a difference to people's lives

5 Post-reading discussion

A Discuss students' reactions to the idea of employing people with disabilities in other situations. You could ask, for example, *'Could a blind person be a teacher? What special aids might they need?'*

You could relate the concept of sign language to the importance of general body language in conveying meaning, asking students to explore how we communicate through facial expressions, gestures, movement, posture, etc., and also how we form opinions of people based on their body language.

B When students discuss the contrasting rewards and stresses of people-orientated jobs and product-orientated jobs, they will be generalising to some extent. It may be quite a difficult abstract concept for those who have not had employment experience. Prompt them if necessary, to elicit ideas along these lines:

In a people-orientated job, you have to learn to cope with many different kinds of personalities and expectations. People may have more needs than you can satisfy, and so the work might feel outside your control at times. You can gain rewards through a feeling of being valued and respected by the people on whose behalf you work.

In a product-orientated job, you have the satisfaction of producing something that you can, in a sense, stand back and admire at the end of the day. On the other hand, the work can be more monotonous as it does not have the unpredictable element that a people-orientated job brings.

C It will be interesting to hear students' views on 'mentoring'. You could develop the idea to include mentors in the family or social sphere, such as aunts and uncles who support younger relatives who need someone to confide in and who may feel isolated in their immediate family.

6 Vocabulary study

Students can work in pairs for this exercise.

Answers

A hyperactive, energetic, lazy/indolent

B loving, affectionate, supportive, friendly, indifferent, cold, critical

C placid

7 Similes

You could ask students to read their sentences aloud.

You may like to point out that in informal English *like* is sometimes used instead of *as if/though*. Example: *Her face turned red like a tomato.*

TEACHING SUPPORT

Like metaphors, *similes* are an example of figurative language. However, there is an important difference: with similes we make a direct comparison between things, actions and feelings, using words such as *like, as* and *as if*. You could introduce similes by putting a few common examples on the board, e.g. *sing like an angel, work like a dog, fight like cat and dog, sleep like a log, as busy as a bee, as strong as an ox, as cold as ice.* You could **challenge** students by asking them to come up with a few of their own to describe the qualities of family and friends, the classroom and so on. This they can do alone, before they share them with a partner. You could then bring the whole class together at the end and ask students to share a few of the similes they came up with.

LEARNING SUPPORT

If you are including '*it was like* + gerund', which may be unfamiliar grammar for some students, follow up the exercise with a drill offering further targeted practice of that structure. For example: *It was so hot it felt like being in an oven. It was so cold it felt like ... It was raining so hard it felt like ... The road was so slippery it felt like ...*

Possible answers

1 an oven

2 ice

3 it hadn't been cleaned for years

4 she had won the lottery

5 being in prison

6 life wasn't worth living

8 Spelling: -able or -ible?

Before students start the spelling exercise, you could write up *preventable* and *responsible* and highlight the endings. Then you could elicit other words with these endings. Unfortunately, there are no clear and simple rules for the spelling patterns, so remind students of the importance of learning the endings by heart. The word *responsible* is commonly misspelled by students. You can also remind students that usually if the word ends in -e, this is dropped when adding -able or –ible, but sometimes it is kept, e.g. in the word *likeable*.

Answers

A 1 available

2 invisible

3 curable

4 responsible

5 incredible

6 sensible

7 reliable

8 advisable

9 inaccessible

10 irritable

B 1 washable

2 inedible

3 digestible

4 desirable

5 approachable

6 excitable

7 bearable

8 incomprehensible

9 Phrasal verbs

Answers

1 gets by

2 carry out

3 turn down

4 leave anyone out

5 drawn up

10 'Eye' idioms

Answers

An *eye-opening experience* is one which makes you realise things for the first time.

1 H **2** G **3** F **4** A **5** C **6** E **7** B **8** D

E Preparing for work

1 How well does school prepare you for work?

A Students may not have a specific idea of their future career, but you could invite them to think of the positive ways school is preparing them, in general, to be successful in employment. Their ideas could range across the subjects of the curriculum, e.g. good communication skills and being numerate and computer-literate are essential for work in many areas, an understanding of science helps you use technical equipment safely, etc. Moreover, personal qualities which are needed at work such as team leadership, being a good team player, creativity and imagination are developed at school by many subjects including sport, art and extra-curricular activities.

Some schools arrange work experience, so you could discuss what students gain from this – learning about how the organisation works, teamwork, relating to employees of different ages and backgrounds, mastering some basic tasks that might be given to them on work experience, getting a 'feel' for a job to help them decide whether this field of work would suit them, etc.

B Holding a position of responsibility at school also develops personal qualities. Encourage students to identify strengths which they have gained, e.g. confidence, good organisational skills, empathy, self-discipline.

2 Before you read

The pre-reading task leads into a reading and writing exercise.

Before students begin the task, it's useful to clarify the concept of Head Boy or Girl, as not everyone will be familiar with this position, especially if their school does not have them. Explain that it's a position filled by a student in the final year of school who has shown outstanding qualities of leadership. A head boy or girl may be elected by the students or chosen by the teachers. He/she does such things as negotiate with teachers over matters of discipline and student grievances, and is trusted by the teachers to act as an 'ambassador' to the other students, explaining the teachers' point of view on unpopular rules, etc.

You could also discuss the disadvantages of the head student system. It is sometimes thought to encourage resentment among students and has been stopped in some UK schools for this reason.

If the school does not have the prefect system, you could discuss the pros and cons of alternative systems such as a student council. Elicit the idea that the council is composed of elected students who meet to discuss ideas or problems. Councils usually elect representatives who talk to the teachers about the wishes of the student council. They discuss matters such as changes to the school uniform, school dinners, new student clubs or new facilities that are needed.

3 Reading, analysing and writing

Luke's article is suitable in terms of its style. It begins well, uses a range of structures, shows awareness of its audience, and is well organised into paragraphs which follow a logical progression of ideas.

Students should work together to identify how Luke has used complex sentence constructions, collocations describing qualities and skills, etc., before they decide how his article could end. Point out that a good conclusion would offer a short summary of what has been said before and might, in its final sentence, include one new point.

Example answer

> Matthew is the best candidate and would be an ideal Head Boy. He has good all-round skills and he has proved his ability to work for the school and get on with all kinds of pupils. I would definitely trust him to represent our point of view to the teachers.

4 Comparing two styles

Students should not have too much difficulty in recognising the weakness of Leila's style. You could ask *'Which article carries more authority/would influence you more? Why?'*

A suitable answer would be something like:

'The short, simple sentences, plain tone, abrupt register and lack of organisation make the article much less authoritative than that written by Luke.'

5 Developing your writing style

TEACHING SUPPORT

See the Introduction for a general approach to helping students with Writing tasks.

Rewriting Leila's article is quite challenging, and you may like to invite students to work on various possible drafts in groups until they have produced a draft everyone is satisfied with. Remind them that Luke's article should give them some ideas of structures, etc.

LEARNING SUPPORT

Students who need more support with writing may enjoy choosing a few sentences from Leila's report and connecting them with clauses or linkers. Demonstrate with one or two examples, eliciting ideas from students, then let them continue on their own or in pairs. For example: *She set up a social club. She worked after school every day. She worked on Saturdays as well. = She set up a social club, <u>where</u> she worked after school every day <u>including</u> Saturdays.*

Example answer

HEAD GIRL ELECTIONS

My personal choice for Head Girl is Nicola Wilson. She has worked extremely hard for all of us and her behaviour is a shining example to the rest of the students.

Do you remember how many of us were being bullied and afraid to come to school? She tackled this problem very effectively and the bullying is no longer an issue. It was also Nicola's idea to start a 'Welcome Day' for new students, which has really helped new students integrate quickly and happily.

The fact that we have a brilliant social club is due to Nicola's hard work too. She worked round the clock to set one up. We now have a wonderful place to meet our friends and unwind after school.

In addition, she negotiates confidently with teachers. Her discussions with the headteacher led to the girls being given permission to wear trousers in winter, which is much more comfortable for us and something we had wanted for a long time.

Her work visiting patients at our local hospital who do not normally receive visitors has developed her understanding of people's needs. This is a great asset in a big, mixed comprehensive like ours.

Nicola is not as egotistical as many of the other prefects, and I know I speak for many of us when I say 'Vote for Nicola'. She is trustworthy, hardworking and, what is more, likeable!

6 Brainstorming

Unemployment may not be a big problem for your students in their particular situations. Nevertheless, students should be developing an ability to discuss issues of global concern. This exercise is a good opportunity for them to think about the problem of unemployment in their own country. As always, encourage them to give local examples, so that they develop the ability to adapt a composition question to a local situation. If you have an international class, it's nice to share ideas about the various economies students come from.

Asking students to read a newspaper article or watch a TV programme about unemployment a day or two before you intend to cover the topic will focus on some of the issues and give them food for thought. Alternatively, they could interview their parents or other adults they have contact with about the causes of unemployment and possible remedies.

Encourage students to write down all their ideas during the brainstorming, no matter how unusual they seem!

7 Reading an example email

The example email follows on from the discussion about unemployment. It raises some ideas which could be followed up after the reading, e.g. Should unemployed people receive welfare payments to provide the necessities of life? What is life like for unemployed people in your country? Why might some people genuinely prefer unemployment to having a job?

Answers

1 Young people need effective careers guidance.

2 A mentoring scheme would be helpful.

3 A partnership of local firms and schools could be set up to teach computer skills.

4 We are aware of the personal effects of unemployment.

8 Analysing the email

Answers

Defining clauses

Paragraph 1: *I read your report which suggested …*

Paragraph 2: *schools should start a 'mentoring scheme' which would match pupils …*

Paragraph 3: *to develop training schemes which would enable us to …*

Comparative structures

Paragraph 2: *school leavers need much more detailed careers guidance*

Idioms

Paragraph 2: *an eye-opener*

Similes

Paragraph 5: *like a high wall you have to climb*

Linking devices

Paragraph 2: *Moreover*

Paragraph 3: *Furthermore, whereas*

Paragraph 4: *I would also like to add that …*

Opening sentence

I do not usually write to newspapers but …

Conclusion

Young people need all the help they can get, not criticism.

Style and register

The overall impression is formal, which is appropriate for a formal email/letter to a newspaper.

9 Writing an email of reply

Remind students that the reply should be formal but not excessively so. IGCSE students are fond of language such as '*I am honoured that you have read my letter*', which is too formal. The right tone should be that of two equals sharing views.

10 Correcting a report for the headteacher

Students should enjoy a pre-task discussion of the text, which states that high exam grades are not everything and personal skills and qualities are just as important. It will be intriguing to find out what students think of this idea. Hopefully, it will give some encouragement to less academic students by emphasising the sometimes overlooked truth that being effective at work is not solely dependent on academic ability, as many other qualities are just, if not more, essential.

Answer

The extra words which should not be there are highlighted in bold and crossed through.

Mr Chen's talk was the most interesting careers **the** event we have attended. He began by explaining how he had built up **with** his factory, 'Chen's Engineering,' from a small company to a large business. He explained that when he was growing up, he helped **them** in the family engineering business. Mr Chen most enjoyed **it** repairing motorcycle engines. At a young age, he realised he liked working with machines, and got a lot of satisfaction from making a damaged engine **to** work well again. Most of all though, he learned **him** about giving good customer service. His saw that his parents **they** were always patient and pleasant to customers, no matter what the effort. His father **he** would say, 'A man without a smiling face should not open a shop.' Mr Chen says he has never forgotten **of** those words, as they have been essential to the success of his business.

Mr Chen then told us what he looks for in when he recruits new employees. He said that job applicants think high exam grades are everything, but they are **in** wrong. He chooses people, including school leavers, because they are polite, enthusiastic and willing **them** to learn. He expects **it** employees to speak in a professional way to customers, and not to say, for instance, 'Hi you guys, wanna have a coffee?' He said everyone can **you** learn to be respectful, talk confidently on the phone, take notes and ask for help when necessary.

We appreciated ~~and~~ Mr Chen's careers talk very much, especially the emphasis on communication skills at work. As a result of the talk, some of us now want to get wider ~~our~~ experience. We are thinking of doing voluntary work or getting ~~us~~ a part-time job in the holidays.

Peter Lee

Head Prefect

11 Choosing appropriate vocabulary

You may like to reinforce the message about rubric error because, sadly, some students do misinterpret questions. Question interpretation is a tricky area because the questions nearly always have some cultural content. Problems arise because the interpretation is too literal, or because students are put off by the artificiality of the exercise and can't think into the situation quickly enough.

Sometimes misinterpretation can be deliberate: students try to stretch the definition of the task to exploit previously prepared material. Remind them that what they write must be relevant to the question set and that going off the point is not a good idea.

TEACHING SUPPORT

To help students understand the point of this exercise, do a few examples on the board. Begin with basic topics (e.g. family, school, free time) and then move on to more specific topics (e.g. school sports day, a job interview). Finally, you could move on to abstract concepts (e.g. love, loss and happiness). To add extra **challenge**, encourage students to think of vocabulary relevant to each of the subjects. Make sure that they understand that this can be any part of speech, i.e. noun, verb, adjective. Stress the point of Exercise 11, which is to ensure that the words you use are appropriate to the topic.

Answers

The unlikely language students should delete is:

Question 1

sales figures

share prices

Question 2

disappointed

irritated

isolated

saddened

12 Timed writing

Timed writing is important because students find concentrating their thoughts and producing coherent compositions in a short space of time very challenging. Let them have more classroom practice on other questions if necessary.

Allow students to read their compositions aloud either to their group or in pairs. Emphasise the value of honest but constructive criticism. Insist that each 'listener' finds two positive things to say about the compositions before suggesting criticisms and positive ways the writing could be improved.

13 Listening: Four work scenarios 🔊 CD 2, Track 16

Answers

1	a Friday morning	b	seeing the specialist
2	a none	b	patience and stamina
3	a very good experience	b	next week
4	a good news	b	pilot

AUDIOSCRIPT

*You will hear four short recordings. Answer each question using no more than **three** words for each detail. You will hear each recording twice.*

1   **a**   Maria is ringing up to change the time and date of a job interview. What alternative is she offered?

       b   What is Maria doing on Tuesday?

'You said the interview was Tuesday at 4 p.m. and that's when you're seeing the specialist? Yes, well if you think you can get here on Friday morning, we can fit you in then.'

2   **a**   According to the careers talk, what special qualifications are needed to enter training schemes for the police force?

       b   What two personal qualities are needed?

'Well, many of you will be surprised that, apart from a good standard of general education, no special qualifications are needed for our basic entry scheme. More important, in fact, are patience and stamina, as the hours are often long and the work is demanding.'

3   **a**   What did the headteacher think about your friend's idea of helping at the children's clinic?

173

b When does your friend want to visit the clinic?

'I told the headteacher I wanted to help at the children's clinic. She agreed it would be very good experience for me, and she encourages us all to do something for the community. But she felt I should visit the place first – so I've decided to ring the clinic and ask if I can visit next week.'

4   a Has the speaker received good news or bad news?

b What job does he want to train to do?

'I'm really sorry – I won't be able to make it. Do give my love to everyone. I've just received a letter saying I've been accepted onto a trainee pilot course. You know I've always wanted to fly, so I'm off to Rome to meet the other trainees.'

Grammar spotlight

> **TEACHING SUPPORT**
>
> See the Introduction for a general approach to helping students with Grammar exercises.

1   Superlatives of long and short adjectives

You may like to write two sentences on the board first, to contrast the use of superlatives for short and long adjectives, and elicit other superlatives, e.g.

We have had the warmest / coldest / hottest/ driest summer for years.

He was the most ambitious / competitive / supportive / annoying man she had ever met.

You could also point out that superlatives are often used with the present perfect and past perfect tenses, as in the examples above.

There is a practice exercise in the workbook (Exercise 22).

Answers

The best candidate, the youngest senior prefect, the most fantastic negotiating skills

2   Adverbs of degree

Students will have some familiarity with adverbs of degree and, as always, the *Grammar spotlight* enables them to explore their intuitive knowledge. If you have more advanced students, you may like to elicit the idea that the adverbs *a little* and *a bit* are used with adjectives which have a negative meaning. We can be

a little disappointed or *a bit tired* but not *a little happy* or *a bit interesting.*

There is a practice exercise in the workbook (Exercise 23).

Answers

Sales Executive: too sophisticated, very child-orientated, too expensive

Marketing Executive: rather bored, extremely competitive, high enough

Exam-style questions

See the Overview of *Cambridge IGCSE English as a Second Language* section at the beginning of the Student's Book for the mark scheme and criteria for marking the writing questions.

Writing

1 Work experience – article

Below are two additional prompts which you may like to provide if you think your students need them:

'It is an exciting idea which will help me mature.'

'I prefer to concentrate on my future studies, not work experience.'

3 Careers event – report

You could discuss the topic of the report first to ensure students understand what is required. Then add two further prompts for Core students and write them on the board, or use the prompts suggested below.

'It made me much more aware of the jobs I can apply for.'

'I still don't understand what I need to do in order to get a job.'

This is one possible response to the question. Detailed knowledge of careers events are not expected; any reasonable response to the question would be sufficient and, as always with the exam-style questions, they can draw on the careers-based topics, examples and language studied in the unit. Students should aim to express their reasons clearly and back up their opinions with some examples. Students can use the comments given, but they are free to make up their own ideas. The report should sound formal or semi-formal.

Example answer

> Our school trip to the careers event was exciting. Mrs Azar took us into a large room where local business people were sitting at tables. She explained that we could ask them for information about the company they represented. She said they wouldn't mind if we didn't know what we wanted to do in the future, and would be happy to answer any questions.
>
> This made us all feel confident. I would like a job in art and design and I was told by a food manufacturer that they have designers who design appealing packaging for their products. She showed me some amazing examples on their website. She also said no one starts their first job after school with a lot of experience, so I shouldn't worry. When they choose new employees, they select applicants who are polite, enthusiastic and willing to learn.
>
> All in all, it was a rewarding and eye-opening day. Some of us would have liked to find out more about possible training courses, so if the visit is repeated for next year's group, it would be useful to have someone from the local college who could tell us about those. (194 words)

(Reading & Writing, Exercise 6: 16 marks (Extended).)

Below are two additional prompts which you may like to provide if you think your students need them.

'Online learning is more flexible, which is useful now we are near our exams.'

'International companies recruit at local events, so we will hear about opportunities overseas.'

Wider practice

1   You could ask students to bring in examples of articles from the internet or from print media which, in their view, distort statistical information. They could argue their case in their groups.

2   Students might like to devise a questionnaire to use with local firms to find out more about their employment policies, e.g. working conditions and pay, health and safety, equal opportunity issues, recruitment, training schemes. Alternatively, a human resources officer or senior member of a firm could be invited to talk about their approach to employment. You could arrange for this to take place at the same time as a careers lesson, if possible.

3   This exercise is designed to take students minds off the stress of exams. Write the following incomplete sentences on the board:

The way I relax during exams is …

When my exams are over, I'm going to …

Give each student a piece of paper, on which students write a completed sentence, e.g. *When my exams are over, I'm going to go to the beach!* Ask students not to write their names on the paper.

The papers are then dropped into a box and shuffled, and each student selects one from the box. They walk around the room, stopping and asking each other open questions such as *'How do you relax during exams?'* until they find the person who wrote the original. They share their views and then choose another piece of paper.

4   As a change from brainstorming ideas for a topic, why not try brainwriting? Each student writes an idea about the topic on a slip of paper. No names are used. The slips of paper are collected and each anonymous idea is discussed in turn in the group.

5   Students can research employment opportunities online and present a short talk to the class on an area of work that interests them.

Unit 1: Happiness and success

1 Quick language check

1	for	6	have
2	realise	7	do
3	I pass	8	on
4	pay	9	she was
5	eat		

2 Formal and informal styles

1 children
2 dismissed
3 bored or unhappy
4 enthusiastic about, prefer
5 high-priced
6 newspaper
7 glasses

3 Adjective suffixes: -*ful* and -*less*

2	colourful	7	speechless
3	pointless	8	harmful
4	thoughtful	9	thankful
5	priceless	10	heartless
6	peaceful		

4 Job suffixes: -*ant*, -*er*, -*ist*, -*or*

1	drummer, footballer	5	assistant
		6	psychologist
2	director	7	accountant
3	supervisor	8	ecologist
4	painter, decorator	9	operator
		10	translator

5 Text completion

1	vital	7	believed
2	afford	8	miserable
3	wealth	9	predicts
4	happier	10	blame
5	pressure	11	loneliness
6	youth	12	replacing

6 Figurative language

1	very proud	4	disappeared
2	very sad	5	reminders
3	based on	6	very noisy

7 Homophones

1	warn	5	weather
2	fought, War	6	grown
3	ate	7	break
4	flaw	8	great

8 Text completion

up, in, possible, taught, excuse, imaginative, passionately, made, yet, inspired, forgave, prevent

9 Comparing information in charts

1 true
2 true
3 true

10 Sentence correction

2	give **up** smoking	7	**as** big as
3	**on** the radio	8	breaks **up**
4	**did** you finish	9	**an** appointment
5	**had** been done	10	I **have** been
6	**to** marry him		

11 Apostrophes: Omission of emails

1	haven't	5	Let's, It's, I've
2	you'd, You're	6	doesn't, they've
3	She's, who's	7	Aren't
4	Don't, you'd, it's	8	coffee's

12 How important is literacy?

Dear Editor

Literacy is very important for people's happiness and (for) the development of the/our country. Studies show / have shown that people who are unable to read or write are more likely to be dissatisfied with their lives. They lack confidence and find it difficult to get jobs / a job. In addition, they can't/don't help their children with their schoolwork or play an active part in their community. They find it difficult to do ordinary things like reading (the) newspapers or filling in forms. Many cannot use the internet or social media. Some (of them) feel ashamed. They cover up their problems and pretend (that) they can read.

I think it is very important that people who can't read or write get help. In our area, there is a literacy scheme which helps / to help adults (to) improve their skills in reading and writing. Schemes like this (can/will) help the government to achieve its/their goal of 100% literacy in/for our country.

Yours faithfully,

Vicki Sansa

13 *Would* and *used to*
1 *Both are correct.*
2 *2nd sentence is incorrect.*
3 *Both are correct.*
4 *2nd sentence is incorrect.*
5 *2nd sentence is incorrect.*
6 *2nd sentence is incorrect.*

14 Describing character
1 absent-minded
2 good-natured
3 untidy
4 ambitious
5 placid
6 optimistic
7 artistic
8 private

15 Vocabulary check
The following sentences should be marked ✗:

1, 3, 6, 7

16 Negative prefixes
unhappy, untidy, unprepared, unlock, unenthusiastic, unconscious, unsympathetic

illegal, illiterate

impatient, impossible

insecure, incorrect, insignificant

irresponsible, irregular

disappear, disobey

misunderstand, misbehave

17 Developing your writing style
Possible answer:

The first thing you notice about my grandmother is her brown eyes, which twinkle when she smiles. She is small and fair-skinned, and her hair is snow white. Despite a painful arthritic knee, she still enjoys life and is very artistic. She paints beautiful pictures of nature scenes. Around her neck she wears a gold locket which my grandfather gave her when they first married. I know she treasures it. Ever since I can remember, my birthday has been made more special by the thoughtful presents she buys me.

18 Sentence correction
1 her
2 to
3 it
4 would
5 of
6 in
7 they
8 such
9 but *or* Although
10 there

19 Text correction
is Charlotte Brontë
She **was** born
pleasure in **walking**
she **began** writing
put **in** her books
school **where**
responsible **for**
Charlotte **was**
looked after
who were also
to **express**
most famous
universal.
delicate-**looking**
as **a** governess
after she got married
at **their** height

Unit 2: You and your community
1 Open and closed questions
2 a open
  b closed
3 a open
  b closed
4 a closed
  b open
5 a closed
  b open

177

2 Forming open questions
Suggested answers:

1 How long have you lived in your neighbourhood?
2 What changes have there been?
3 How do you feel about growing up there?
4 What are your friends like? / Tell me about your friends.
5 What clubs do you belong to? / Tell me about any clubs you belong to.
6 Where can you spend free time near you? / What places are there to spend free time near you?

3 Vocabulary check

1 inspiring
2 sporty
3 down-to-earth
4 adventurous
5 close-knit
6 curious
7 courageous
8 hospitable
9 keep
10 sociable

4 Text correction
The words in bold should be crossed out:

at the decorative iron bridge

and **of** skill

last **long** for generations

used to meet **there**

and chat **us**

see **more** into the market

catch **up** fragrant whiffs

the atmosphere **well**

we could **do** relax

be **a** beautiful

moving **over**

we got **us** out of touch

pass **to** the bridge

5 Language to describe places
1 c   2 b   3 c   4 b

6 Word formation
2 converted
3 own
4 traditional
5 reductions
6 relaxing
7 light
8 charm
9 inspiring

7 Using adjectives
1 sleepy, picturesque
2 breathtaking
3 fascinating
4 spacious, luxurious
5 shady, sweet-smelling

8 Developing your writing style
Possible answer:

I'm lucky enough to have my own bedroom, and to me it is a very special place with a tranquil atmosphere. The room overlooks the garden and, if I lean out far enough, I can touch the walnut tree which grows just under the window. In autumn I can even pick walnuts from the tree. When I get in from school, I love curling up on my soft comfortable bed to read, relax or just dream. There are lots of cushions on the bed and a beautiful Indian silk bedspread. I find its soft colours particularly relaxing.

9 Choose the best word
1 b   2 c   3 a   4 b   5 c   6 b   7 b   8 a   9 d   10 a

10 Sentence correction
1 going to buy
2 as long as
3 lunch of green vegetables
4 I will go to bed
5 on his own
6 won't be able
7 chance of meeting
8 If we had known
9 have you been saving
10 It was snowing

11 Text completion
1 of
2 from
3 For
4 words

5	to	12	sure/clear
6	such	13	a
7	fought	14	by
8	with	15	in
9	the	16	are
10	to	17	is
11	they	18	to

12 Colloquial language round-up
1 a   2 c   3 b   4 b   5 b   6 b

13 Correcting an email
Dear Isabel,

It was lovely to hear from you, and I apologise for not getting in touch sooner.

Unfortunately, we've had some family problems. Dad has had a pain in his back for quite a long time, and the doctor has just told us he's going to need an operation. He'll have to stay in hospital for a while, and when he comes out he'll need complete rest.

I'm sorry to disappoint you, but I think we had better postpone your holiday with us until Dad is better. Mum and I will have to go to the hospital every day, and it wouldn't be much fun for you to be left at home alone. Also, the trips we had hoped to do would have to be cancelled, as neither Dad nor Mum will be able to drive us anywhere.

I am so sorry again to disappoint you. I was really looking forward to your coming over. Everyone hopes you will be able to come next summer, and then we really will have a great time.

All the best,

Kelly

14 Improving the tone of an email
Possible answer:

Dear Ahmed,

I'm really looking forward to your visit to our home. My family consists of my mother and father and my younger brother, Joseph. He's only ten so he can be mischievous at times, but don't worry – he's really friendly too.

I've arranged for you to come to school with me and I think you'll enjoy it. Most of the other students are easy to get on with. I'll explain everything you need to know about the school timetable, like when to bring your gym kit, for example. Our form teacher is Mrs Tait. She's usually pretty kind, and, like most of the other teachers, only a tiny bit strict.

I've got lots of exciting activities planned for after school, like swimming, badminton and trips to the cinema.

We've also got email at home, so you can keep in touch with your family as often as you like.

I can't wait to meet you.

Best wishes,

Oliver

15 Understanding information in a table
1	Coulden	5	Williams
2	Morel	6	Lilkova
3	Carter	7	Bloome
4	Khan		

16 Language round-up
a world
b miss seeing
c **in** touch
d te**m**plate; using **it**
e give up
f to send
g enjoy choosing
h confiden**tial**

Unit 3: Sport, fitness and health
1 Is sport always fun?
1 c   2 b   3 d   4 c

2 Linking ideas
1 b   2 c   3 f   4 e   5 d   6 a   7 g

3 Making comparisons
1 a fish
2 an angel
3 a horse
4 a log

4 Sentence correction

1	had scored	5	had fallen
2	Have you ever won	6	did you buy
3	replaced	7	take care
4	tell you	8	I twisted

5 Compound nouns

The correct words are:

carrier bag, wedding cake, football pitch, tennis court, school leaver

6 More compound nouns

2 an application form
3 a football shirt
4 a cycle helmet
5 shin pads
6 a football stadium

7 Newspaper headlines

1 Romantic novel tops bestseller list
2 New weapon against heart disease
3 Rare whale species close to extinction
4 Hundreds join in carnival fun
5 Mobile phone users in cancer scare
6 City firm wins jobs contract

8 Noun or verb?

1	verb	5	noun
2	noun	6	verb
3	noun	7	verb
4	verb	8	noun

9 Vocabulary check

1	consultation	6	court
2	tops	7	take
3	truancy	8	excluded
4	danger	9	get
5	peers		

10 Grammar and spelling

1	enjoys, approaches	2	stresses

3	splashes, punches	7	passes
4	sings, accompanies	8	mashes
5	fixes, goes	9	focus(s)es, worries
6	tries	10	guesses, hopes

11 Sentence correction

1 that **it** is
2 **was** taken
3 I **will/could/might**
4 the key **to** living
5 easier **than** I expected
6 I **will/could/might** buy
7 lent **them** to her
8 **on** the environment

12 Five-minute note-making practice

1 social media campaign
2 videos to schools promoting mental benefits
3 structured training courses
4 supervised training for safety
5 only friendly competition is allowed
6 qualified instructors
7 instructors trained in first aid
8 redecorated club house
9 hot showers, hairdryers, lockers, mirrors

13 Five-minute summary writing

Possible answer:

The steps taken to ensure the success of the club include a campaign on social media and sending out a video to schools promoting the mental benefits of kung fu. The training courses are carefully planned to cater for all levels of experience. The training is carefully supervised to ensure the safety of club members, and Dan only allows friendly competition. All the instructors must be qualified and have received first-aid training. The club house has been pleasantly redecorated, and the changing rooms all have modern conveniences, including hot showers.

14 Using fewer words

2 Raul goes to a co-educational school.
3 He is a specialist in chronic skin diseases.

4   The car accident was a traumatic experience for my brother.

5   The champion was given a medal.

6   Marisa has a great deal of anxiety about the future.

7   The doctor gave the injured sportsman a painkiller.

8   She nibbled a chocolate biscuit while she drank her coffee.

15 Redundant words

The following words should be crossed out:

2   by bike, of water

3   which is where they play their games

4   that he got while playing sport

5   and not eat any fat

6   to run in

7   so he thinks everyone should work together as part of a team

8   in many different colours

9   own, telling people his life story

10 so that it's better recognised and known about

16 Vocabulary check

1	beating	6	fresh
2	lines	7	encouragement
3	inconceivable	8	slump
4	immersed	9	stop
5	key	10	blog

17 Informal expressions

1   strength to strength

2   got out of hand

3   hooked

4   top of the world

5   all day long

6   snacked

7   get rid of

8   keep clear of

18 Text completion

1   of

2   has/contains

3   So/Therefore/Consequently

4   which

5   the

6   can/may/will

7   addition

8   on

9   from

10 one

11 in

12 by

13 to

14 than

19 Understanding pie charts

1	swimming	4	basketball
2	table tennis	5	keep fit
3	basketball	6	judo

Unit 4: Our impact on the planet

1 Vocabulary check

1	guarantee	5	luggage
2	skilled	6	pace
3	engineer	7	addressed
4	numerous	8	invention

2 Choose the best word

1	on	5	opposed
2	standardised	6	rate
3	distrust	7	novelty
4	immobilised	8	wider

3 Phrasal verbs with *take*

1	take up	4	took it off
2	taken in	5	taken on
3	take them up	6	taken out

4 Logical reasoning

1 e 2 d 3 h 4 g 5 b 6 c 7 i 8 a 9 f 10 j

5 Sentence completion

Possible answers:

1 there'll be time to watch the new video Dad rented.

2 he might be seeing quite a lot of the dentist in future!

3 what are you going to put on your cereal in the morning?

4 sea levels will rise.

6 Linking words: Reason and consequence

Suggested answers:

1 The roads are getting more crowded because the number of cars manufactured is increasing.

2 My parents won't allow me to have a motorcycle because/as (they think) it is too dangerous.

3 (The) swimming lessons were / have been cancelled because / as the pool was / is leaking.

4 Train travel became more popular because safety checks were introduced.

5 Therefore they would land / were going to land in Manchester.

6 Consequently, many people feel inadequate.

7 As a result, house prices have risen / are rising.

8 … so she bought a new one.

7 Text correction

a lot **of** dangerous drivers

time **for** breakfast

on their way

More **of** us

a fuel-efficient model**?**

reach **for** the lead-free variety**?**

suffering **from**

by bus

why aren't you using it**?**

contributes **to**

journeys **by** car

8 Word formation

1	beautiful	7	pollute
2	necessary	8	refreshments
3	donate	9	sponsor
4	own	10	diversity
5	Participants	11	guide
6	register	12	popular

9 Grammar: Future simple in the passive voice

1 An official sponsorship form will be sent to participants.

2 You will be guided on the route by experienced riders.

3 The route of the cycle ride will be planned by experts.

4 Children's health will be damaged by increasing traffic fumes.

5 Threats to the surrounding area will be highlighted by the campaign.

6 The campaign will be helped by these funds.

7 Extra trains will be provided.

8 Participants will be met at the start of the route.

9 People will be encouraged not to use cars.

10 Prizes will be given to the teams / The teams will be given prizes.

10 'Walk to school' campaign

2 An article will be published in the school magazine.

3 Emails will be sent to parents.

4 Students will be told to walk in pairs or threes.

5 Senior students will be asked to look after junior pupils.

6 (The) money saved on petrol and fares will be used to improve the school's cycle racks.

11 Linking words: Addition and contrast

Suggested answers:

1 Moreover, most people use bikes to get to work.

2 However, it is a quite / quite a dangerous form of transport.

3 Nevertheless, many people say they are scared of flying.

4 In addition, there were long queues to get on the rides, and some of the rides were not working.

5 Furthermore, a factory would encourage more people to move into the village and as a result, (the) local shops would get more customers.

12 Presenting the pros and cons

Listing: Secondly

Contrast: but, however, However

Reasoning: because, Therefore, as

Emphasis: in particular, as surely

Addition: Another point to consider, Moreover

Consequence: As a result, Consequently

Opinion: In my view, I think

Summing up: On balance

13 Word game

2 road
3 halt
4 plane
5 trip
6 town
7 area
8 crowd
9 train
10 sign

14 Understanding graphs

1 $50 000
2 March
3 $70 000
4 May
5 Up

15 Choose the best word

1 a **2** c **3** c **4** c **5** a **6** c **7** b **8** c **9** d **10** b

16 Relating to your target audience

Internet users   **C**

Residents   **F**

Teenage magazine readers   **E**

People looking for a job   **A**

Parents   **D**

A penfriend   **B**

17 Paragraphing and punctuation

Report to the School Management Committee

At the end of the spring term our class held a fundraising barbecue. We decided after some disagreement, to donate the funds to the local hospital. Some students argued that the school needed the money to help replace our classroom laptops. However, in my opinion we made the right decision to donate the money to a good cause.

Although organising the event was hard work and time-consuming, I think most of us enjoyed selling the tickets and cooking the food. In addition, the nurses told us our donation helped to buy oxygen cylinders for emergency use which made us feel very proud. The majority of us agreed saving lives is more important than state-of-the-art computers. Nevertheless, a few students disagreed and I understand their point of view.

On balance, I think that, although most of our fundraising efforts should continue to benefit local charities, we should have one event each year just for our school. If the headteacher gives permission, perhaps we could use the money we raise to have our classroom computers replaced.

Please let me know if you require any further information about our fundraising activities and plans.

Jordan Inara

Student Representative to the School Management Committee

18 Linking words round-up

b, h, j, o

19 Text completion

1	because/as	6	but
2	will/would	7	where
3	with	8	when
4	been	9	which/that
5	which	10	Finally

20 Report on the school visit to the Alternative Energy Centre

Example answer:

The school visit to the Alternative Energy Centre was very enjoyable.

We were given very interesting talks about alternative energy sources and we also watched a fascinating film on wind power. We were given lots of useful handouts, although unfortunately some students did not bring folders with them, so they had difficulty looking after their papers and some students lost theirs, which was a shame.

At the end of the day, we visited the gift shop and saw an intriguing range of inexpensive recycled goods. Most of us bought some gifts to take home.

The atmosphere on the bus home was extremely positive. Most of us felt we had learnt a good deal. This will help us in our studies, especially science, and we are also all more aware of the importance of renewable energy sources and what we can do to save energy and care for the planet.

We would love another visit to this cutting-edge centre, as there is still so much we could learn.

Unit 5: Entertainment

1 Film vocabulary

1	heroine	5	characters
2	costumes	6	scene
3	reviews	7	genres
4	cast	8	box office

2 More film vocabulary

1	special effects	6	message
2	Oscars	7	performance
3	settings	8	recommend
4	role	9	star
5	suspense		

3 *So ... that* and *such ... that*

Possible answers:

1	a powerful performance
2	an exciting story
3	an amazing actor
4	convincing/appealing/attractive
5	violent
6	poignant
7	long
8	beautiful/magnificent
9	sad

4 Word formation

2	excitement	9	entertainment
3	responding	10	powerful
4	performance	11	expressions
5	atmosphere	12	imagination
6	emotional	13	director
7	substitute	14	isolated
8	lonely	15	convenient

5 Collocations

Words in brackets are possible, but less likely, collocations.

stylish: shoes (animation, horror film, documentary)

atmospheric: horror film, documentary (animation)

witty: animation (horror film, documentary)

violent: animation, documentary, murder

thought-provoking: documentary (animation, horror film)

skilful: animation, horror film, documentary

6 Odd word out

sumptuous

7 Describing films

1 e 2 h 3 a 4 b 5 d 6 i 7 g 8 c 9 f

8 Describing plots

1 Max **introduces** Annie
2 **becomes** a weapon
3 to **begin** a new career, but can he **do** it
4 then nearly **ruins** it, who **detects**
5 Zoe **falls** in love
6 **knocks** on the door, why **does** she have
7 **catches** fire, that **defies**

9 Choose the best word

1 b   2 b   3 a   4 d   5 a   6 b   7 c

10 Prepositions

1 about
2 in
3 in
4 on
5 by
6 of
7 into
8 on
9 in

11 Choose the best word

1 a   2 b   3 b   4 d   5 a

12 Text completion

1 for
2 is
3 to/with
4 of
5 as
6 Furthermore
7 if/when
8 with
9 one
10 to
11 up
12 When/If
13 take/carry
14 than

13 Sentence correction

1 waste **of** time
2 better **than** mine
3 **has** shown
4 growing **up**
5 **is** fun
6 right **to** privacy
7 **a** discussion

8 was **not** able
9 brought him **up**
10 who **are** good
11 as modern **as**
12 reading **a** story

14 Understanding pie charts

1 false
2 true
3 true
4 true
5 true
6 false

Other possible sentences:

(Books of) poetry and plays were twice as popular as foreign-language books.

Novels accounted for nearly half of all books borrowed.

The most popular kind/type/category of books borrowed was novels.

Short stories were slightly more popular than poetry and plays.

15 Vocabulary check

1 compassionate
2 integrity
3 aspirations
4 lend
5 identify
6 burst
7 twists and turns
8 shortcomings

16 Developing your writing style

1 a   2 j   3 f   4 i   5 h   6 c   7 d   8 g   9 e   10 b

17 Language round-up

Only the following sentences make sense:

3, 5, 11, 12, 14

Unit 6: Travel and the outdoor life

1 Vocabulary check

1 fully equipped campsite
2 brochures
3 culture and customs
4 holiday resort

185

5   nightlife

6   scenery

2   Paragraphing and punctuation

Recently our class looked at a website advertising an activity holiday. We identified the persuasive techniques advertisers use to convince potential customers to choose this kind of holiday.

Firstly, we looked at the photographs showing young people doing interesting activities. The activities looked very appealing and succeeded in the advertiser's aim of making us want to find out more about the holidays. The target group for this kind of holiday is teenagers, and we noticed how, in order to increase a sense of identification, young people of similar ages and backgrounds to ourselves were chosen for the pictures.

We also studied the information given on the website. This was also very persuasive, as comments such as 'every minute of the day is filled with fun' were used to look like real facts, rather than just the advertiser's opinions.

I think by choosing scenic locations, happy-looking people and exciting activities, the holiday company achieved their aim of making the holiday seem attractive. In addition, they cleverly disguised any negative aspects of the holidays.

If you are thinking of booking on a holiday webite, remember the advertiser wants you to buy the holiday and will only show its good points. So think of its potential drawbacks for yourself before making up your mind.

3   Text completion

1	flexibility	12	emergency
2	strain	13	flexible
3	costume	14	invest
4	trunks	15	map reading
5	supervised	16	compass
6	sensitive	17	distances
7	risky	18	skid
8	warnings	19	balance
9	sea	20	cracked
10	shallow	21	gates
11	lifesaving	22	escape

4   Position of adverbs

I've just finished …

No one ever goes … and I'm certainly …

sometimes staying … / days sometimes …

I'll probably feel … but it's definitely going to be …

I occasionally did … / pay occasionally.

5   Sentence correction

1   a (great delight)

2   the (France)

3   at (the top)

4   it (causes)

5   there

6   will

7   him

6   Grammar revision

being, since, exploring, where, identifying, capture, from looking, a, like, who, which

7   Expanding notes into sentences

2   We went fishing in a nearby lake, but we didn't catch anything.

3   We were caught / got caught in a thunderstorm and, as we had no coats with us, we were soaked to the skin.

4   We went to a country market where I bought a brand new DVD dirt cheap.

5   We went on / did a terrific walk through a pine-scented forest and had a picnic near a waterfall.

6   We met a man in the forest who lent us his binoculars to look at a deer.

7   We spent a whole hour watching a breathtaking sunset until the sky went completely dark.

8   'Body' idioms

2   behind my back

3   blew my mind

4   give me a hand

5   off my chest

6   old head on young shoulders

7   itchy feet

8   a straight face

9 Adjective suffixes

1   memorable

2   poisonous

3   dramatic, basic

4   changeable

5   courageous

6   spacious

10 Text completion

arranges, According to, with, observe,
study, to, do, disturb, argue,
where, on, even,

11 Building an email from prompts

Hi Nancy,

Just a quick email to tell you about our wonderful
holiday touring the beautiful islands of Sicily and
Sardinia. They are places I had never been to but
had always wanted to visit.

Sicily has a grand but turbulent past. We saw traces
of Arabic and Greek influence in the buildings and
ruined temples (which/that) we visited. We spent
two nights in the capital, Palermo, which was full
of life. We also hired bicycles and cycled through/
to sleepy villages. We were impressed by the gentle
pace of life and the warmth of the people.

The highlight of our trip was a picnic in a magical
mountain setting. We sat near a stream. Far below
(us) we could see the Mediterranean gleaming in
the sunshine. The only sound was the rustling of the
wind in the trees.

It was a holiday I'll never forget!

Write soon!

Love,

Esther

12 Understanding maps

1   Palermo, Messina and Catania

2   Naples

3   Sardinia

4   Mount Etna, 3323 m

5   false

13 Using fewer words

1   mosaics

2   distinctive

3   hospitable

4   remote

5   well-preserved

6   enthusiastic

14 Sentence correction

1   **of** that island

2   if I **had** known

3   **too** tired to eat

4   **as** her brother

5   the house **where** / lived **in**

6   preferred **to** go

7   the train **will** leave

15 Using adverbs as intensifiers

1   incredibly painful

2   exceptionally interesting

3   frantically busy

4   dazzlingly bright

5   hardly recognisable

6   bitterly cold

7   completely exhausted

8   historically accurate

9   heavily in debt

10 mentally tiring

16 Developing your writing style

Possible answer:

Tranquil Paradise Island has everything: stunningly
white, palm-fringed beaches, a dramatic, rocky
coastline, sparkling sea full of fish. The air has the
scent of exotic flowers, and often the only sound is
the song of the birds. In the evenings, the setting
sun turns the sky a deep pink and the starlit nights
that follow are especially beautiful. Forget pollution,
traffic and tower blocks. This diamond-shaped
island is truly special and you'll want to return. I
promise you.

17 Vocabulary building

2   ✓ building, ✗ cathedral

3   ✓ jewel, ✗ valuable

4   ✓ tourism, ✗ colony

5   ✓ weather, ✗ surf

187

18 Grammar: Adjective plus infinitive

1   hard to believe
2   marvellous to visit
3   awful to live in
4   expensive to heat
5   idealistic of me to think
6   easy to maintain
7   pleasing to look at

19 Compound nouns with *snow* and *sun*

sunshine, sunhat, snowflake, snowdrift, sunburn, snowball, sunstroke, snowstorm, sunroof, snowplough, snowboard, sunlight, sunscreen, sunbathe, suntan

20 Spelling revision

1   thundery
2   smoky
3   icy
4   windy, rainy

21   Text correction

tourists **visit**, activit**ies**, we **had** eaten, to see **everything**, explained **to** us, to **make** the exhibits, he **showed** us, let us choose, I **chose**, had finish**ed**, went outside again, **climbed** 100 steps, the **best** part of the trip, **You'll** be surprised

Unit 7: Student life

1 Challenges of student life

1 h   2 a   3 d   4 j   5 k   6 f   7 g   8 b   9 i   10 c

2 Vocabulary check

The following sentences should be marked **✗**:

1, 5, 8, 9, 10

3 Compound nouns

1   coffee table
2   pillowcases
3   frying pan
4   ironing board
5   oven gloves
6   bin liner
7   washing machine, laundry basket
8   duvet cover

4 Prepositions

1   about
2   with
3   on
4   with
5   by/to/for
6   for
7   for
8   to

5 Problems and advice

1 b   2 d   3 a   4 c

6 Developing your writing style

Possible answer:

Dear Hilary,

I'm really sorry, but I won't be able to come to your party as I've already accepted an invitation to Barry's party at the University Social Centre. It's such a shame, as I would have loved to come to yours.

Good luck with your party. I will be thinking of you. It's wonderful that you managed to persuade your parents to go out for the evening! If we give a party at home we always put away any ornaments that might get broken. It might be worth your doing that too, just to be on the safe side, as I know your mother loves her glass animal collection!

Have you thought about what music you want to play? You've got such fantastic taste that I'm sure you'll find just the right music for the atmosphere you want to create.

You mentioned your parents were giving you some money for your birthday. How about visiting that new boutique in town? It's got a great range of stylish clothing. Why not browse around and see if anything takes your fancy?

Have a wonderful party. I'm only sorry I won't be there to enjoy it with you.

Lots of love,

Samira

7 Choose the odd one out

e   at a loose end

8 Confusing words

1   diary
2   bored
3   resit
4   librarian

5	impressive	7	social
6	text	8	lecture

9 Sentence correction

1	dependent **on**	5	will **be** eighteen
2	meant **to** write	6	**had** already left
3	I **was** living	7	**a** minute
4	right **by** the sea	8	in **the** USA

10 Talking about exam pressure

1 e 2 k 3 b 4 a 5 d 6 c 7 i 8 j 9 h 10 g

11 Informal expressions

1 loads
2 push me
3 nag you
4 stick to
5 get on
6 make up
7 do my best
8 too much on his mind

12 *Should, ought, need* and *had better*

1 You shouldn't have forgotten Mum's birthday.
2 You needn't buy any milk when you go out.
3 You'd better take warm clothes with you.
4 I should have gone to bed earlier last night.
5 You oughtn't to leave your revision to the last minute.
6 You needn't have booked a taxi.

13 Understanding visual information

1 true
2 false
3 false
4 true
5 false
6 true

14 Homophones with silent letters

2	(h)our	4	wei(gh)t
3	rei(g)n	5	(k)ni(gh)t

6	w(h)ich	9	s(c)ent
7	w(h)ether	10	(w)rote
8	wei(gh)		

15 Capital letters

Mr Jones, Joseph, University of Colorado, Baltic Sea, Wednesday, Chinese, September, India, River Nile, Asia, Harvey Street, BBC, Himalayas, Professor Grivas

16 Punctuating a text

Having just marked her last revision test, I am concerned that Jennifer's poor English is holding her back. Fortunately, she is seeing Mr Barnes, the Language Support teacher, every Tuesday afternoon for help with grammar, spelling, vocabulary and handwriting. She needs to make a special effort to improve in these areas.

17 Idiomatic expressions

The following sentences should be marked ✗:

2, 3, 5

18 Guessing meaning

Try to do better / improve your work.

19 Choose the best word

1 b 2 a 3 c 4 d 5 a 6 d 7 a 8 c

20 Word formation

2 embarrassed
3 advice
4 training
5 occupation
6 appointments
7 earning
8 wonderful
9 choose
10 discuss
11 organise
12 effect
13 confidential
14 positive

189

21 Sentence correction
The words in bold should be crossed out:

1. started on **to**
2. **the** time
3. too little **of** studying
4. some **do** regular exercise
5. counsellor **is** available
6. make you laugh **at**

22 Tone and register round-up
1 c 2 d 3 c 4 c 5 c 6 d 7 a 8 a

Unit 8: The search for adventure

1 Sea vocabulary

1	e	5	a
2	d	6	i
3	f	7	b
4	g	8	c

2 Vocabulary check

1	docks, cargo	4	snorkelling
2	horizon	5	smugglers
3	tide	6	dinghy

3 More sea vocabulary
1. whales
2. skipper
3. oceans
4. voyage, pirates, cargo
5. coastguard
6. lighthouse, swimmers
7. dolphins
8. shells/stones
9. vessel
10. dinghies, yachts

4 Onomatopoeic words
1. squelching
2. splashed
3. howling
4. screeching

5 Describing problems and challenges
1 f 2 e 3 b 4 j 5 h 6 d 7 c 8 a 9 g 10 i

6 Narrative tenses
1. they had not eaten a proper meal …
2. he was / had been devastated …
3. the ferry we were going to catch …
4. *This sentence is correct.*
5. before it sank.
6. and asked if I had lost anything.
7. when I fell over …

7 Forming questions
1. Did you ever give up hope?
2. How big is the Pacific Ocean?
3. Are you in good health now? / Are you now in good health?
4. How much longer do you think you could have survived?
5. What preparations did you make for the journey?
6. How big is a sperm whale?
7. What are your plans for the future?
8. What did you think about while you were on the raft?
9. What do sharks taste like?
10. Are you still keen on sailing?

8 Collocations

1	film	4	screech
2	air	5	drown
3	potatoes	6	insult

9 Ordering events
The correct order is:

g, i, e, b, h, a, f, d, c

10 Understanding visual information
Possible answer:

Starting in San Diego, we flew down to La Paz in the south of Baja California. From there, we took a boat to Manzanillo on the Pacific coast of Mexico, via Mazatlán. From Manzanillo, we continued by bus down to Acapulco, and then flew inland to Mexico City. From Mexico City, we took a train across to the port of Veracruz, from where we went by boat through the Gulf of Mexico to New Orleans. Finally, we took a plane back to San Diego.

11 Text completion

been, staying, cancelled, woke, delightful, quietly, glorious, violent, crashing, drowned, cruelly, recovering, screeched, splashed, reminding, collection, inspect, passing, astonishment, decided

12 Vocabulary check

1 sheer
2 bouncing
3 condition
4 convinced
5 chase
6 comfort
7 stranded
8 initially

13 Reporting verbs

1 boasted
2 admitted
3 congratulated
4 offered/agreed
5 apologised
6 estimated
7 agreed/offered
8 explained
9 complained

14 Sentence completion

1 down
2 up, for/at
3 off/from
4 up, of
5 on
6 of, from
7 in, of, into
8 on
9 in
10 in, of

15 Sentence correction

The words in bold type should be crossed out:

1 on **a** holiday
2 we rented **it**
3 **there** on the journey
4 regained **in** their health

5 and **before** they had left
6 too little **of** exercise

16 Defining relative clauses

Possible answers:

1 there is plenty to see and do.
2 lives in the sea.
3 daughter was lost at sea.
4 helps guide larger boats into and out of ports.
5 you came to stay with me
6 can cause an incredible amount of damage.
7 had coordinated the rescue of his pet.
8 to do in case of emergency?

17 Adverb formation

2 suitably
3 romantically
4 steadily
5 extremely
6 responsibly, immediately
7 simply
8 dramatically

18 Obeying the rules of a narrative

The text should be marked ✓ (all the rules have been followed)

19 Text completion

1 in
2 which/that
3 best/most
4 bought
5 trips/excursions
6 too
7 passengers
8 jumped/leaped/stepped/climbed/went
9 spent/had
10 for
11 wish
12 managed
13 show
14 horror/surprise/amazement
15 forgotten/failed
16 more

191

17 worried/anxious/desperate

18 man

19 back

20 light

20 Text correction

Last October, Mr Bains, our science teacher **1** told us about the Young Explorer competition. He **2** was driving to school listening to the radio when he **3** heard an interview with an explorer. At the end of the programme, the competition was announced. To enter the competition, Mr Bains explained that we had to make a model of equipment which would be useful on an expedition. Our club **4** got really excited about the idea, although we were a bit nervous about it too, as it was the first time we **5** had entered a competition.

We decided to make our model from toy construction bricks which we could **6** borrow from younger brothers and sisters. First of all, we **7** brainstormed our ideas and after some disagreement, we **8** decided to make a sled for carrying equipment on an Arctic expedition. We wanted the sled to be original and Finlay Hudson **9** suggested making a sled that could also be used as a life raft. We all liked the sound of that!

We **10** experimented with different approaches and finally we **11** built a model we were happy with. We **12** used very small bricks to make the ice axe, skis and storage boxes.

We **13** packed our model carefully and **14** sent it off. The club then **15** forgot about it, because we were busy with exams. To our delight, Mr Bains got an email last week saying our club **16** had won an award for the most inventive model. We were all so proud as none of us **17** had ever won a prize before. The club will get an Explorer's Survival Kit which **18** includes sleeping bags, ropes and a compass.

Please let me know if you require further information.

Hugo Yi

Year 11

Unit 9: Animals and our world

1 Parts of animals

bird: beak, feathers, wings, claws

cat: paws, fur, claws

horse: hooves, mane

camel: hump, hooves

elephant: tusks, trunk

goat: horns, hooves

fish: fins, scales

2 Vocabulary check

The following sentences should be marked ✗:

3, 4, 5, 8

3 Text completion

1	historians	7	result
2	empire	8	for
3	private	9	from
4	until	10	active
5	classify	11	Nevertheless
6	it	12	but

4 Odd word out

foal

5 Linking ideas

1 but nothing could be further from the truth

2 Furthermore

3 Despite

4 As a result

5 After weighing up the pros and cons

6 Medical science

1	vaccine	7	asthma
2	ethical	8	anaesthetic
3	lungs	9	antibiotics
4	blood	10	vitamins
5	hormones	11	virus
6	veins	12	laboratory

7 Prepositions

1	between	6	by/at
2	of	7	behind, of
3	from	8	in
4	for, into	9	to
5	for	10	against

8 Understanding graphs

1	false	4	false
2	true	5	true
3	true	6	false

9 Expressing strong opinions

1 d **2** e **3** f **4** c **5** b **6** a **7** g **8** h

10 Adding adjectives for emphasis

1	innocent	4	apologetic
2	absurd	5	anxious
3	magical		

11 Odd word out

ewe

12 Vocabulary check

1	humane	6	deprived
2	harmless	7	distressed
3	contempt	8	uncomfortable
4	wild	9	refuse
5	appealed	10	historical

13 Sentence correction

1 **to** look after
2 for **their** beauty
3 **should/must** be cleaned
4 **before** lighting
5 **an** operation
6 can **be** cared for
7 **if/when** we go away
8 pick up **a** peanut

14 Verb forms

1 Dinosaurs became …
2 early man kept …
3 Lizards feed on …
4 the rabbit had bitten …
5 Ruben sold …
6 the camel has been used … *(because it is still used)*
7 are often criticised …

15 Vocabulary check: food production

1	orchard	6	organic
2	poultry	7	free range
3	herds	8	harvest
4	rear	9	pesticides
5	contaminating	10	processed

16 Text completion

1 was
2 be
3 it
4 which/that
5 have
6 where
7 where
8 much/far
9 only
10 what
11 say/claim/argue/protest/believe/think
12 feel/experience
13 in
14 for
15 is
16 in
17 so
18 to
19 while
20 of/for
21 which
22 there
23 for
24 to
25 but

17 Sounds right?

1	miaow	7	howling
2	hissed	8	croaking
3	roared	9	buzzing
4	clucking	10	giggled
5	squawks	11	chimed
6	purred		

193

18 Proofreading a report for the headteacher

Our class visit to the animal sanctuary to see ~~with~~ the giant panda and the newborn twin giant panda cubs was so thrilling. We were all looking ~~very~~ forward to it so much. All of us felt we knew ~~so~~ a lot about the cubs before the visit. In our biology lesson, we had learnt that they ~~had~~ were sleeping in warm cots called incubators and special techniques were needed to care for them.

Mrs Lun had ~~been~~ told us about the way in which in the wild, a mother who has twins may struggle to feed both babies and may abandon one of them. In the zoo, however, staff will take one cub to the incubator while the mother ~~her~~ feeds the other one. It was amazing for ~~to~~ see this happen in real life. The zoo staff ~~they~~ used a stick of sugar cane to distract the mother while a member of staff took one of the cubs away.

We all wanted to take photographs, and everyone was able to get ~~there~~ fantastic pictures of the cubs. We also saw ~~how~~ the cubs trying to move by pushing their legs backwards. We were told they only weighed about 113 grams when they ~~been~~ were born, which is about the same as our phones. We don't know their names yet, because the cubs will not be named until they are 100 days ~~of~~ old.

On the way back to school, we decided to upload ~~on~~ the photos onto the school website. Mrs Lun suggested we also write a fun online quiz based on the notes ~~from~~ the staff gave us.

We all appreciated the experience so much and we are going to treasure ~~it~~ the memories for the rest of our lives.

19 Developing your writing style
1 b 2 c 3 a 4 d 5 i 6 e 7 f 8 g 9 h

Unit 10: The world of work
1 Who does what?
1 dentist
2 novelist
3 interpreter
4 interior designer
5 firefighter
6 journalist
7 cellist
8 company director
9 nursery teacher
10 labourer
11 carpenter
12 miner
13 chauffeur
14 midwife
15 plumber
16 choreographer

2 Word formation: Feelings and abilities
1 disappointed
2 frustrating
3 intrigued
4 enthusiasm
5 determination, initiative
6 creativity
7 discipline
8 patient
9 dexterity
10 courage
11 imagination

3 Vocabulary check
1 research
2 packaging
3 formula
4 competitive
5 investing
6 profitable
7 consumers
8 launch
9 campaign
10 products
11 brand
12 manufacturing

4 Choose the best word
1 a 2 b 3 b 4 a 5 b 6 d 7 c 8 d 9 c

5 Sentence correction
The words in bold should be crossed out:
1 develop **the** new
2 developed **as**

3   a few **of**

4   **a** new products

6 Approximations
The following sentences should be marked ✗:

1, 2, 4, 6

7 Questioning information
1 d   **2** h   **3** e   **4** a   **5** c   **6** f   **7** i   **8** g
9 j   **10** l   **11** b

8 A training scheme for young people
Suggested answer:

A new training scheme is / has been offering high-quality training to/for school and college leavers aged 16 and upwards in a wide range of occupations. Some employers were initially reluctant to take part, and say/said they were / had been worried that teenagers were / would be a bad employment risk. However, they now say (that) the media image of young people is a total distortion of the truth.

The scheme gives training opportunities in engineering, hairdressing and manufacturing, and shows that teenagers are hardworking, enthusiastic, reliable and quick to learn. (The) employers themselves designed the scheme so that it was/is genuinely useful to them. Around 76% of local employers recruited teenagers to/for the scheme, and next year it is hoped to reach the government target of 85%. Employers say (that) two out of three youngsters make / have made 'better progress than expected', and that there was / has been a drop-out rate of less than 10%.

A recent government report concluded that the experience was/is invaluable to/for those taking / who took part. Four-fifths of (the) trainees say/said (that) it is/was the only way to earn and learn at the same time. Most are/were very impressed with/by the scheme and plan / are planning to recommend it to their friends.

9 Comparing information in charts
1   true

2   true

3   false – the least popular was fashion design

4   true

5   true

6   false – it decreased in popularity with male students

10 Employment vocabulary
1	staffing	5	disciplinary
2	knowledge	6	qualities
3	promoted	7	recruit
4	realistic		

11 Punctuating a text
Jan Benson is employed as an assistant to a human resources officer for a big clothing chain in Scotland. 'HR work is often stereotyped as lacking in excitement,' says Jan, 'but it can offer a fulfilling career to anyone who has a genuine desire to make organisations more efficient.'

Jan took a degree in economics at Mumbai University before deciding she was interested in working in human resources. 'I started as a human resources assistant last August and have been studying for my qualifications in HR management in the evenings,' explains Jan. 'It's hard work but worth it, as I'm able to go on earning while I'm gaining qualifications.'

The aspect Jan most enjoys about her work is the challenge of gaining the respect of the store managers. 'I'm learning from my boss, Mrs Shah, that it's essential to try to understand the managers' needs, rather than just imposing my views,' she explains.

12 Odd word out
Hating because the other words describe positive emotions towards people.

13 Guessing meaning from context
1 failed / went out of business
2 do different kinds of things to make money
3 someone who buys from the manufacturer and then sells to the consumer
4 shared the running of the business with someone else

14 Vocabulary check
The following sentences should be marked **✗**:

1, 2, 4, 6, 7, 8, 10

15 Choose the best word
1 at a loss
2 groundbreaking
3 left out
4 cautiously
5 relieved

16 Phrasal verbs with *up, down* and *out*
1 turned down
2 let down
3 drew up
4 put him down
5 drew out
6 turned up

17 Sentence correction
1 **in** the workplace
2 loving **to/towards**
3 he **had** gone
4 to **be** a cook
5 **if** you study
6 **have** you decided
7 inaccessible **to**
8 looked **like**
9 **as** it could

18 Collocations
1 brother
2 smile
3 person
4 ocean

5 mother
6 website

19 Sentence completion
1 how
2 who
3 as
4 which
5 why
6 who
7 which
8 when/while
9 that

20 Text completion
1 is
2 give/offer
3 to
4 are
5 such
6 information
7 if
8 know
9 an
10 to
11 have
12 of
13 help
14 to
15 might
16 in
17 which
18 how
19 found
20 include
21 part
22 of

21 Colloquial language round-up
The following sentences should be marked **✗**:

1, 3, 5, 6, 8, 9

22 Sentence completion
1 the most sophisticated
2 the worst
3 the cleverest

4 the most successful

5 the laziest

6 the best

23 Sentence correction

1 good enough

2 not very realistic

3 *This sentence is correct.*

4 a little noisy

5 rather bad-tempered

6 a bit disappointed

24 Adding capital letters and full stops to a report

We all really appreciated our work experience at Le Yung Motorcycles. At first, students did not want to do work experience because we had a stereotyped idea of what working in a factory is like. We thought the factory was going to be noisy and dirty and we would be desperate for the day to end. In fact, we found out that in a modern factory like Le Yung Motorcycles, nothing could be further from the truth. The factory itself was clean and pleasant, and the machines were quiet.

After being shown around the factory, to our surprise, we were told we could operate some of the machines ourselves. We felt proud as we walked through the door marked 'Staff Only' and were given our special work uniforms. I personally loved working with the supervisor, Mr Zu, who operated a large machine used to repair damaged engines, and I know other students had similar good experiences.

Everyone in the company encouraged us to think of engineering as a career with many possibilities. Since doing work experience, I have become interested in doing an engineering degree and others in the group are thinking of jobs in marketing, design or sales for an engineering company.

Fatima Al-Sultana

Year 11